BRITISH MILITARY
OPERATIONS
IN
ADEN AND RADFAN

Also by Nick van der Bijl

Pen & Sword Military Books
Nine Battles to Stanley
5th Infantry Brigade in the Falklands
Victory in the Falklands
Confrontation; the War with Indonesia 1962-1966
Commandos in Exile; The Story of 10 (Inter-Allied) Commando
1942-45
Operation Banner; The British Army in Northern Ireland 1969-2007
The Cyprus Emergency; The Divided Island 1955-1974
The Brunei Revolt 1962-1963
Sharing the Secret

Osprey
Argentine Forces in the Falklands
Royal Marines 1939-1993
No. 10 (Inter-Allied) Commando 1942-1945

Hawk Editions
Brean Down Fort and the Defence of the Bristol Channel

BRITISH MILITARY OPERATIONS IN ADEN AND RADFAN

Nick van der Bijl

Pen & Sword
MILITARY

First published in Great Britain in 2014
By Pen and Sword Military
an imprint of
Pen and Sword Books Ltd
47 Church Street
Barnsley
South Yorkshire S70 2AS

ISBN 978 1 78303 291 4

Printed and bound in England by
CPI Group (UK) Ltd, Croydon, CR0 4YY

Typeset in Times New Roman by
CHIC GRAPHICS

Pen & Sword Books Ltd incorporates the imprints of
Pen & Sword Aviation, Pen & Sword Family History, Pen & Sword Maritime,
Pen & Sword Military, Pen & Sword Discovery, Wharncliffe Local History,
Wharncliffe True Crime, Wharncliffe Transport, Pen & Sword Select,
Pen & Sword Military Classics, Leo Cooper, Remember When,
The Praetorian Press, Seaforth Publishing and Frontline Publishing

For a complete list of Pen and Sword titles please contact
Pen and Sword Books Limited
47 Church Street, Barnsley, South Yorkshire, S70 2AS, England
E-mail: enquiries@pen-and-sword.co.uk
Website: www.pen-and-sword.co.uk

This book is dedicated to the wives, children and families of members of the Armed Forces, in particular to those who lost their lives to terrorism in Egypt, Malaya, Cyprus, Aden and Northern Ireland, for their resilience, patience and support during Britain's campaigns since 1945 in often difficult circumstances.

Contents

Foreword and Acknowledgements

Aden, on the southern tip of South Arabia in the country now known as Yemen, was in 1839 the first colonial acquisition of Queen Victoria's reign. It soon became an important staging post to and from India and the Far East. It remained largely unaffected by international affairs until the Ottoman Empire re-aligned its territories during the late nineteenth and early twentieth centuries. Aden began to attract headlines after the Second World War when decolonization, the spread of Soviet and Chinese communism, Persian Gulf oil security and the Arab unity promoted by Colonel Nasser of Egypt upset the status quo in the Near and Middle East. Although the British Government was determined to leave Aden and the states to the north, known collectively as the Federation of South Arabia, as a stable democracy, the territory soon became a prime target for Egyptian subversion and terrorism. After three years of pointless violence, the British withdrew in a carefully planned operation, leaving Yemen to endure years of instability and to become a cockpit of international terrorism.

This book is an account of the British military presence in Aden between 1839 and 1967 and is designed to be a companion to other books that I have written on British military campaigns between 1945 and 1990. The work is not a researched history but a collation of information from those 'who were there' and from existing books, publications and pamphlets.

I am indebted to a number of people for their encouragement and helpfulness: to Alex Taylor, the Editor of *The Dhow*, the Middle East Command Service newsletter and now the Journal of the Aden Veterans Association; to the Aden Veterans Association; to Brigadier Richard Mountford, who served with the Royal Horse Artillery in Aden, for his provision of a mass of valuable information and photographs; to Colonel Nicholas Beard for his account of the ambush on the Royal Corps of Transport on 20 June 1967; to Major David Riddick and Jim Carroll for their recollections of serving with the Royal Northumberland Fusiliers, with particular reference to the events of 20 June 1967; to Rod Leonard, who served with 3rd Royal Anglians and Brian Downey, who served with 45 Commando; to Ray Deacon for helping with RAF matters, in particular 8

Squadron 'Aden's Own'; to Lieutenant Colonel David Pepperell, who served with the Royal Army Service/Royal Corps of Transport; to Ray England for his assistance with SAS operations in Radfan; to Jenny Hill (née Wileman) for describing her role at HQ Middle East Command with the Women's Royal Army Corps; and to Cliff Lord, who filled in the considerable gaps in my knowledge of the Aden Protectorate Levies and Federal Armed Forces.

Museum and military archives are crucial to the maintenance and development of naval and military history. Captain J.M. Holtby AMA, Curator, the Queen's Royal Lancers & Nottinghamshire Yeomanry Museum, provided information on the 16/5th Lancers. I also owe thanks to Graham Dyson, Assistant Curator the Prince of Wales Own Regiment of Yorkshire Museum and Archive, and to Lesley Frater, Museum Administrator, Fusiliers Museum of Northumberland.

In relation to photographs, Brigadier Mountford and Brian Harrington Spier, who served with 3rd Royal Anglians, permitted me access to fascinating photographs of Aden then and recently. Others have given me photographs that have lacked any sort of copyright trail and therefore I am uncertain about their origins. As always, I would be pleased to hear from anyone who can help, for future reference in the event of a reprint.

I am indebted to George Chamier, who was insistent, patient and inquisitive during the crucial editing process – for the second time. Brigadier Henry Wilson and Matt Jones at Pen & Sword Military Books, were, as always, invaluable for their encouragement and administration during the final production. Peter Wood, of GWR, who served in Aden with a Royal Engineer topographical squadron, has again produced the maps. John Noble, former Royal Navy, who flew home from Aden in 1963 at low level in a Beverley, has again produced an exhaustive index.

As always, my wife Penny has proven a rock of patience and understanding throughout this, and other projects, by proofreading. The wonders of e-mail also saw our daughter, Imogen, contribute from her flats in Khartoum and Beirut.

Nick van der Bijl
March 2014

THE FEDERATION OF SOUTH ARABIA

RADFAN OPERATIONAL AREA

Legend:
- 1914 Boundary Line
- 1934 Treaty Line
- Undemarcated
- State Boundary
- Protectorate Boundary
- Roads

Created by Peter F Wood, FRGS, FBCartS

Kms 0   100   200   300   400 Kms

ADEN AND THE PROTECTORATES

Created by Peter F Wood, FRGS, FBCartS

Kuria Muria Is.

MUSCAT AND OMAN

EASTERN ADEN PROTECTORATE

Qishn

HADHRAMAUT

Al Riyan
Al Mukalla

WAHIDI

SAUDI ARABIA

YEMEN

SA'ANA

Harib

BEIHAN

UPPER AULAQI

LOWER AULAQI

Ahwar

DATHINA

WESTERN ADEN PROTECTORATE
(The Federation of South Africa)

UPPER AUDHALI

FADHLI

Zinjibar

LOWER YAFA

UPPER YAFA

SHAIB

DHALA

Lahej

ADEN

MAFLAHI

ALOWI

HAUSHEBI

LAHEJ

Karmaran I.

Hodeida

RED SEA

Perim I.

DJOUBUTI

FRENCH SOMALILAND

ERITREA

SOMALILAND PROTECTORATE

SOMALIA

Berbera

ETHIOPIA

ADEN

GULF

OF

Socotra

N

Kms 0   100   200   300 Kms

RADFAN

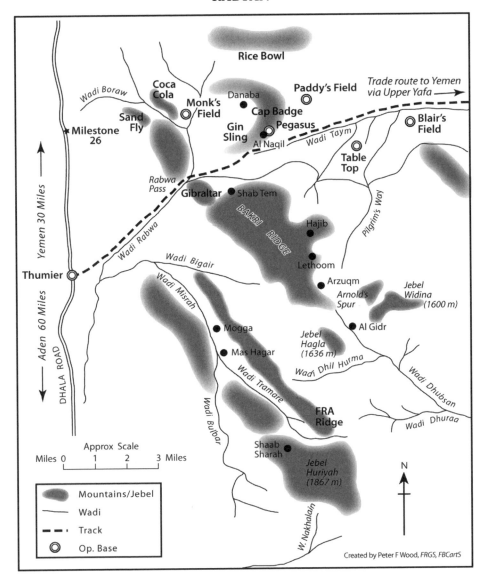

Rice Bowl

Coca Cola

Wadi Boraw

Danaba

Paddy's Field

Trade route to Yemen via Upper Yafa →

Monk's Field

Sand Fly

Milestone 26

Cap Badge

Gin Sling

Pegasus

Al Naqil

Wadi Taym

Blair's Field

Table Top

Yemen 30 Miles

Rabwa Pass

Gibraltar

Shab Tem

BAKRI RIDGE

Hajib

Pilgrim's Way

Wadi Rabwa

Wadi Bigair

Lethoom

Thumier

Wadi Misrah

Arzuqm

Arnold's Spur

Jebel Widina (1600 m)

Aden 60 Miles

DHALA ROAD

Mogga

Al Gidr

Jebel Hagla (1636 m)

Mas Hagar

Wadi Tramare

Wadi Dhil Hurma

Wadi Dhubsan

Wadi Bulbar

FRA Ridge

Wadi Dhuraa

Approx Scale

Miles 0   1   2   3 Miles

Shaab Sharah

Jebel Huriyah (1867 m)

N

W. Nakhalain

	Mountains/Jebel
	Wadi
	Track
◎	Op. Base

Created by Peter F Wood, *FRGS, FBCartS*

CRATER

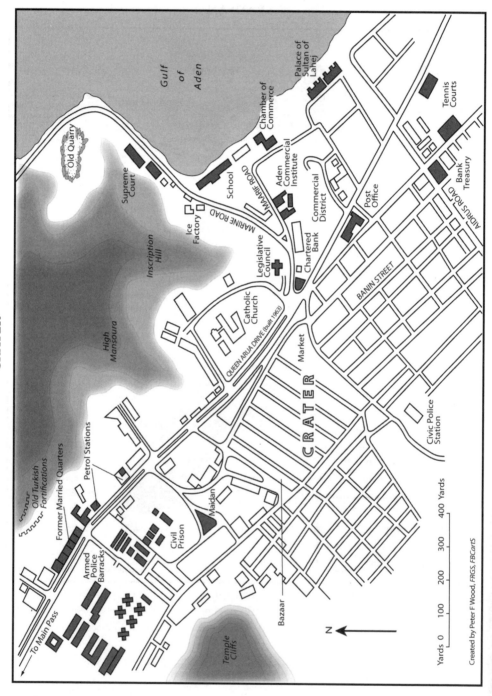

Created by Peter F Wood, FRGS, FBCartS

CHAPTER ONE

The Annexation of Aden

L ocated 100 miles to the east of the Straits of Mandeb linking the Red Sea and the Indian Ocean is a south-facing inlet protected by two headlands that are overlooked by a partly collapsed volcano, leaving the remaining cliffs to contain the desert heat.

When Lieutenant Stafford Bettesworth Haines of the Indian Naval Service, surveying the East African and South Arabian coasts, first saw the inlet of Aden in 1819, he found several hundred Arabs, Somalis, Jews and Indians living in reed huts dotted in the once prosperous town and surviving from piracy, but at risk from raids by desert tribes. He described the place that had once been known as the 'eye of the Yemen':

> The little village (formerly the great city) of Aden is now reduced to the most exigent condition of poverty and neglect. In the reign of Constantine, this town possessed unrivalled celebrity for its impenetrable fortifications, its flourishing commerce, and the glorious haven it offered to vessels from all quarters of the globe. But how lamentable is the present contrast! With scarce a vestige of its former proud superiority, the traveller values it only for its capabilities, and regrets the barbarous cupidity of that government under whose injudicious management it has fallen so low.

Known in the first century as Eudaemon and described as 'a village by the shore', its harbour later became a focal point for pilgrims using the road north to Mecca and for camel caravans transporting spices, frankincense and perfumes from East Africa, South East Asia and India to Europe. Christian Abyssinia governed the area between the fourth and early sixth centuries until it was ruled for three hundred years from the seventh century by Islamic caliphs in Damascus and Baghdad. A powerful influence in the area that became known as South Arabia was the religion practised by the Zaidi branch of the Shi'ite sect, electing their Imams for their knowledge of

Islamic scholarship and proven skill in diplomatic and military leadership. Sixteen years after the Portuguese had opened up the Indian Ocean by navigating around the Cape of Good Hope in 1497, the Portuguese diplomat Alfonso d'Albuquerque, en route to Goa, recognized the strategic value of Aden and also landed on Perim Island at the mouth of the Red Sea. Perim is three and a half miles long by two and three-quarter miles wide, with a maximum altitude of 65 metres. The absence of fresh water prevented permanent settlement, except for a fishing hamlet on the southern coast. Vegetation is scarce.

The Italian traveller Ludovico di Varthema, the first European to enter Mecca as a pilgrim, wrote in the early sixteenth century:

> Aden is such mighty and powerful that I have hardly seen another city of its might during my life . . . all big ships anchor at the port coming from India, Ethiopia or Persia.

The Ottoman armies that conquered Egypt in 1517 and annexed South Arabia twenty years later used Aden as a base for raids against Portuguese enclaves in India and defended the harbour with forts and artillery.

During the fourth voyage of the East India Company in 1609, a storm separated Captain Alexander Sharpaigh, commanding the *Ascension*, from a pinnace off the African coast. A Gujerati ship guided Sharpaigh to Aden, and while he was waiting for the pinnace, a merchant on board named John Jourdain travelled to the coffee trade centre at Mocha and recommended trading with the town. He did not favour Aden because merchant ships did not call there.

As the British expanded their influence in India during the eighteenth century, passengers could take a ship to Alexandria in Egypt, travel overland to Suez and board ships for the onward voyage. During the Napoleonic Wars, Perim was occupied by an East India Company garrison after the Battle of the Nile, to deter the French from sending troops from Egypt to India. In 1802, Sir Home Popham negotiated a treaty with the Sultan of Lahej, in whose domain Aden was, to cede the settlement, but nothing was agreed with the ruling Zaidi Imam.

By the time that the British required coaling stations for steamships sailing to India, Sir Robert Grant was Governor of Bombay, a Liberal with expansionist ideas that suited the imperial, commercial and industrial ambitions of Great Britain. The Bombay Presidency, one of the three East India Company Presidencies, stretched from western and central India and modern Pakistan to the Arabian Peninsula. Captain Haines, who had been involved in negotiating the use of Socotra, a small archipelago 150 miles east of the Horn of Africa, also recommended using Aden. A reason was now needed to annex it.

In January 1837, the merchantman *Doria Dowllitt*, which was owned by the Nawab of the Carnatic and licensed in Madras, was beached and then plundered by the local villagers; they had also refused to rescue survivors, robbed those who reached land and subjected several women on pilgrimage to Mecca to suffer 'brutal and shameful indignataries'. Although substantially over-insured, the ship was sailing under the Union Flag and it was this that gave the Bombay Presidency a reason to demand Aden as compensation from the Sultan. In negotiations with Haines, in December, the Sultan agreed to cede 75 square miles in compensation, including the inlet.

In October 1838, Haines returned in his ship, the *Coote*, to take formal possession and was being rowed ashore with Lieutenant Western of the Indian Engineers, who was tasked to assess the fortifications, when they came under small-arms fire. After exchanges of cannon fire between a fort and the ship and letters to and from the Sultan, it emerged that his son and several minor sheikhs opposed the agreement, to the extent that, in mid-January, Haines learnt the son planned to kidnap him. This threat, and concerns that the Ottoman governor of Egypt might seize Aden, led to the Presidency hurriedly assembling a fleet that by mid-January 1839 was hovering off Aden with orders to seize the settlement. Its strength was as follows:

Naval forces (Captain J.H. Smith)
• East India Company 3-gun Indian Navy schooner *Mahi*
• Mortar-boat *Chaki*
• Barque *Anne Crichton*
• 28-gun sixth rate HMS *Volage* commanded by Lieutenant Patrick Campbell
• 18-gun sloop HMS *Cruizer*
• The transports *Lowjee Family and Ernaad*

Landing Force (Major T.M. Baillee (24th Bombay Native Infantry Regiment)
• 350 sepoys of the 24th (Bombay) Regiment
• 4th Company, 1st Battalion Artillery
• 6th Company, Golundauze Artillery with ten coastal artillery guns

Intelligence indicated that the defence forces consisted of about 1,000 Arabs deployed in the Turkish forts along the volcanic rim of the crater and Sirah

Island. After the defenders rejected a call to surrender on 19 January at 9.30 am, HMS *Volage* silenced a battery on the island within half an hour. HMS *Cruizer* bombarded the forts, and then both ships reduced a 60ft watchtower to rubble. Shortly after 11am, a landing force commanded by Major Baillee in rowing boats beached north of Sirah Island and within two hours had defeated the Arabs, at the cost of five soldiers killed and ten wounded, most during a disagreement about the disarming of prisoners. Great Britain had gained its first colony in the reign of Queen Victoria.

Appointed by Bombay to govern Aden Settlement as Political Agent, over the next eighteen months Haines defeated several attacks by the Amir of Dhala, in one instance, in 1841, by counter-attacking a coalition of sheikhs blockading the water supply from the oasis of Sheikh Othman and then negotiating a peace treaty. The threat from the north led to one of the two British battalions that rotated annually in India being posted to Aden for a year before it returned to Britain, usually in February. This rotation lasted until 1914, and then again from 1919 to 1928. Aden lacked the lure of India and was an unpopular posting. The other battalion went to the settlement of Singapore.

In 1877, in his detailed *The British Settlement of Aden in Arabia,* Captain F.M. Hunter of the Bombay Staff Corps and Assistant Political Resident wrote:

Aden is a peninsula situated on the south coast of the Province of Yemen in Arabia Felix. The British territory includes the peninsula and extends to a creek named Khor Maksar, about two miles to the northward of (the Turkish) defensive works across the Isthmus. The adjoining peninsula of Jebel Ihsan, generally called Little Aden, is within British limits, as is also the harbour. The area of the land may be approximately stated at about thirty-five square miles. The inhabited peninsula is about fifteen miles in circumference of an irregular oval form, five miles in its greater and three in its lesser diameter; it is connected with the continent by a narrow neck of land 1,350 yards in breadth, but which is in one place nearly covered by the sea at high spring-tides.

Aden is a large crater formed of precipitous hills, the highest peak of which has an altitude of 1,775-feet; these, on the exterior sides, slope towards the sea, throwing out numerous spurs, which form a series of valleys, radiating from a common centre. A gap exists opposite the fortified island of Seerah, the position of which would induce the belief that the circle was at one time complete, but that some convulsion of nature produced the gap. Aden West Bay, more generally known as Aden Back Bay, is formed by the peninsula of Jebel Ishsan on the west and Jebel Shum Shum on the east. It is about eight miles broad from east to west, by four miles deep; and is divided into two bays by a spit, which runs off half a mile to the southward of the small island of Aliyah: the entrance between Ras Salil on the west and Ras Tarshyne on the east is three and a third miles in width. The depths of water in the Western Bay are from three to four fathoms, decreasing gradually towards the shore, across the entrance the depths are four and a half to five fathoms, and at a distance of two miles outside ten to twelve fathoms; bottom, sand and mud, both inside and outside the bay. There are several islands in the bay.

The climate during the north-east monsoon, or from October to April, is cool, and in the months of November, December, and January, pleasant and agreeable. During the remainder of the year hot sandy winds, known as 'Shamal' or north, indicating the direction from which they come, prevail within the crater; but on the western, or Steamer Point side, the breezes coming directly off the sea are fairly cool, and that locality is accordingly much preferred by European residents. The months of May and September are especially disagreeable, those being the periods of the change of monsoons, when the wind almost entirely ceases, and the air is close and oppressive, more particularly during the earlier part of the night: towards morning a cool and refreshing land breeze generally springs up. The vegetation of Aden closely resembles that of Arabia Petrasa; it is eminently of a desert character, the species being few in number. Some of the remains of its former magnificence are still visible in the ruins of the forts which crown every summit and the far-famed tanks.

Haines was largely left to govern as he saw fit, because those in London and Bombay who had supported Aden's annexation had been replaced by others less convinced of its value, particularly in India, where the focus was on the consequences of catastrophic defeats in Afghanistan in 1841. With a romantic vision of restoring Aden to its former glory, Haines immersed himself in its politics and that of the hinterland. He enjoyed the reputation of being approachable, recruiting his administration from Indians, destabilizing opposition by offering bribes and creating an efficient intelligence network using Jews. Within about seven years, the population had grown to 25,000 living in a modern town in which Haines had offered advantageous rents to those agreeing to build in stone. Shipping was focused at Steamer Point, where three steam condensers and an aqueduct from Sheikh Othman supplied water. The district in the volcanic throat became the commercial centre, known as Crater.

But Haines' repeated requests for experienced auditors were ignored, and while his commitment was crucial, his fatal flaw was that in an age of patronage, he had none. Thus, when auditors eventually arrived and found a deficit of £28,000 in the Treasury, he was recalled to Bombay in February 1854 to answer charges of fraud. He was acquitted, but Governor Lord John Elphinstone demanded immediate repayment and when Haines refused to surrender his property and offered his salary instead, Elphinstone rejected it and confined him to a debtor's jail. Haines was freed six years later by the new governor; however, his health was ruined and he died on the day that he was released, on board the ship taking him to England. Meanwhile, Haines's vision was vindicated when telegraph cables linking Britain to India were routed through the Settlement in 1855.

CHAPTER TWO

The Settlement of Aden
1854–1914

A succession of Army officers followed Captain Haines as Resident. When relations with rulers to the north deteriorated, Colonel W. Coghlan (1856–62) raised a camel troop to patrol the Settlement border south of Sheikh Othman, collect intelligence within forty miles and map the hinterland, although his Arab cameleers did not take to military discipline. The Bombay Presidency then raised a troop from three Indian cavalry regiments, but it was first diverted to accompany the British military expedition to Persia in 1856 and was then involved in the 1857 Indian Mutiny. This became known as the Aden Troop. When in March 1858 the Sultan of Lehaj intercepted a diplomatic column conveying the Imam to meet Coghlan, the Resident ignored orders from Bombay not to deploy outside the Settlement and defeated an Arab force at Sheikh Othman. In December 1865, a force punished the Fadhlis after they had plundered a caravan near the oasis by attacking their coastal capital at Shugra. When the Fadhlis then massacred the crew of a dhow under British protection, their capital was attacked again.

Perim Island was added to the Settlement in January 1857, and the Khuriya Muriya Islands eleven years later. Most of the 300 people living on the islands were employed by the Perim Coal Company, protected by an outpost of 50 soldiers. Water was initially delivered from Aden until a reservoir was built in 1861 to collect rain and a condenser installed to produce distilled water. Meanwhile, the Suez Canal was being dug, and the consequent increase of shipping passing through the Red Sea prompted the Bombay Presidency to build a 38ft-high, dark blue lighthouse south-west of Obstruction Point. It was raised to 81ft in 1912 and could be seen for 22 miles in clear weather. In 1858, the French Navy revolutionized naval warfare by launching the steam ironclad *La Gloire* at Cherbourg and, at a stroke, won the strategic naval balance in the English Channel. Prime Minister Lord Palmerston immediately ordered a chain of forts be built to defend Great

Britain and her empire overseas. At the same time, the British were also developing rifled breech loading artillery that extended range and accuracy. Three options therefore emerged for Perim:

1. A 'Cronstadt' redoubt. Cronstadt was an island covering the approaches to St Petersburg captured by the Russians from the Swedes in 1703 and converted by Peter the Great into a fortress.

2. Colonel Coghlan and Major General Waddington, Chief Engineer in Bombay, proposed a second fort to cover the harbour. Coghlan proposed it should be circular and above Lang Point, equipped with six guns, three of which could be brought to bear on any target, and that the garrison accommodation should be below ground level to take advantage of shade and cool temperatures.

3. A small fort to prevent pirates from Africa destroying the lighthouse.

Although the third option was the one agreed, the Chief Engineer in Aden appeared unwilling to prepare a design that included artillery. Ten years later, the designer of the 'Palmerston's Follies', Colonel Sir William Jervois (late Royal Engineers), reviewed forts on his way to take up office as Governor of the Straits Settlement (Penang, Malacca and Singapore); he recommended that Perim should have a small circular fort with iron shields acting as embrasures for 10-inch rifled muzzle-loaded guns. Lieutenant King, the OC Outpost during the visit, challenged the suggestion on the grounds that there would no room for the garrison to live in so small a fort and the barracks needed for the gunners would be exposed. His belief was:

The only land approach to it being via a very circuitous route round the harbour where there is at present no road . . . The hill on which the present lighthouse stands must always be the chief military post on the island as this is the position from which the best command of observation is obtainable and from which one can most easily communicate by signals with passing steamers.

King concluded that two artillery detachments would be required. In the event, a second fort was not built.

In late January 1869, the officer of the watch on a French Messageries Imperiales Line steamer passing Perim saw signal flags flying from the fort:

'Short of Provisions'. An officer sent ashore with biscuits, cheese, pale ale and port returned with a despatch to Major General Sir Edward Russell, the Resident (1867–1870), from Lieutenant Davie, the Outpost commander, that the garrison was short of *dhal* (Indian pigeon-pea puree), *ghee* (clarified butter) and beef. Less than amused, because of Anglo-French rivalry, and embarrassed that Davie had accepted help from a French ship, Russell ordered that supplies be sent without delay and then reprimanded Davie, requiring him to refund the costs from his own pocket. However, an inquiry by the Aden Garrison Commissariat noted that Davie's signal had been 'short of' and not 'out of' and that the contract to supply three months provisions due for renewal on 31 December had not been signed because of a long-running disagreement with the contractor.

When Captain Hunter wrote his *British Settlement of Aden in Arabia*, the Suez Canal had opened (in 1869) and the Settlement had expanded into streets of characterless white-washed stone and mud houses, many two-storey, and cantonments of wooden bungalows of a type regularly seen in India. Major W.L. Merewether (1863–1870) raised the Aden Levy in 1867 from the three Indian regiments on the understanding that it would be used only to defend Aden from its base at Khormaksar. Immigration from Yemen increased during the early 1870s as refugees fled Ottoman rule and others sought employment. Crater remained the focal point, buildings of note including the Courthouse, the Treasury, the Protestant Church and the two barracks housing the British and Indian regiments. The Roman Catholic Good Shepherd Convent sheltered freed slave girls. The department store Muncherjee Eduljee competed with shopkeepers selling cloth, grain, confectionery, groceries, and with general dealers and water-sellers. The Government commissariat monopolised slaughterhouses. A few businesses trading with ships had licences from the Conservator of the Port and a Government Steam Bakery to undercut commercial bakers. Jewellers and bookbinders were mostly Jews. The Indian community generally provided blacksmiths, carpenters, masons, mechanics, cobblers and tailors. While wealthy Arabs traded in coffee, others were boat-builders, water-carriers and occupied in the lucrative industry of lime-burning to make mortar, plaster and paint. Arab and Somali women sold cakes, bread, cups of buttermilk (*katib*) and sweetmeats. Somali women were also renowned for their reed mats. Africans from East Africa were labourers and coal-coolies. Usually single men, they ate in cook-shops and slept in coffee-shops or the open. Road sweepers were generally low caste Indians and outcast Arabs. Hunter observed that in spite of their 'small size in stature, and not [being] very powerfully built', Jews and Arabs were generally porters of luggage and consignments. Day labourers, including children, were employed in construction, road-making and much other unskilled labour. Hunter continues:

> There were a few houses in the higher parts of the Colony to take advantage of cool breezes during the summer. A tunnel led from Crater into the Isthmus position. To the north lies the Main Pass through which the harbour is reached with a steep hill forming the approach to this entrance on the town side. On the harbour side was a considerable decline of Z-bends before sea-level is reached and the road turns in a westerly direction. About half a mile from the foot of the Main Pass lies the village of Ma'alla, which consisted partly of stone houses and partly of mat huts occupied by Somalis. A pier runs from the foreshore. There is also a Custom House.

Steamer Point was a crescent of two- and three-storey private houses occupied by comparatively wealthy English, American, German, French, Italian, and Indian businessmen and agents for shipping companies; there were also two hotels, a police station, a post office and several consulates. Most households had butlers, gardeners and carriage drivers. Indian domestic servants commanded higher wages, and many of the cooks and nannies were the wives and camp followers of Indian soldiers. Public carriage-drivers were licensed but the trade had been monopolized by several Somali families who saw off competitors. Donkeys were hired for recreational riding. Above the crescent were a barracks, the Turkish Fort Morbut and, at Ras Tarashyne, the Residency and the Royal Artillery Officers Mess. On the foreshore of Aden Bay were coal bunkers, a covered jetty and offices of the shipping companies. Most regional commerce was conducted by Arab and Indian businesses trading in livestock, dates, rice and cloth, with the fair winds between October and May regarded as the trading season. Hunter noted that the British regime was so relaxed that Arab and Somali hawkers and brokers took every opportunity to indulge in chicanery.

When investigating sources of water north of Khormaksar, Major Walter Ducat RE noted low-lying desert and scrub that extended to Sheikh Othman and skirted the foreshore and the coastline eastward in a belt of varying thickness, sometimes running right up into the sand-drift, at others only a few hundred yards from the coast. Ducat wrote:

> The water, which is to be met with at a depth below the surface varying from three feet to about eighteen feet throughout this tract, is

directly influenced by the rise and fall of tide; and is, of course, brackish to a degree, being in fact almost, if not quite, simple sea-water. Between this salt belt and the hills is an alluvial plain falling from the hills towards the sea, with a slope near the foot of the hills of about thirty feet in a mile, easing off to about seventeen feet in a mile, till it reaches the salt belt, which is very nearly dead level. Throughout this alluvial tract of country a slightly brackish, but drinkable water, is met with at a depth of sixty to seventy feet. The water-bearing stratum seems nearly parallel to the surface of the soil when the latter has fairly taken its incline after leaving the coast. The soil of this part of the country is composed of sandy clay, very retentive of moisture, and capable of high cultivation.

Numerous wells under official control at the heads of the valleys in Crater and to the west of the town dug to a depth of between 120ft and 190ft supplied good quality water. The sweetest water was extracted from the Banian Well near the Khussaf Valley. Outside British control, water from the Sheikh Othman well and from the northern shore of the harbour was carried in leather skins. In 1867, the Sultan of Lahej agreed to the construction of a seven-mile aqueduct from the oasis wells to reservoirs.

The opening of the Suez Canal in November 1869 led to the Ottoman Empire claiming South Arabia and then declaring Sana'a to be the capital of Yemen Province. But garrison life was so grim that Anatolian folklore suggested a soldier posted to Yemen was as good as dead. When Turkish forces threatened Lahej in 1872, British and Indian troops marched to the area the next year to deter a weak incursion. When ships loaded with Turkish troops entered several ports, including Aden, the Royal Navy proved to be a regional deterrent.

A total of 651 soldiers from the 14th Foot (West Yorkshires) and 165 accompanying dependants relieved the 56th Foot (Essex Regiment) as the garrison in 1878. Formed in 1685, the 14th had fought in the Napoleonic Wars, India, the Crimean War, the Maori Wars in New Zealand and, most recently, the Second Afghan War (1878–1880). London and Bombay regarded Aden as important to the security of imperial interests in the western Indian Ocean and Persian Gulf, and even though the prospect faded of converting its port into a prosperous commercial venture on a par with Singapore, the Settlement was converted into Fortress Aden, with four 9-inch guns guarding the port, while defence treaties with nine rulers to the north acted as a buffer from incursions. The oasis of Sheikh Othman was purchased from the Sultan of Lehaj in 1881.

In 1882, the 22nd Bombay Infantry Regiment was the first Indian unit to reinforce the garrison on yearly rotations. At about 30 officers and 723 other ranks, with companies segregated by tribe, caste and religion, Indian regiments were smaller than British battalions of 29 officers and 970 other ranks. The Indians were generally organized into four double rifle companies, each numbering 190 all ranks and twice the size of a British company. Since battalions seldom had more than ten British officers, companies were also commanded by Indians. When the 2nd East Yorkshires arrived in 1888, Lieutenant Wilson was appointed as the first aide-de-camp to the Resident; and, as was becoming common, well educated soldiers were employed in the Colonial administration. The Duke of York's Own, as it was sometimes known, was formed in 1685 and, as the 15th Foot, had fought in the War of the Spanish Succession, the Seven Years War, the American War of Independence, the Napoleonic Wars and two campaigns in Afghanistan. On leaving Aden after a year, it handed over to another Yorkshire regiment, the 1st West Ridings (later known as the Duke of Wellington's Regiment). In 1895, the 2nd West Yorkshires spent a year in Aden.

In 1891, the Hamid al-Din family succeeded in gaining the Imamate in Yemen and expanded their influence to become a near-feudal monarchy and although Islam was revitalized, the failure to trade with Aden and other outlets meant that Yemen remained politically and economically backward. In mid-1900, hostile Haushebi tribesmen crossed the border and built two forts near the village of Ad Dareja astride the principal caravan route. The Resident, Brigadier General O'Moore Creagh (1899–1901) despatched an official, Mr G. Wyman Bury, to the area, and he discovered that they had been built by a sultan, Muhammad Nasir Muqbil, on land that, according to a British Survey map, was British. The Turks persuaded him to return to Yemen; nevertheless, by December, the sultan had returned to Ad Dareja, with about 175 Turkish troops and more across the border. The Resident, Brigadier General Pelham Maitland CB DSO (1901–1904), who had been a member of the Afghan Boundary Commission and was one of several Army officers experienced in negotiating borders, attempted diplomacy on 27 June, but it failed. On 14 July, therefore, he formed a column from the 1st Royal East Kents (The Buffs), 5th (Bombay) Light Infantry, a half-company of 4th Bombay Sappers and Miners, twenty Aden Troop, thirty horsemen and a similar number of camel sowars (cavalry) supplied by the Sultan of Lahej and six screw guns manned by No. 16 Company, Royal Garrison Artillery. The new 10-pounder pack gun, or 2.75-inch mountain gun, was known as the screw gun because the barrel consisted of two 3ft tubes that screwed together. It could be dismantled into six horse-loads and brought back into action within two minutes. Mainly used on the North West Frontier, it had a range of 6,000 yards, and since the shells used cordite as a propellant, the risk of the gun position being identified was lessened. The Royal Garrison Artillery (RGA) had responsibility for fortress and coastal artillery, large calibre guns and howitzers, mountain artillery and the land-based Royal Marines Artillery.

The column concentrated at Sheikh Othman but delays were experienced because of the need to purchase more camels and the Buffs' commanding officer collapsing from heat exhaustion. Maitland instructed Major Rowe, the Buffs' second-in-command, to take over, but the planned seven-day approach march stretched to eleven days as the midsummer heat, the sand and the unfitness of the troops took their toll. Nevertheless, on 26 July, the column destroyed both forts at the cost of four killed and five wounded. Interestingly, the Buffs complained of the unsuitability of leather boots and recommended that British battalions should acclimatize with route marches into the desert.

By October, Great Britain and the Ottoman Empire had agreed to Border Commissions of surveyors with escorts of no more than 200 troops; but at the first meeting in February 1902 at Dhala, the Turks adopted a hardline approach by surrounding the British camp on three sides, harassed the survey parties and strengthened their garrison at Qataba with men and artillery. In 1903, Maitland formed the Aden Movable Column as a flying column out of British reinforcements from India and sent it to Norbat Dakim. His 2,200 troops on the border and 1,400 in Fortress Aden outnumbered the Turks on the border but could not match the 30,000-strong VII (Yemen) Corps, then tied down by another Zaidi insurrection. Meanwhile, Bengal Sappers and Miners improved the road from Aden and laid a field telegraph. Diplomatic protests in Constantinople induced the Turks to withdraw to Qataba in March; nevertheless, the Aden Movable Column remained on the border training the retinues of the rulers and punishing tribesmen from the bleak Radfan volcanic mountains and deep wadis who raided the Dahla Road.

As the weather cooled in September, the Commissions started surveying the border of the state of Shaib. Although an Indian surveyor was shot near Rubiatain, British surveyors, protected by the 1st Hampshires, crossed Wadi Bana to survey high ground and when, on 12 September, heliograph signals reported that 1,000 Yafa'is had crossed into Shaib, they were intercepted at the cost of a private killed and four wounded. The dispute was resolved and, on 11 October, the first boundary pillar agreed. When the Nobat Dakim base and lines of communication were attacked by the Quatabi from Radfan, Maitland ordered the first punitive expedition to the area at the cost of nine killed, twenty-one wounded and the destruction of the village of Nakhlain.

By 1904, boundary pillars marked the border in the State of Dhala and good progress had been made in Haushebi territory. Anxiety in the State of Shaib led to Maitland reinforcing the Boundary Commission with the Shaib Column of 600 British and Indian infantry and two screw guns. Concerns about a watchtower overlooking the State of Maflahi were resolved by 6 Mountain Battery shelling it. Within the year, the border had reached Shaikh Said on the Red Sea, where the Turks had a fort at Turba, but the negotiations had cost ten soldiers killed and twenty-five wounded in skirmishes and ambushes, as well as thirty-four non-battle fatalities. Guarding the border were 1,640 infantry, eight mountain guns, forty-five sappers and 130 troopers in garrisons.

Zaidi opposition was a persistent threat to the Ottoman occupation in Yemen, and although revolts had been crushed in 1872 and 1892, another broke out in December 1904 after successive poor harvests. When Turkish reinforcements from Middle East provinces began arriving at Hodieda, intelligence reports suggested two battalions had refused to embark because they had not been paid for a year. The provincial capital of Sana'a was then besieged.

When unease emerged in Radfan, in mid-February 1905, Captain Howard Jacob, the Acting Political Resident at Dhala, tried to send a heliograph message to Aden that the Imam's forces were within six hours of Qataba and that the Turkish District Officer was seeking sanctuary in Aden, but poor weather intervened. Commissioned into the Army in 1887, and married to a daughter of Lieutenant Colonel Hunter, Jacob had spent most of his career in the Indian Political Service, mostly in South Arabia. Fluent in Arabic, he used his knowledge of the Koran when dealing with Arab officials and complainants. When a despatch rider delivered his message, the Resident, Major General Harry Mason (1904–1906), advised him instructions from India were that any Turk crossing the border was to be detained but that this did not apply to Royalists seeking sanctuary. When Jacob learnt that the Imam intended to cross the border and that Mason proposed to withdraw two of the four guns from Dhala, he urged that more guns to be sent, a notion that Mason rejected because he wanted to maintain a stance of neutrality.

When the British Embassy in Constantinople reported that the Turkish reinforcements being sent overland from Syria were being hindered by drought and a high mortality rate amongst camels and donkeys, and that ships were being considered to transfer brigades from Central Europe, London warned Turkey that it would defend the border and despatched two cruisers to Aden. Although delayed in Aqaba by discontented soldiers, the Yemen Commander-in-Chief designate, General Ali Riza Pasha, arrived from Libya and disembarked at Hoideda in early March. Two days later, he set off to relieve Sana'a with 6,000 men divided into seven infantry battalions and eight mountain batteries. But after a 10-day march, he reached the city with a force crippled by desertion because of lack of supplies, unfamiliarity with their Mauser rifles and sympathy with the Iman. Sana'a surrendered to Royalist forces in mid-April and Riza agreed a one-year armistice.

When Jacob learnt from a Turkish district officer that Sana'a had fallen and that Royalist forces were approaching Qataba, General Mason returned the two guns to Dhala, requested an Indian battalion as reinforcements and instructed the Dhala Local Defence Committee to erect field defences. He rejected a suggestion from Jacob that he personally warn the Imam against any ambitions he might have on Aden, but authorized him to write to the Iman. He also reminded Jacob that commanders on the spot would decide operational responses. Meanwhile, Colonel Mansell, the British Military Attaché in Constantinople, reported that some Turkish officers believed the Imam should be bought off and Yemen given up to enable Turkey to preserve the security of its Central European border. Instead, Marshal Ahmed Fezi Pasha, the commander of IV Corps in Baghdad and with thirty years experience of Yemen, during which he had quelled a Royalist revolt with considerable severity, was appointed to command VII (Yemen) Corps.

In mid-May 1905, Mason informed India that the Qataba district officer was seeking sanctuary in Aden and since Jacob had reported that Royalist forces were a day's march from the town, a 3rd Rifle Brigade platoon had been sent to Sanah to reinforce the border. Jacob learnt from the Qataba garrison commander that his force consisted of a mix of about 500 Turks and Syrians but he was censured by Mason for crossing the border without authority. By the first week of June, 19,000 Turkish reinforcements, mostly Albanian and Anatolian reservists, were suffering from typhoid, dysentery and heatstroke. Brigadier General Mason left Aden on sick leave in early July and was replaced by his deputy, Colonel Scallon, as Acting Political Resident. India agreed that two Turkish officers could purchase food for the Qataba garrison and added that any such request from the Royalists was to be rejected, a principle that Jacob strongly believed to be a breach of the policy of neutrality.

After waiting for animal transport, in mid-July, Marshal Feizi advanced toward Sana'a in three columns at the head of eight Albanian battalions from Menakha. When his line of communications to Hodeida was cut, he turned about and stormed the Royalist position. Meanwhile, forty-five of seventy Yemeni dissidents exiled to Rhodes arrived at Hodeida after offering to use their influence to end the rebellion. While the Imam indicated that he favoured a settlement, several Royalist leaders rejected the proposal. The assassination of about twenty saw these objections disappear. In mid-August, sheikhs governing land astride the road from Menakha to Sana'a switched sides, and a fortnight later, Feizi recaptured the city and ended the rebellion. Lieutenant Colonel Mansell reported that 68 battalions had been sent to reinforce the 32 battalions of VII (Yemen) Corps that now numbered 110,000 troops. Turkish casualties he estimated to be about 27,500. Nevertheless, intelligence about the Corps order of battle and its combat efficiency was sparse until Lieutenant Colonel Arthur Solly Flood, during a visit from the War Office to the Boundary Commission in 1911, was impressed by their quality, despite their isolation by the vast desert to the north. It consisted of the 39th and 40th Infantry Divisions, both of which had reformed in 1908 after the Balkan War. The 39th Infantry Division covering the Taiz Operational Region consisted of:

- 115, 116, 117, 119 and 120 Infantry Regiments.
- About half of 26 Cavalry Regiment.
- 7 Model Regiment of Arab irregulars.
- An artillery component of thirty-eight guns of varying types.

An Overseas Defence Committee in 1907 assessed the naval threat to Fortress Aden as bombardment by three light cruisers. By 1912, this was escalated to the German China Squadron of five cruisers entering the Indian Ocean from the Pacific. As a result, four coastal 10-inch rifled muzzle-loaders were replaced by two modern 6-inch breech-loading guns on the Steamer Point battery controlled by Fire Command at Ras Tarshyne. Plans were drawn up to replace eight obsolete 10-inch guns at the Fort Morbut Battery, where 61, 70 and 76 Companies, RGA manned the artillery. Howard Jacob was promoted Lieutenant Colonel in 1913 and became the Chief Political Officer to the Aden Field Force in the event of war.

CHAPTER THREE

Aden in the First World War

When war broke out in Europe on 4 August 1914, Aden became an important strategic lynchpin in lines of communication between India and Europe. Aden Field Force consisted of 1st Royal Irish Rifles, until the battalion was recalled to Great Britain and replaced by a company of the 1st Lancashire Fusiliers, then based in Karachi, and 109th Infantry Regiment. In command was Brigadier General David Shaw. Commissioned into the 67th Regiment (South Hampshire Regiment), he had transferred to the Punjab Cavalry in 1884 and fought in Afghanistan, Waziristan and the North West Frontier. In October, shipping was warned to respond to signals or risk fire from the coastal batteries, and telephone cables to defensive positions and water supplies were checked.

As intelligence emerged that VII (Yemen) Corps was assembling on the border, Perim coaling station was assessed to be at risk from the four Krupp 6-inch guns of Fort Turba at Sheikh Sa'id. As Britain and Turkey stumbled towards war, expatriate families were evacuated to India on 1 November. In an operation conceived by the Chief of the General Staff (India), but not immediately shared with the War Office and Fortress Aden, on 3 November, the 11th Indian Division, en route in two convoys from Bombay and Madras to Egypt to defend the Suez Canal, was instructed to destroy the fort within 36 hours of H-Hour. Brigadier General Herbert Cox, commanding the 29th Indian Infantry Brigade, was given the task. Under command he had three Indian infantry battalions and 1st Battalion, 23rd Sikh Pioneers (1/23rd Sikh Pioneers) of infantry trained to work with assault pioneers. Cox was refused 'naval cooperation' (naval gunfire support), but this changed the next day when the two convoys escorted by the battleship HMS *Swiftsure,* the armoured cruiser HMS *Duke of Edinburgh*, and a ship of the Royal Indian Marine, merged. A suggestion from Shaw that Lieutenant Colonel Jacob should accompany the attack so that he could assure local tribes of British intentions received no answer; so he applied a strict 'need to know' rule that only he, Major Bradshaw, the Field Force Brigade Major, and Major General

J.A. Bell, Resident since 1910, should be cognisant of the operation. On 5 November, the British declaration of war on Turkey was not reciprocated. Cox transferred his headquarters to the fastest troopship and, reaching Aden three days later, was briefed by Major Bradshaw. HMS *Duke of Edinburgh* joined the assault force with three transports.

Meanwhile, the German naval threat to the Indian Ocean had disappeared. After passing through the Panama Canal, officers of the German China Squadron meeting at Pagan Bay in the Mariannas on 14 August concluded that since coaling in the Indian Ocean presented considerable logistic difficulties, operations would focus on the Pacific and the light cruiser *Emden* would disrupt British naval operations in the Indian Ocean. On 9 November, *Emden* was trapped while attacking the Cocos Keeling Islands cable and wireless station. The 1912 intelligence assessment had proved accurate.

The assault force arrived off Fort Turba at about 3 am on 10 November, but strong winds led to the landing being switched to an alternative beach in a sheltered bay almost underneath the fort. HMS *Duke of Edinburgh* silenced the Turkish artillery at dawn and then, in an amphibious assault that predated Gallipoli, two Punjabi battalions in ship's boats were towed ashore by two tugs commandeered from the Perim Coal Company and a third brought from Aden. Wind and sea conditions, the unreliability of the tugs and the shallow water meant that it took fours hours to land the 3,000 men and then attack the garrison, at the cost of four killed and sixteen wounded. Demolition parties then destroyed the guns and a large ammunition dump. The operation was complete by mid-afternoon, and while 1/23rd Pioneers and Major Bradshaw returned to Aden, 29th Brigade rejoined the 11th Infantry Division convoy. Brigadier General Shaw reported to India that the attack had been a success but had antagonized local rulers and the Turks. Indeed, it was a factor when Turkey finally declared war. There were further bombardments on 7 January and 12 March 1915. Meanwhile, the Aden Field Force was designated the Aden Brigade.

As the severe fighting in France sucked in troops, several reservist Territorial Force (TF) battalions were sent to India to defend it from external attack and maintain internal security. The 44th (Home Counties) Division, which had been formed in 1908 as a wholly Territorial Force formation, was being used to replace the battalions. The 1/1st Brecknockshire Battalion (4th South Wales Borderers) recruited from the Dale area of Pembrokeshire and was part of the South Wales Brigade in the Welsh Division. It had completed annual camp at Portmadoc on 25 July and was mobilized on 4 August to its primary task of defending Pembroke Dock. It was then transferred to 132nd (Middlesex) Brigade in October, and with almost the entire unit of about

1,000 men volunteering for overseas service, it arrived in Bombay on 3 December. Within the fortnight, it replaced the Lancashire Fusiliers company in Aden. The company later landed at Gallipoli on 25 April 1915. The battalion reorganized from eight into four company defensive sectors and began a period of acclimatization and training controlled by a British officer to each company, but the change from exercises in the Welsh mountains to operations in Aden and the necessity to keep troops in defensive positions proved problematic.

The landward defence of Aden hinged on the rulers inland defending their states, the most important being the Amir of Dhala, who protected Aden's northern 'backdoor'. Intelligence on Turkish military activity was patchy. On 23 December, Lieutenant General Sir Percy Lake, the Chief of the General Staff in India, agreed that a telegraph line should connect HQ Aden Brigade to Lahej and that the three main tracks north should be improved. Two days later, after the Amir reported that five Turkish battalions and five guns had deployed to Qataba, Shaw selected the government well at Ath Thalub as a defensive position. When two officers checking the eastern track from Bir Salim to Bir Amir reported deep sand three miles south of Lahej in which camels would be needed to tow artillery, 1/23rd Sikh Pioneers spent six weeks improving the tracks. Shaw reformed the Aden Moveable Column and reinforced it with an enlarged infantry company and a 15-pounder field artillery battery to be based at either Nobat Dakim or Lahej. When an Indian battalion took over the Brecknockshire sectors in January 1915, an HQ Aden Brigade assessment concluded that the Welshmen needed more training. A further assessment in May questioned whether they were sufficiently acclimatized.

On 17 February 1915, Colonel William Walton arrived as Deputy Commander from France, where he had commanded 9th Royal Berkshires during the Battle of Loos. Commissioned into the Royal Scots Fusiliers in 1884, he had transferred to the Indian Army two years later, had been aide-de-camp to the Governor of Bombay between 1895 and 1897 and had commanded the 104th Wellesley's Rifles between 1908 and 1914, which included active service in the Persian Gulf in 1911. While serving in the Intelligence Branch for three years from 1903, he recommended to India that dhows taking telegrams, mail and money from Jeddah to the VII (Yemen) Corps headquarters in Sana'a be intercepted. When he recommended that Kamaran Island, 200 miles to the north of Perim, should be defended, the India Office in London, the Admiralty and the Commander-in-Chief at Port Said agreed it should be used as a 'naval base for small vessels'; however, the Viceroy of India claimed its occupation would be misunderstood by Muslims and providing a garrison would weaken the defence of Aden.

Meanwhile, reports from the 109th Indian Infantry company on Perim that 3,500 Arabs were planning to land on the island added credibility to intelligence on VII (Yemen) Corps intentions. After Lieutenant General Sir John Nixon, Commander, Southern Army, had visited Aden in February, he instructed that no offensive operations were to be conducted north of Sheikh Othman except in a 'grave emergency' and only after agreement from HQ Southern Army and the Government of India. Aden Brigade now consisted of:

• 1st Brecknocks.
• 108th Infantry.
• 126th Baluchistan Infantry with two double companies on line of communication to Lahej (it had detachments in France).
• 1/23rd Sikh Pioneers split between Perim Island and Aden.
• Aden Troop, commanded by Captain Norbury with Indian officers commanding the Horse and Camel detachments. Norbury was also the aide-de-camp to the Resident and responsible for organizing his Mess when the latter was in the field.

However, nationalism fermented by German subversion had bred discontent in the Indian Army through a newspaper, *Ghadr* (Mutiny). As the subversion spread to Rangoon and Singapore, the counter-intelligence technique of censoring mail limited the paper's distribution. On 26 March, eight sepoys in the Brahui company, 126th Indian Infantry fired at their officers, and three days later, Sapper Basakha Singh of the 1/23rd Pioneers was arrested after murdering a *subadar* major and a *subadar* (senior NCOs) while they were sleeping. Eleven other mutineers were also arrested. As had been standard since the 1857 Indian Mutiny, ammunition magazines were always guarded by British troops.

In early April, when four 10-pounder field guns arrived for the Sultan of Lahej, a British artillery officer taught his retinue how to use them. By early May, Turkish confidence was high, particularly as British, Australian, New Zealand and French forces had been pegged to their Gallipoli beachheads and the British confined to Egypt. The next objective was Aden. After Lieutenant General Lake had queried, in May, the impact of the unusually hot weather in Aden, HQ Aden Brigade instructed the Aden Moveable Column to shorten their training marches.

After a visit to Lahej, Lieutenant Colonel Jacob and Captain Paige, the Brigade Intelligence Officer, briefed Brigadier General Shaw that while elements of VII (Yemen) Corps were at Ad Dareja, there was no need to deploy the Aden Moveable Column. Jacobs suggested to Delhi and Brigadier

General Bell that friendly Arabs should be armed, particularly as Turkish subversion of several hinterland sheikhs was proving largely successful. An intelligence report on 11 June indicating that Turks had reached Mauia was confirmed by the Sultan of Lahej. Shaw's request to Lake for 1,000 reinforcements from Somaliland was rejected; nevertheless, he responded to an appeal from the Sultan two days later by agreeing that the Aden (Camel) Troop should move to Nobat Dakim and patrol the caravan routes to Dhala. Heliograph communication to the station on Jebel Shamshan in Aden was intermittent because midday haze made signalling difficult.

Meanwhile, Captain A.G.C. Hutchinson, the Perim Outpost commander and a 1/23rd Sikh Pioneer company commander, learnt that a Turkish force that had reoccupied Sheikh Sa'id were intent on invading the island, where he was accompanied by his wife, their baby and an Indian nurse. On 13 June, artillery damaged the barracks and cracked the lighthouse lantern, and after dark, twelve dhows each carrying about twenty soldiers and approaching the north coast were engaged by a picquet. A star shell fired by the battery on Gun Hill helped the *Empress of Japan*, the Perim guardship, to sink two of the dhows. Of some concern was that telephone lines between the Outpost HQ and the battery had been cut, it was believed by discontented sepoys after the conviction and hanging of Singh the previous week. Two days later, 500 men of 108 Indian Infantry reinforced the defence.

On the 17th, Brigade HQ instructed the Camel Troop to rejoin Aden Troop at Lahej, and after Captain Norbury had inspected the position assigned to the Sultan of Lahej's forces south of the town, he replaced Captain Paige as the Brigade Intelligence Officer. A week later, HQ Southern Army complained to Brigadier General Shaw that the quality of intelligence was poor, which was hardly surprising because he lacked air photographic reconnaissance and the embryonic wireless intercept information was emerging in Egypt. Furthermore, as the intelligence officer Captain Aubrey Herbert noted on this way from Egypt to Mesopotamia, having just served at Gallipoli, the garrison possessed no Turkish linguists. Brigade HQ also lacked an Intelligence Branch to collate, analyse and disseminate intelligence and was reliant upon Lieutenant Colonel Jacob collecting Human Intelligence from his contacts with the rulers.

Three days later, the 3rd Double Company, 1/23rd Sikh Pioneers, commanded by Captain Nicholas, reinforced Perim; since Nicholas was senior to Hutchinson, he took over as OC Outpost. When he reported that 1,600 Turks had left Sheikh Sa'id and were heading for Qataba, other intelligence indicators suggested that VII (Yemen) Corps was assembling in the town. Although Jacobs disagreed, Brigadier General Shaw sought confirmation from Lieutenant General Lake that 'grave emergency' was constituted by a Turkish advance to Lahej, particularly as the reports were suggesting that the Sultan of Haushabi had defected and that 39th Infantry Division had crossed the border at Ad Daraj. The Sultan had an historical grievance against the Sultan of Lahej, complaining that his neighbour was benefiting from the profitable caravan routes and the delivery of fish and bread from Aden. The defection was worrying because the State of Haushabi stretched from the border to near the coast east of Aden and could give the Turks an easy advance.

In the event of a 'grave emergency', and intending to use the motorable track to Fiyush as his axis, Shaw appointed Lieutenant Colonel Pearson to be Temporary Commander Aden Mobile Column; his Adjutant, Captain Squires, was designated to be the Staff Officer at Brigade HQ and 1/23rd Sikh Pioneers provided Column Headquarters, supported by an Indian Pack Wireless detachment. Instructing that a Tactical Brigade HQ be formed, Shaw instructed Captain Norberry to resume his duties as his aide-de-camp and, in so doing, deprived the Aden Troop of a British officer. He then divided Brigade HQ into:

Advance Guard
• The Aden Moveable Column reinforced by two 109th Indian Infantry double companies. Under normal circumstances, the advance guard would have usually been a British battalion, but the Welsh were not ready and Shaw asked Lake to transfer the remainder of the Regiment immediately.

Main Body
• HQ 126th Baluchistan Indian Infantry and a double company from 30th Indian Infantry Brigade.
• HQ 1/1st Brecknocks and two companies numbering about 400 soldiers.
• 23 (Fortress Company), 3 Bengal Sappers & Miners
• Detachment 1/23rd Sikh Pioneers providing two Maxim machine-gun sections, a weak platoon protecting the 15-pounder battery and 13 signallers for Brigade HQ.
• 15-pounder battery of six field guns.
• 10-pounder battery of four pack guns.
• 1st line transport and reserve of water.

In spite of the doubts put forward by Jacob, Brigadier General Shaw pushed the Aden Moveable Column forward to Sheikh Othman on 1 July. Lack of hard intelligence was alleviated the next day when an agent at Sheikh Sa'id reported to Captain Nicholas that 39th (Turkish) Division intended to attack Lahej in three columns from the general direction of Dhala. When Jacob learnt from the Sultan of Lahej during the evening that the Turkish advance guard was at Al Milah, about five miles north-east of Nobat Dakin, Shaw instructed Pearson to cover the approaches to Lahej but told him not to enter the Radfan. Next day, the Battle of Lahej opened with patrols reporting that the Turkish division was about to debouch from Radfan and would reach Lahej before the Aden Moveable Column arrived.

During the day, India advised Brigadier General Shaw that the rest of 108th Infantry Regiment had left Bombay. He arrived at Sheikh Othman at about 6 pm to review progress and, rejecting protests that the march from Aden had exhausted the men, particularly the Brecknocks, insisted the advance would continue at 3am next morning, Normal speed in abnormally hot weather was 15 miles a day, with troops marching at the last possible moment after being paraded. Shaw instructed Pearson to use the frequency of wells along the centre track to Bir Nasir and take up positions to defend Lahej. Returning to Aden, he then reported to Lake that the Advance Guard with several Maxim machine guns would join the Aden Troop, but did not mention the heat problems.

Early on Sunday, 4 July, the Main Body began the 25-mile advance to Lahej along sandy tracks, but the unusually searing heat and lack of water took its toll, particularly among the Brecknocks. One problem was that the medical services were not ready, and it would not be until the early evening that they could offer any kind of assistance. Seven Ford cars carrying packs of ice from Aden became stuck in sand. Jacob returned to Brigade HQ to dissuade Shaw from visiting the Aden Moveable Column until 6 July, because he believed that the Turks would not attack Lahej. Shaw disagreed and told Captain Paige that that he believed they would attack and that he intended to leave at about 4 pm; but as more reports reached Brigade HQ, he left in mid-afternoon by car and visited the heat exhaustion casualties evacuated to the Keith-Falconer Mission hospital at Sheikh Othman. Then, learning that Pearson had reached Lahej, Shaw left with some reinforcements in ten cars. But eight were unable to negotiate the sand and he instructed they be used to evacuate casualties to the hospital while he headed toward Lahej.

Meanwhile, Pearson had used his double company commanded by Captain Barr to take up a defensive position north of the town with the second company in reserve. His left flank was covered by a Maxim machine gun and two British Camel Battery 10-pounder field guns – the Sultan's battery had been crippled by desertion. Turkish shelling during the afternoon wreaked havoc, and then during the early evening, the 39th Division spilled from the mountains and advanced across fields and through orchards toward Lahej against the delaying screen provided by the Aden Troop. The Sultan was fatally wounded by friendly fire as he galloped into the town to meet Pearson and died in Aden on 13 July.

Captain Norbury met Brigadier General Shaw in mid-afternoon with a despatch from Pearson that the Turkish attack was heavy and he could not hold the town. When Shaw learnt that the positioning of ammunition, medical support, food and water could not be completed because the mule transport and camel drivers had deserted, as the Main Body began arriving at about 7 pm, the troops were inserted into defensive positions near Brigade HQ and the 15-pounder Camel Battery. The RGA had been forced to stop by the lack of extra camels to extract the guns from the deep sand. Shaw sent a despatch by an Aden Troop rider to advise Pearson that the Main Body would not reach Lahej and that he should withdraw to Bir Nasir; however, the rider failed to reach Pearson. With no news coming from the fighting in the town, at about 7.15 pm, Shaw and his escort rode towards Lahej but were intercepted by several Baluchi sepoys, who seized his horse's bridle and told him the Turks were south of Lahej. Soon after Shaw returned to Brigade HQ, Lieutenant Bingham, the 109th Infantry Regiment Staff Officer, arrived with a second despatch from Pearson that he had heavy casualties and intended to withdraw to the Government Guest House on the southern outskirts. Shaw sent an Assistant Surgeon to help evacuate the wounded. Advised at about 8.30 pm that the reserve company had withdrawn to the Guest House, Captain Barr withdrew through the town at about 10 pm and during confused fighting in the main street, his men captured a Turkish machine-gun crew. Captain Squires was killed while clearing houses, the only British officer to die in the fighting. Shaw wrote:

> During the night, hostile attacks from the West were beaten off, some hand-to-hand fighting taking place. But some parties of the enemy, who had penetrated Lahej from the north, continued practically throughout the night to attack with shell and rifle fire our troops and the hospital which was situated in a garden to the south of the town.

By dawn, it was clear to Shaw that Lahej had been captured by the 39th Division and Aden now needed to be defended. At about 5 am on the 5th, he ordered the Main Body to withdraw to the wells at Bir Nasr, two miles to the south and that the transport should be used to evacuate the wounded.

Captain Paige controlled the withdrawal and at Bir Nasir directed the troops into the shelter of acacia trees astride the road, where they were supplied with water. Shaw again:

> Using the only available means of transport for carrying the wounded and sick, three-quarters of the ammunition, all kits and equipment together with two 10-pounder guns and some .450 machine guns were abandoned at Lahej. I left Bir Nasr at 09.30 a.m. and, in view of the fact that our troops were suffering very severely from great shortness of water and food, withdrew the force to the next water supply at Bir Amr. The enemy did not follow up and the retirement was continued at 4 p.m., Sheikh Othman being reached at 9 a.m. on 6 July.

Many of the Brecknocks spent the day sheltering in grass huts at Bir Amir. Shaw believed that his casualties and loss of ammunition meant that the position at Sheikh Othman could not be held without exposing Aden, 'which is of Imperial importance', as was the Admiralty Wireless Station at Steamer Point. Consequently, he withdrew to a defensive line across the isthmus at Khormaksar. He paid tribute to the RGA, who had withdrawn with all their guns.

After ensuring that his casualties had been evacuated and having heard nothing from Shaw, Pearson decided to retire to Sheikh Othman. In effect, the Aden Moveable Column was now the brigade rearguard. With Captain Barr bringing up the rear, his thirsty troops reached the wells at Bir Nasir at about 8 am with eight prisoners, including a major and a captain, and then withdrew to Sheikh Othman.

In Aden, Lieutenant Colonel Warren, commanding the RGA and Deputy Commander, prepared for the worst and asked the French Consul if troops on the *Elkantara*, due in Aden that evening, could be landed as a precaution until reinforcements arrived from Bombay. The Senior Naval Officer moved the *Empress of Asia* to the east of Aden in order to threaten the Turkish pursuit. A Royal Navy priority throughout the war was to protect the cross-Channel lines of communication to France. To compensate for the lack of warships, several commandeered liners were armed with 4.7-inch guns and classified as Armed Merchant Cruisers. The Canadian Pacific Line 16,800-ton *Empress of Asia* had been duly requisitioned and had arrived in Aden on 9 December 1914. In March 1915, she went into dry dock at Bombay for about two months. The Royal Indian Marine transports *Northbrook* and the *Minto* took up positions in the inner harbour as guardships, and three Maxims from the

Fortress machine-gun section, as well as another Maxim section landed from *Northbrook*, joined the defence line. Owners of motor cars helped evacuate casualties from Keith-Falconer Hospital.

After receiving reports sent by Shaw to HQ Southern Army and the Secretary of State (India) in London, India concentrated on the loss of ammunition and equipment, the logistic lapses in organizing transport and water and the fact that troops, especially the Brecknocks, had not been properly acclimatized. Colonel H.F. Cleveland of the Indian Medical Service and Assistant Director Medical Services (India), concluded that the 118 heatstroke casualties over four days, and fifty battle casualties, had essentially degraded the Brecknocks as a force and, observing that their caps offered no protection from the sun, recommended Cawnpore *topis*. He despatched a British and two Indian sections from 105 Indian Field Ambulance to Aden as an advance guard of medical support that would include five British, Indian and Combined field ambulances, a casualty transport unit, casualty clearing stations, depot of medical stores and a British and Indian hospital. The Ordnance Branch (India) sent 1,000 rounds of 15-pounder shrapnel and a million rounds of .303 ammunition. The Director of Military Operations, HQ Southern Army drew up plans to reinforce Aden Brigade, diverted the troopship *Teesta* carrying drafts for Egypt and landed 500 men, including 9th Gurkha Rifles. A double company was slotted into Khormaksar's defensive position and a company defended the Wireless Station, but their weapons were not immediately available and they were equipped with spare .303 rifles from the 109th Infantry Battalion armoury and obsolete Martini-Henris from the stockpile held to reward loyal rulers. Assurances were given that British Somaliland could provide two naval guns, ammunition and about 375 troops, of whom 150 could be sent immediately. Half an Australian battalion and an Indian battalion were also available from Egypt. Next day, Shaw reported to Southern Army that the Turkish strength at Lahej was eight battalions and 20 guns.

After receiving Shaw's assessment, on 9 July, the Viceroy of India telegraphed the Colonial Office that Lahej must be recaptured to restore British prestige and agreed with Lake that Aden must be reinforced. Asked to comment on the availability of water to support an enlarged brigade supported by four artillery batteries, two cavalry squadrons and an engineer company, Shaw replied that there were sufficient wells to support two battalions between Sheikh Othman and Lahej and in Lahej itself, but not enough to support an infantry division. There was, however, a river at Nobat Dakin.

Secretary of State for War Lord Kitchener immediately instructed that the 28th Indian Infantry Brigade, then in Egypt and commanded by Brigadier

General George Younghusband, and two artillery batteries should be despatched to Aden. Younghusband had joined the Army in 1878 and had transferred to the Guides, which had won its reputation on the North West Frontier. He had also served in Afghanistan, the Sudan, Burma, the Boer War and the 1898 Spanish-American War in the Philippines. Kitchener queried a suggestion of sending cavalry because of the water situation. When the Turkish 39th Division seized the Sheihk Othman wells, water for the garrisons at Lahej, Sheikh Sa'id, Subar and Waht was rationed. The Turks had long lines of communication, and if the 1905 Yemen civil war had proved one thing, it was the weakness of their logistic organisation.

Since Brigadier General Shaw intended to defend Aden from the Khormaksar defence line, he requested the support of the monitors, HMS *Severn* and HMS *Mersey*, which were in East African waters, to defend his flanks, but his request for aeroplanes was refused. His imposition of martial law caused further anxiety in India. The arrival of the 108th Indian Infantry during the day allowed him to cancel the reinforcements from Somaliland. In India, 1/4th Hampshire Howitzer Battery (TF), 24th Hazara Mountain Battery and 51/1st Field Company, Bengal Sappers and Miners were earmarked for Aden.

Next day, Lake told Shaw he was being relieved by Younghusband and he was to remain at his disposal until further notice. Jacob would remain as senior Political Assistant. Captain Paige had written in the Garrison Diary that 'Political Officer [Jacob] should have accompanied Column'. Shaw was permitted to keep for Aden two 5-inch coastal guns earmarked for Perim. Younghusband arrived on the light cruiser HMNZS *Philomel*, which had been lent by the Royal Navy to New Zealand and was the foundation on which the Royal New Zealand Navy was built. Meanwhile, one of the prisoners volunteered that the Turkish forces consisted of five weak battalions of about 350 men each, a mounted infantry squadron, ten mountain guns and about 400 Arab irregulars. Intelligence was then received on 14 July that the Turks did not intend to attack Aden during the month of Ramadan. The next day, 28th Brigade arrived with 3,500 men plus 567 mules and 532 horses. It consisted of:

- 51st Sikhs (Frontier Force).
- 53rd Sikhs (Frontier Force).
- 52nd Punjabis.
- 56th Punjabis.
- B Battery, Honourable Artillery Company (TF).
- Berkshire Battery, Royal Horse Artillery (TF).
- 5/1st Field Company.

The Berkshire Battery, based at Reading with a section at Ascot, was equipped with eight Quick Firing (QF) 15-pounders. In 1914 1/1st and 2/1st Berkshire Batteries had been merged to form the battery. B Battery initially supported the 22nd Mounted Brigade. The QF 15-pounder had a range of 6,400 yards and was the first British gun to have an on-carriage recoil system. First-line ammunition stocks included 600 rounds per gun.

While Younghusband regarded Aden a sideshow to operations in Mesopotamia and Palestine, its defence guarded the lines of communications to India and tied down VII (Yemen) Corps in South Arabia. He disagreed with the Viceroy of India's instruction that British prestige should be restored by recapturing Lahej, a view agreed in London, because he believed it would require a division to recapture and garrison the town and secure the lines of communication to Aden. He assured Southern Army:

> There is no cause for any alarm or despondency in situation here. Practically impossible for any hostile forces which could be brought against Aden to take it. I consider arrangements (by Shaw) quite secure and suitable but as soon as troops arrive from Egypt. I shall occupy Sheikh Othman as a detached post, strongly entrenching around water supply. I do not recommend any further military operations in this season.

On 21 July, he counter-attacked the Turks at Sheikh Othman and drove to within five miles of Lahej until heat and sand forced the pursuit to be abandoned. The oasis and its water then became the focus of the defence of Aden. No.138 Combined Field Ambulance set up at the Keith-Falconer Mission, and within twenty-four hours, the Bengal Sappers and Miners had repaired the aqueduct. Engineers also produced detailed maps, constructed a light railway from the port to Hatum, laid a water pipeline connecting a condensing plant at Sheikh Othman to tanks at Steamer Point and located several searchlights to aid the coastal artillery. Telephone lines and semaphore connected the gun lines at Sheikh Othman to HQ Aden Infantry Brigade in Crater. Sand tyres fitted to cars and lorries facilitated the moving of equipment. In the last three months of the year, 109th Infantry Regiment fortified the oasis.

Younghusband kept the Turks off balance by attacking with flying columns and ensured the sheikhs were allies or neutral. Tactically, both sides settled into skirmishing in the spring, patrolling and intelligence-gathering in the summer and combat operations in the cool of the autumn and winter. When HQ 5th (Mhow) Division replaced the Brecknocks in August with the

1/1st The Buffs (TF), it set in motion until 1918 the principle of Territorial Force battalions from Cornwall, Surrey and Hampshire serving one-year tours in Aden. The Buffs recruited from the Canterbury area and had mobilized with the Kent Brigade in the Home Counties Division. The Brecknocks rejoined the Mhow Brigade and remained in India until 1918.

Although the climate plagued the garrison, the medical support provided by Colonel Cleveland proved a wise decision. In mid-October, Lieutenant Colonel Baldock, commanding 108th Indian Infantry on Perim Island, died within three days of contracting dysentery. In fighting at Waht, the Buffs suffered eight fatalities, six of them to heat exhaustion. When the Battalion returned to Aden after a short period at Sheikh Othman, 145 officers and soldiers were hospitalized with a mysterious fever that had defeated the commandant of No. 10 British Stationary Hospital. Cleveland queried the quality of drinking water and the ablution and latrine arrangements at Sheikh Othman. When scurvy broke out among Indian troops in November, lime juice and tins of jam were distributed. An outbreak of venereal disease among Indian soldiers, attributed to local prostitutes, led Colonel Cleveland recommending that women found with the disease should be deported. Additional work was carried out on Perim to improve the fort and water condensers.

A proposal that 28th Indian Infantry Brigade should join 7th (Meerut) Division in Iraq in 1916 was rejected; thus it avoided involvement in the disastrous attempt by Major General Charles Townsend to seize the junctions of the rivers Tigris and Euphrates at Kut al Amara. Captain Morice Lake, of 109 Indian Infantry, formed the irregular 1st Yemen Regiment of 600 men recruited largely from the Arab Legion then defending the Suez Canal and the Arab Labour Corps building the Sheikh Othman defence line. His intention was to collect intelligence and dominate no man's land between Sheikh Othman and Lahej. When Major General James Stewart arrived as Resident, Aden Brigade, he did so as a soldier's soldier from East Africa. Commissioned into the Gloucestershire Regiment in 1881, he transferred to 5th (Royal) Gurkhas Frontier Force two years later and saw service in the North West Frontier, Burma, China and Tibet. The Malay States Guides Battery, which arrived in June, was quickly stricken by diarrhoea and dysentery. The British air presence in the region began in June 1917, when Royal Naval Air Service seaplanes, which had been delivered by the converted freighter HMS *Raven II*, bombed Turkish positions. An airstrip was then built at Khormaksar.

As the fighting in the Middle East tipped in favour of the Allies in 1917, Colonel Jacob, now promoted, joined General Edmund Allenby's staff as an adviser on South West Arabian affairs and became acquainted with Lawrence of Arabia. Allenby commanded the Egyptian Expeditionary Force and was planning to attack Turkish forces in Palestine. Jacob was instructed to lead a diplomatic mission to visit the Iman in Sana'a but was captured by tribesmen soon after landing at Hodeida. He failed to hand over the diplomatic negotiations to Major A.S. Meek, which had been agreed in order to secure the mission's release, and negotiated an agreement with the tribesmen without Foreign Office authority. The mission was released after several months of comfortable captivity.

When the Armistice was signed on 11 November 1918, demobilization and the Spanish influenza epidemic meant that the British were incapable of forcing Turkey to comply; and Turkish commanders in South Arabia were reluctant to surrender until protracted negotiations eventually led to a Turkish detachment surrendering on 6 December. British impatience led to the 2/101st Grenadiers landing a week later at Hodeida, where it became involved in street fighting with Turks and Arabs, but stalemate prevailed. An advance to Lahej by the Aden Moveable Column and more landings at Hodeida eventually led to the repatriation of the Turkish garrisons being completed in March 1919. The railway proved valuable in moving Turkish prisoners to Aden for repatriation by ship. It was only then that the demobilization in Aden began.

CHAPTER FOUR

The Colony of Aden
1919–1945

From the collapse of the Ottoman Empire in 1918 emerged the state of Yemen. It was governed by Imam Yahya, who extended his control of the country by rejecting the 1904 Boundary Commission on the grounds that the territories protected by the British had been 'marked on maps by infidels'. He also claimed Aden Settlement.

In 1920, Britain reluctantly accepted the League of Nations Mandate to oversee the progress of the new states of Iraq, Palestine and Transjordan to full independence. However, the Iraq Mandate was threatened when Emir Feisal I, son of Sharif Hussein bin Ali, who had led the Arab Revolt, established a government in Damascus, an act opposed by nationalists, who declared his older brother to be King of Iraq. By midsummer the country was in a state of anarchy, except the cities of Mosul, Baghdad, and Basra, where the bulk of the British garrison was stationed. Remembering that, earlier in the year, a rebellion in Somaliland led by Mohammed Abdulhah Hassan, nicknamed the 'Mad Mullah', had been quelled within three weeks by twelve DH-9 aircraft sent from Great Britain on board the aircraft-carrier HMS *Ark Royal* to support the Camel Corps, Secretary of State for Air Winston Churchill asked the Chief of the Air Staff, Air Marshal Hugh Trenchard, to examine air power as a suitable alternative to ground forces. After other instances of the deployment of aircraft in Sudan and Transjordan, Trenchard wrote to Churchill in October 1922:

> Air power is of vital concern to the Empire, and in Iraq, under the control of an air officer; further evidence is accumulating of its great potentialities. A continued demonstration, until its effectiveness is beyond dispute, may have far-reaching results, in that it may lead to still further economies in defence expenditure, not only in Iraq, but also in other Eastern territories where armed forces are required to give effect to British policy and uphold British prestige.

Churchill replied that he was convinced that British responsibilities and Imperial prestige could be met by the extended use of air power with a minimum of expenditure both in lives and money. The strategy became known as Air Control, or Proscription. It had first been used in February 1917 when No. 31 Squadron bombed rebellious tribesmen near the Khyber Pass as an alternative to sending ground forces across difficult terrain. With the Army insisting on retaining internal security control in India, when Churchill agreed at the 1922 Cairo Conference that the RAF should control peacekeeping in Iraq, Air Vice Marshal Sir John Maitland Salmond was selected to take charge of Iraq Command. Noted for his imaginative use of air power, he had joined the Royal Flying Corps in 1912.

Air Control was designed to sustain government authority with a simple set of rules of engagement. Sir Bernard Reilly described the official line:

> A time limit would be imposed for the payment of the fines, and the offenders would be warned that if they were not paid within the time limit allowed, they should move themselves, their women and children and their livestock from a specified village or group of houses and the surrounding ground as certain buildings would be demolished from the air. A *dar* or tower belonging to the leader would be knocked down by air action. The operation might sometimes have to be repeated on another named target but provided that the warning to evacuate had been obeyed, it would be bloodless, which a ground operation might not have been. This point should be realized by critics who are disposed to regard any form of air action as being unduly harsh.

Air photographs helped target acquisition. Reilly was, in order, the last Aden Political Resident reporting to the Government of Bombay in 1931, the only Chief Commissioner and then first Governor of Aden between 1930 and 1940. Air Control was seen by some not as a cost-effective mechanism designed to maintain law and order in usually inaccessible areas but rather as the bombing of defenceless people. The strategy did prove cost-effective, however, and once recalcitrant rulers had shown remorse, engineers, medics and police could help repair damage, improve infrastructure, treat the sick and infirm and restore order. When Air Control failed, ground forces were sent in. In some respects, Air Control equates to modern drones.

Because of the distances and difficulties involved in supporting the desert rulers with whom it had defence treaties, the British Government had been considering withdrawing into Aden Settlement. However, Air Control offered a flexible solution, particularly as the War Office was seeking savings. During a meeting of the Middle East Committee at the Colonial Office in October 1922, Major General T.E. Scott, the Political Resident (1920–25), tabled cuts that included withdrawing HQ RGA, a suggestion that the Army Council rejected on the grounds that the defence of the oil refinery on Little Aden and the port should not be degraded. The disbandment of the HQ Aden Brigade Signals Section was agreed, but only in proportion to other reductions, which included reducing the two Indian battalions to one and replacing the Royal Artillery Pack battery with a camel battery.

In early 1926, much to his delight, Lieutenant Colonel Lake, who had formed the 1st Yemen Regiment (which had been disbanded in 1925), was recalled from India and instructed to raise a force to defend RAF Khormaksar and Perim and Kamaran Islands until the Aden Armed Police were strong enough to do so. The Aden Police, which had reported to the Bombay Provincial Police Department since 1857, had been reorganized to include the paramilitary Armed Police, then based in the former barracks in Crater and raised from the hinterland tribes. The Government of India regarded the initiative as experimental and sent police officers until the local constabulary was ready. Assisted by four NCOs from 2nd South Wales Borderers, the resident British battalion, Lake contacted tribal rulers and former Yemen Regiment members and raised the Aden Protectorate Levies (APL) of six platoons, each of one Arab officer and 34 other ranks, and a Camel Troop of three mules, 11 baggage camels and 37 trotting camels.

At the Middle East Committee meeting, agreement was reached that RAF Khormaksar would be retained. No. 8 Squadron was reformed at Helwan, Egypt and, in October 1920, replaced the Aden Flight to earn the title of 'Aden's Own'. Within four years, about thirty airstrips were constructed south of the border to support Air Control and form part of the air bridge to RAF bases in Iraq. Guarding them were the APL and the RAF Armoured Car Wing of two Rolls Royce armoured cars and a Crossley six-wheeler. The airstrips led to an extension of treaties through Colonial Service political officers advising rulers on spending government funds and collecting intelligence on internal security. In a country in which roads were far between, the RAF also provided a 'flying doctor' service to remote areas. Indeed, they were the only medical help for some communities. By January 1928, the squadron was equipped with the general purpose Fairey-3s (F-3); they were replaced by Vickers Vincent Army Co-operation aircraft in 1935. Sandstorms stirred up by the south-west monsoon between May and September often made flying difficult by suddenly blotting out the ground. On 14 August 1928, an F-3 crashed killing Flight Lieutenant Edward Norman Edwardes and injuring

Leading Aircraftsman Albert Jones. It was one of two aircraft that crashed in that month.

Aden appears to have been a somewhat tedious posting. In 1926 Sapper Robert Whiffin joined 20th Fortress Company RE on his first posting. Prickly heat was a constant torment. There was little to do except train in building fieldworks, shoot at the Gold Mahur Range, enjoy the soldiers' zoo and pay visits to the hinterland. An outbreak of smallpox during 1929 led to the Company being re-vaccinated; nevertheless, bazaars, Crater and the port were placed out of bounds for several weeks. Mr J. Campbell wrote of his experiences with the RAF Khormaksar Engine Repair Shop in 1937:

> The camp was divided into two parts, with one side the domestic side and across the road the working side containing the hangars and workshops. The camp was guarded by Aden Levies and Native Labour, mainly Somalis. We would go to work just after 6 am, returning for breakfast around 8 am, and on returning to work, finish around noon. The temperature was usually around 98 with the humidity the same. Afternoons usually meant a couple of hours in bed, after which we indulged in sport. Despite having arrived from Iraq, we were not allowed to compete in any sporting activity for the period of one month. Each hut had a native servant and boy to look after every need, such as cleaning shoes or fetching tea in the morning, and if memory serves we each paid about eight annas per week for this service. Laundry was collected each morning and returned the same afternoon, immaculate. Swimming was played in a wired-off enclosure in the sea and had a platform on which a lookout stayed watching for sharks or barracuda. Sometimes after a liner passed, the rollers would sweep over the wire and bring in unwanted visitors. The Royal Engineers then cleared the place before it was safe to swim again.

On 4 April 1928, the Air Ministry assumed responsibility for the defence of Aden from the War Office, and the Army withdrew the 1st Welch, 5/10th Baluchs and 7 Heavy Battery RA. In October, Lake handed over command of the APL to Captain F. Robinson (York and Lancasters), who, over the next eleven years, trained the Arab soldiers using the philosophy of 'Keep it simple': enhancing discipline, undertaking long 'flag' marches into the hinterland and exercising alerts. The Camel Troop proved itself on ceremonial duties and on long escorts using the Dahla Road.

The British had become increasingly impatient with Imam Yayha and incursions across the border. When, in 1927, negotiations collapsed, with Yemen claiming a large share of the fertile Dhala plateau, Air Control was extended to defending British interests; No. 8 Squadron bombed the Yemeni Regional HQ at Taiz and border garrisons, breaking up troop concentrations and supporting ground forces by forcing the Yemenis to withdraw from the border states of Dhala, Haushabi, Shaib and Audhali. Nevertheless, concern was expressed that bombing would not disrupt mass attacks, something that artillery could do. When British realization that the stipends paid to rulers to keep the peace had been ineffective led to cuts in aid and the Haushabis then protested at the reduction in weapon issues, a visit from No. 8 Squadron dampened their objections. The close relationship between the Squadron and the APL developed in April 1931, when Lieutenant Colonel Robinson arranged for a flight of nine Fairy-F3s to help a patrol that had clashed with hostile tribesmen in Wadi Rukuh in the Sheikhdom of Hatib. Although low cloud prevented direct support, their mere presence encouraged the tribesmen to melt away. A month later, after a Levy had been murdered and two colleagues injured during the robbery of their camels and property while they were going on leave, Air Control bombed the village of the offenders.

Friction in Palestine between Jews and Arabs had little effect in Aden, largely because Jews had been integral to South Arabia for generations and local newspapers were not reporting the unrest. Nevertheless, there was some migration by Yemeni Jews to Palestine. In May 1932, several waiting for ships were sleeping under the stars in Crater, as most people did, but unknowingly had used part of a street on which there was a nondescript mosque for their night-time ablutions. This accidental disrespect sparked serious riots, and an APL company had to enforce a curfew in their first foray into internal security.

In February 1934, the Anglo-Yemen Treaty finally encompassed a 40-year agreement under which both sides recognized the status quo of the border as agreed by the Boundary Commission. Lieutenant Colonel Lake, who was highly respected by the Imam, signed on behalf of the British. Even so, the phrase 'status quo' caused further dispute, because Yahya referred to the political status of the border, as opposed to the tribal dispositions. When Italy annexed Abyssinia in 1935, 203 Squadron deployed to RAF Khormaksar to deter Italian raids on Aden and the Protectorates.

One Air Control mission during the year was against the Quteibi, who lived in the Radfan Mountains near Thumeir. Although the Amir of Dhala claimed sovereignty over the tribes living in *wadis* of Rabwa, Taym and Misrah, the village sheikhs were independently-minded and regularly raided the Dhala Road to collect 'dues'. An APL operation tasked to support Air

Control in March fell foul of influenza among the camels and of Ramadan, which restricted the working hours of the Levies. When several APL of Quteibi origin failed to return to barracks, the Amir intervened and successfully appealed to their sense of duty.

In 1937, Aden Settlement was converted into a Colony and the three states in the inhospitable Hadhramaut desert to the east of Aden were formed into Eastern Aden Protectorate and governed by a British resident. The remaining seventeen rulers' territory became the Western Aden Protectorates, governed by a British agent. Each was supported by a political officer. Sapper Robert Whiffin wrote:

> Another of my memories being the sight of the Political Agent, a Captain Sullivan, I believe, with his Red Coats awaiting a flight up country to settle some tribal dispute. The Red Coats, so called as each man had a red blanket, were rumoured to be the dregs of every tribe and each had a rifle lovingly oiled and wrapped in cloth. They looked a tough bunch. If a chieftain or tribe was in default or whatever, this merry lot would call on them and that was usually enough, but if they failed, then they would be bombed.

The rulers were encouraged to raise Tribal Guards from their retinues as armed rural constabularies, usually commanded by family and friends. In the Western Area Protectorate, rulers were also supported by the Government Guards as a *gendarmerie* based in border forts perched on high ground and commanding spectacular desert views. They also protected key points, in particular wells. In spite of occasional lapses, the APL continued to develop so that by 1937, it was conducting co-ordinated operations with No. 8 Squadron in the Tor Al Baha area, where the trade route to Hodeda was frequently harassed by the Haushebi, who, like the Quitebi, were distinctly independent-minded.

When Italy declared war on Great Britain in June 1940, the principal threat was air and naval operations from Italian East Africa. In June 1940, 5th Coast Regiment reformed as 1st Heavy Anti-Aircraft Regiment with 15 and 23 (Gun) and 24 (Searchlight) (Hong Kong and Singapore Royal Artillery) Batteries. Defence of the port was undertaken by 9 (Minden) Coast Battery from 1940 to May 1945, with18 and 27 Mountain Batteries briefly providing field artillery. Other units included 20th Fortress Company RE, 3/7th Rajput Regiment from 1940 to 1944 and the RAF Independent Armoured Car Flight. The APL formed part of the Pennine Chain defence line south of Sheikh Othman against the threat from Yemen and guarded the garrison ammunition compound. It also helped the Aden Police intern Italians. The APL provided the Light Anti-Aircraft Battery of four 40mm Bofors and the motorized Machine-Gun Troop. When the Bofors were sent to North Africa to replace losses, a proposal to form an artillery troop was rejected and the Light Anti-Aircraft Battery became a machine-gun company. The garrison at Socotra was equipped with two 75mm Pack Howitzers for coastal defence. Two days after the Italian declaration of war, Aden experienced the first of several air raids and an APL patrol captured the crew of an Italian aircraft that crashed near Ras Imran.

Aden became an important staging point for British, Indian and Northern Rhodesian units staging to and from the fighting in Abyssinia. RAF Khormaksar quickly became a busy airfield. The motorized elements of the Aden Home Guard patrolled in three reconditioned RAF armoured cars. The Aden Labour Corps was reformed. Major J.V.L. Kell (South Staffordshire Regiment) formed 1401st (Aden) Company, Pioneer Corps in November 1940 to support operations in East Africa and, since recruiting was so good, then raised 1402nd (Aden) Company. Both companies helped Royal Engineers build roads from beaches and unload equipment and stores from lighters in port operations and at airstrips. They returned to Aden in 1943 and were disbanded. In 1942, Captain D.N. Seton (Welch Regiment) formed 1422nd (Hadhramaut) Pioneer Company to build roads in the Eastern Aden Protectorate. It also relieved a pioneer company on Socotra Island, where the troops were employed as stevedores and in road construction until the end of January 1944.

Providing counter-intelligence and port security was 269 (East Africa Command) Field Security Section of the Intelligence Corps. Formed in Cairo in early 1941 and first spread along the border between Somalia and Kenya, in September 1942 it moved to Aden, primarily on Port Security. However, it lacked a launch and was forced to rely on hired motor boats in order to visit ships anchored in the Outer Harbour. Nevertheless, in December 1942, 123 vessels were vetted and their crews probed for information. Ships taking prisoners of war to prison camps in India were screened in 1944, as were two troopships transporting 5,000 Soviet soldiers captured while serving in the German Army to Basra and an uncertain future in the Soviet Union.

The most serious internal threat developed in the Eastern Aden Protectorate, after plans to develop three-year 'peace boards' agreed in 1937 had made little progress because of distrust between the tribes. The failure of the rains in 1943 over most of South West Arabia resulted in a drought, and destitute families poured into Aden. The RAF was prominent in delivering famine relief, while Air Control undermined outbreaks of unrest. After several airmen returning from leave in Dhala were ambushed in October near the picturesque village of Al Sawda and one was killed, Air Control's retaliation proved ineffective because dust and smoke from bombs obscured the valley.

By May 1943, the APL had increased its establishment from 600 to 1,416 all ranks, divided into 25 and 38 British and Arab officers, 20 British other ranks and 1,333 soldiers spread between Regimental Headquarters, ten rifle companies, the Signals Company and the Anti-Aircraft Battery reformed with Bofors.

The Adeni Jews prospered during both world wars, while those in Yemen suffered. Jewish refugees reaching Aden were placed in Hashed Camp to await transport arranged by Zionists that would take them to Palestine. When typhus ravaged the camp in January 1944, 5 Company helped contain the epidemic by providing guards. In May 1944, when the APL became a Regular force, the Royal Indian Army Medical Corps opened a clinic for families at RAF Khormaksar Beach. In September, the APL Wali Road Camp south of Sheikh Othman was renamed Lake Lines in honour of Lieutenant Colonel Lake, the British officer who had raised the Levies.

By April 1942, Aden Command had been formed with roles to protect Aden and the Protectorates against external aggression and to preserve internal security in the Protectorates. Its area of responsibility included the Persian Gulf, the Red Sea and the north-western seas of the Indian Ocean. After supporting operations in East Africa, No. 8 Squadron concentrated on anti-submarine patrols, operating Vincents and then Bristol Blenheim fighter-bombers. Its flight of Free French pilots flew Marylands. Long-range patrols were flown by 621 Squadron Wellingtons between 1943 and 1945, and Nos. 11, 39 and 203 Squadrons, flying Blenheims, patrolled the Red Sea and bombed Italian forces in Abyssinia. Catalina flying boats of Nos. 259 and 265 Squadrons flew from Dar es Salaam on long-range convoy escorts and search-and-rescue. A major air role was to protect ships from interception by German surface raiders and the Monsun Gruppe of U-Boats that sailed from Occupied French ports and around the Cape of Good Hope to conduct joint operations with the Japanese and also transfer strategic war materials, scientists and experts to and from Germany. When U-533 was sunk in the Gulf of Aden by a No. 244 Squadron Blenheim operating from Shaibah, the only survivor escaped from a depth of 200ft and then remained afloat without a lifejacket for twenty-eight hours until he was rescued. A Flight, No. 3 Squadron, South African Air Force provided fighter defence with Hurricane 11cs and Spitfire Vs, while the Aden Protectorate Support Flight took responsibility for Air Control. No. 1566 Flight of Gladiators provided meteorological flights.

It was not until January 1935, that the Royal Navy established a permanent base in Aden, HMS *Norfolk III*. In 1940, she was moved to Tawahi and renamed HMS *Sheba*.

On 16 June 1940, the Italian submarine *Galileo Galilei* sank a Norwegian tanker twelve miles south of Aden, but a search by an aircraft launched from the cruiser HMS *Leander* found nothing. Six days later, the submarine carried out a gun attack on a Yugoslav cargo ship. The action was heard by the Aden-based anti-submarine trawler HMS *Moonstone*, which raced to the scene and, after a lookout had spotted a periscope, forced the submarine to the surface with depth charges. She then used her guns to seriously damage the submarine and kill all the officers except for a midshipman, who continued the fight until the destroyer HMS *Kandahar* appeared. The destroyer towed the submarine to Aden, where the British claim that the her operational documents were captured intact was denied by the Italian survivors, who reported that every document was destroyed before surrender – a claim that appears to have been an attempt to screen the ability of the British to read enemy transmissions. The submarine was later used as a generating station for berthed British submarines in Port Said, until she was commissioned into the Royal Navy in June 1942 as a training boat in the Far East until 1946 as HMS *X2* and later *P711*. Following the incident, HMS *Teviot Bank* laid an anti-submarine minefield to control the approaches to Aden. The only offensive naval action seems to have come from the Government Guards. In 1940, an Irishman named Ham raised a flotilla of four armed motorized dhows that pestered Italian ports in Somaliland, briefly blockaded the Straits of Bal al Mandeb and a sank German ship trying to breach the blockade. The Senior Naval Officer described the flotilla as pirates and ordered them not fly the White Ensign. Ham responded by flying the Cross of St Patrick.

When Great Britain and the USA agreed Lend Lease, several transatlantic air routes were established to ferry equipment and personnel to the Middle East and India. The most southerly was the South Atlantic route formed in July 1941 by 26th Army Air Force Ferrying Wing, later reformed as Middle East Wing, to fly equipment to Burma and China. Aden became an important staging post between Khartoum 859 miles to the west and Karachi 1,669 miles to the east, the latter connecting to the 'Hump' over the Himalayas to Nationalist Chinese forces. When US officers accused APL solders of stealing ammunition from dumps, HQ APL withdrew from guarding their aircraft. 1211th Army Air Force Base Unit providing refuelling and servicing at RAF Khormaksar until 1943, when the Allied victory in North Africa enabled several captured airfields to be used. A US air force signals detachment remained until June 1945.

CHAPTER FIVE

Defending the Border
1945–1955

The Second World War ended with the Japanese surrender in Tokyo Bay on 2 September 1945, and Aden returned to a degree of normality as wartime restrictions were discontinued.

In a transition that unsettled the soldiers, the APL entered the New Year as an RAF unit, using air force terminology and commanded by RAF Regiment officers, some of whom were former Army. Those who did not speak Arabic were encouraged to attend the Command Language School (Aden Peninsula) and its successors. Headquarters moved from No. 2 Standing Camp (Rashid Camp) to Seedaseer Lines, which had been built by 2/5th Mahratta Light Infantry between August 1939 and 1940 and were named to commemorate a battle honour. The Aden Levies Hospital was renamed Khormaksar Beach Hospital. No. 8 Squadron was disbanded but soon reformed from No. 114 Squadron operating Mosquitoes.

The State of Dhala remained the focus of attention, with differences between the Amir and Radfan tribes guaranteed to escalate into conflict. When, in February, a brother of the Amir, Haidara, seized a *jebel* and announced that he now governed the Amirate, there was a feeling that he had been encouraged by Yemen, still niggled by the 1934 border treaty. In a four-day operation in early February 1947, the APL Mobile Wing, supported by No. 8 Squadron, seized the hill. Royal Engineers then demolished several forts. After two tribes clashed in an historic dispute in the Amirate of Beihan, Air Control was conducted on a tribal fort by eight rocket-firing Tempests and one aircraft was possibly hit by ground fire, crashing in Yemen and killing the pilot. Meanwhile, the British policy of supporting rulers with financial stipends to keep the peace came under attack from opponents who saw them as autocratic, corrupt and a bar to the democratic process. Had there been elections, however, most rulers would have won.

The UN declaration in December creating the state of Israel and scheduled for implementation in 1948 drew resigned protests from most Arab nations, but in Aden, tensions between Arabs and Jews erupted into violence as Jewish shops in Crater were attacked. The Armed Police fired at ringleaders and several people were injured during baton charges. Although some Colonial Police officers had served in the Palestine Emergency between 1945 and 1947, the constables were generally unfamiliar with riot control. Governor Sir Reginald Champion transferred internal security to the Aden Fortress Commander and requested support from HQ Middle East Command. The Command had been established in June 1939 as a unified command covering British military interests in the Mediterranean and Egypt, Sudan and Palestine, Transjordan and Cyprus. Its area of responsibility was extended during the war to North Africa, East Africa, Palestine and Lebanon.

The next day, Royal Marines Ships' Detachment from the destroyers HMS *Contest* and HMS *Cockade* landed. The previous August, the APL began training for the Internal Security Scheme; however, 3 Squadron had been stoned when it deployed into the Crater. Champion was writing his report on the disturbances when reports of further rioting and arson in Crater arrived, and the APL were ordered to fire over the heads of the rioters. The riots continued, and when reports of snipers were received at about 9.30 am, 3 Squadron imposed a curfew and the Armoured Car Flight was permitted to use automatic fire against snipers. But the disturbances continued, and during the afternoon the Jews were evacuated to the vacant Rashid Camp. Next day, 5 December, two companies of the 2nd North Staffords arrived from Egypt on RAF Dakotas and immediately based themselves at the Crater football field. Patrols opened fire several times during curfew. A strong wind during the night led to fires, and all available fire appliances were rushed to the district. When a dozen people broke out of a burning house in the Jewish quarter, there was a burst of firing and, although no one claimed responsibility, rumours circulated that the APL was targeting Jews and an Arab soldier was shot dead. A Middle East Command proposal that British soldiers replace the Levies was discussed. So far, an estimated 20 rioters had been shot dead, 100 had been wounded and looting and arson were widespread. Some 50 Jews had been killed, including 14 who had remained in Sheikh Othman after 900 had been moved to Camp Rashid, swelling the numbers inside to 4,000. No incidents were reported in Ma'alla, but in Tawahi five Jews were killed. APL casualties were 34 Arabs and two Indians wounded. To relieve the internal security pressure in Crater, on 10 December, 100 Yemeni Jews were moved to Rashid Camp. Damage to Jewish homes, businesses, synagogues and both Jewish schools was extensive, particularly in Sheikh Othman.

With the necessities of life in short supply and several thousand requiring welfare support in a country that was now hostile, the Jews' predicament was precarious. In spite of the 1948 Arab-Israeli War seeing Egypt threatening the Red Sea and Suez Canal, the Jewish Agency activated Operation Magic Carpet and evacuated an average of 300 a day of those wished to emigrate to a homeland in Israel. Aden's 7,273 Jews listed in 1946 dropped to 821. To buttress internal security, 300 airmen of 58 and 66 Rifle Squadrons, 20th Wing, RAF Regiment arrived in late December. Although there was a feeling at HQ Middle East Command that the APL should be disbanded, an inquiry chaired by Governor Champion concluded that they had shot only at snipers. He expressed sympathy for a force that had come under intense moral pressure not to open fire on fellow Arabs. Nevertheless, twelve APL were court-martialled for looting.

On 19 February 1948, Yemen's elderly Imam Yahya was assassinated in a palace coup engineered by tribal factions opposed to his tight control; however the coup failed in that Yahya was succeeded by his son, Ahmed, who solidified his position by claiming that Great Britain had engineered his father's assassination and that Aden was part of Yemen. In reality, he envied the Colony and its growing sophistication and economic success. Ahmed defeated the rebels in a tough campaign and began modernizing his 10,000-strong army with up-to-date Soviet weapons and sending officers to military academies in Egypt and Iraq. Most returned radicalized and enthused with nationalism and socialism. Yemen was a founder member of the Arab League in 1945 and joined the UN in 1947.

As Yemen became a bolt-hole for dissidents seeking support from Imam Ahmed, British objections were largely neutralized by the growth of Arab nationalism, particularly in Egypt, and anti-imperialism in the UN and Arab League. The border remained a seething pot of tension, particularly during the civil war. Two days after the murder of Imam Yahya, the APL camp at Dhala was occupied by squadrons rotating from Aden to give the Arab soldiers experience of a hostile environment in which their numerical superiority and air support was neutralized by the lack of roads, deep wadis, hilly country, countless ambush positions and inaccurate maps, all of which limited opportunities for tactical deployments.

Over the next ten years, Aden prospered. An oil refinery was built at Little Aden by British Petroleum (BP). The port was deepened and, by 1958, was the busiest after New York. Flats erected in Ma'alla rivalled Crater in size, though not in design. Crater, although airless and hot, remained the commercial centre, with banks, businesses, shops, institutions such as the Public Library, and government buildings nestling among the network of teeming streets and alleys. The dual carriageway that ran through Ma'alla to Queen Arwa Road in Crater was opened in 1963. A causeway across the harbour linked Crater with a road to Little Aden and to Al Mansoura and Sheikh Othman. The oasis at Sheikh Othman had grown into a residential and business suburb. Along the east coast were several barracks. Construction was absorbing about 25 per cent of the workforce, supporting a population that grew from 80,550 in 1946 to 225,000 in 1963. The Colonial authorities were also a significant employer. Compared to the autocracy in Yemen, Aden was sophisticated, and independence beckoned as Great Britain conformed to the UN Declaration on the Granting of Independence to Colonial Countries and Peoples adopted in December 1960, with the proviso that power be transferred to a reliable administration. The educated sons of rulers in the Protectorates and the merchant class in Aden were impatient with the conservatism shown by their elders. The creation of the South Arabian League in 1951 in Lahej promoting independence and a united South Arabia was significant, because it drew general support from Aden and the Protectorates. The forming of the Aden Trades Union Congress (TUC) three years later amplified militant dissent in the port and oil refinery and produced a leader named Abdullah al-Asnag, who formed close links with the British Labour Party.

Psychological operations, 'flag' marches and visits to rulers helped reduce internal security tension. Forward air controllers directed Air Control, although there was growing anxiety that operations were not supported by ground forces. An Intelligence Officer at HQ RAF Aden selecting sites for airstrips faced two major problems: the mountainous terrain and the inaccuracy of maps, some dating to the nineteenth century. Aircrews regularly updated existing maps with sketches. Things improved in early 1958 when Valiants and Canberras of Bomber Command and Canberras of the Middle East Air Force conducted aerial photography coverage, from which map and charts were updated. By 1953, the Aden Protectorate Support Flight flying Austers and Ansons, and later Pembrokes, was capable of operating from gravel landing-strips. In 1957, two Transport Command Blackburn Beverley freighters delivered bulldozers, drilling equipment, guns and armoured cars to the landing strips at Dhala and Beihan. No. 1 Squadron, Royal Rhodesian Air Force inaugurated training courses for Rhodesian airmen in Aden as a contribution to Commonwealth defence.

In March 1949, the Amir of Beihan had built a Customs post on Negd Merqad pass that linked the trade route from Beihan through Wadi Hatib to Dathina to Thumier and Aden to the south. The Yemenis claimed that it violated the 1934 border agreement and built a fort west of Negd Merqad, from which insurgents regularly crossed the border. Insurgency can be described as organized resistance aimed at spreading an ideology through subversion, sabotage and armed conflict in order to overthrow an existing administration. Guerrillas are the faces of insurgency. Government Guards reinforced the Amir's retinue, and then, on 2 September, 8 Squadron Tempests reduced the fort to rubble. As insurgency peppered the Western Aden Protectorate border, the APL adapted with long patrols, one in 1953 lasting 54 days. Nevertheless, Yemeni subversion and arms smuggling meant that some less stable tribes became less willing to cooperate with officials. Ambushes on caravans meant bigger escorts were required, leading to the APL suffering from operational fatigue, desertions, information leaks and apathy, particularly as Air Control was becoming a political embarrassment. To bolster the defence, the establishment of the Government Guards was increased to 500 and a screen of forts was built in depth to add to those on the border.

In mid-April 1953, a colourful bandit named Salim Ali Mawar, who was nicknamed 'Sam' and was head of a sect in the Rabizi tribe, became active in Wadi Hatib in the State of Upper Aulaqui. He and his small band were largely left alone until he accepted weapons from the Yemenis, on the promise that he use them against the British. The Sultan of Aulaqi was determined to end Sam's opportunism, and on 17 November, two APL columns launched Operation Nothing Ventured, to enter the wadi from the north and south, aiming to trap Sam, take hostages and seize grain and livestock. Poor recce, lack of air photographs and decent maps and extremely bad 'going' led to a series of inconclusive, sharp actions; nevertheless, on 6 December, South Force reached Robat and Sam's village. Six days later, the the Government Guards were building a fort when explosives laid against a wall killed six of them. The insurgency escalated in January 1954 after Governor Sir Tom Hickinbottom had suggested to the Western Aden Protectorate rulers that they form a federation, a suggestion that alarmed the Yeminis because such an alliance would be hard to undermine. In spite of sniping by Sam's band, the fort was built. Throughout 1954, the APL and Air Control struggled to eradicate Yemeni insurgency. The failure in October of the Imam to convince Hickinbottom to drop the federation idea led to increased insurgency focusing on Wadi Hatib, with the fort at its centre. Fighter ground attack supported APL patrols and offensive operations, but APL morale dipped and the force now numbered about 100 men, as opposed to the six companies needed.

Propping up Yemeni aspirations was Egypt, where nationalism had challenged the 1936 defence agreement that 10,000 British could stay in the country until 1956 to counter Italian regional aspirations. After the war, nationalist demands led to the treaty being abrogated in October 1951; nevertheless, as serious anti-British disturbances developed, the garrison moved from the comforts of Cairo and Alexandria to the less salubrious Canal Zone, centering on Ismalia and the ill-named Sweetwater Canal. The Canal Zone quickly became a running sore as militant Liberation Battalions attacked Service dependants, ambushed patrols and vehicles, kidnapped and murdered British servicemen and intimidated the 66,000-strong locally employed workforce. The overthrow of King Farouk saw a military council adopting a conciliatory approach to the British withdrawal, until it was ejected by Colonel Gamal Abdul Nasser, whose ideology promoted the concept of Arab socialism and rejected communism as being incompatible with Arab traditions and Islam. In October 1954, GHQ Middle East Command moved to Cyprus, just as the island's Emergency broke out in 1955. When the British left Egypt, the strategic importance of Aden, midway between the Middle East and Far East, grew. The Egyptian General Intelligence Service was formed in 1955 to enforce internal security and conduct external operations. Three years later, Salah Al Nasr was appointed Head of Intelligence during a period when Nasser flirted with the Eastern Bloc and opposed Israel as a state. Al Nasr drew on his experiences gained from the British to spread Nasserism throughout the Middle East, opening an office in Taiz in Yemen and using the highly effective 'Voice of the Arabs' to broadcast a continuous stream of venomous propaganda against the British presence in Aden.

During the morning of 15 June 1955, Wing Commander V.R. Marshall, who commanded 1 APL Mobile Wing, was with the advance guard of a convoy en route to Robat through Wadi Hatib, covered by picquets seizing high ground. The convoy moved tactically and, in the final stages, aircraft attacked several ridges, until it reached the fort without a major contact. The convoy was preparing to leave when a former APL warned Marshall that 'Sam' intended to ambush it at the bend where the desert narrows into a defile. Marshall appeared to be assured that the air support would deter Sam, but as the vehicles entered the defile, Sam sprung the ambush, the first volley killing Marshall, another RAF officer and his radio operator and a senior APL officer. In spite of the loss of command, the junior officers put down sufficient fire to dissuade Sam from following up his success; nevertheless, six APL and three Government Guards were killed and five APL and four Guards wounded. Of concern was that nineteen APL then deserted when orders were issued for another convoy to Robat. When an appeal for military assistance was made to HQ Middle East Command, which had just moved to Cyprus, Brigadier J.A.R. Robertson (6th Gurkha Rifles) arrived by air in July with a Tactical HQ from his 51st Infantry Brigade, 1st Seaforth Highlanders, a Life Guards squadron equipped with Ferret Scout Cars and a Royal Engineers troop from Kenya. In an early example of joint operations, the Seaforths and three APL squadrons were flown to the airstrip at Ataq in the Sultanate of Upper Aulaqi; however, the strip was unable to take Hastings medium transport aircraft, which meant that the fuel and other stores had to be driven in twenty 3-ton lorries, with Ferrets providing the escort. The 345-mile drive took five days and, not for the only time, demonstrated a fallibility of Air Control – the lack of roads. Two Ferrets broke down, and when seven lorries were left with local guards, bandits killed a Seaforth Highlander and wounded an RAF Regiment airman. On 9 July, the Seaforths began the 40-mile advance to Fort Robat; when they were seven miles short they waited outside a defile while a Lincoln bombed the entrance in case there were any lurking insurgents. Then, covered by picquets, they advanced past the wrecked vehicles of the ambush and evacuated the Government Guards from the fort. Three weeks later, the Seaforths, with the RAF Regiment and APL under command, lost another soldier killed and had three wounded while clearing insurgents from the main track running between Lodar and Mafidh, south of Ataq. This was the first time that British soldiers had been in the area, and the Amir of Beihan laid on the traditional Arab welcome of uncontrolled volleys fired into the air and a lavish feast. The Seaforths replied by producing their bagpipes.

No sooner had Brigadier Robertson and his force returned to Kenya in October than Yemeni insurgents infiltrated into the Amirate of Dhala. In October 1955, 1st Kings Own Yorkshire Light Infantry arrived as the Resident Battalion, followed by 1st Glosters in April 1956, both on six-month tours from Kenya. Detachments were sent to Mukeiras, overlooking the border in the State of Audhali, and to Dhala. The 15/19th Hussars sent a squadron of Ferrets from the jungles of Malaya to the desert of the Protectorate primarily for convoy escort to reinforce 10 APL Armoured Car Squadron. As the Army presence grew, an ad hoc brigade HQ was attached to Air Officer Commanding. Operations focused on mobility, particularly in the Amirate of Beihan, generally exacting reprisals for attacks on Government Guard forts. B APL Flight was attached to 1st Kings Own Yorkshire Light Infantry during a strike at the BP Oil Refinery. When the enterprising Shairis in the Amirate of Dhala imposed their own laws, 1 APL Squadron based in Dhala brought them to heel in an operation that included Air Control on part of the village of Jaleila, in order to convince the wavering Amir to reject Yemeni subversion.

When finances were withdrawn from Nasser's pet project, the Aswan High Dam, in July 1956, he nationalized the Suez Canal and forced users to pay dues to his treasury as opposed to the Anglo-French Consortium which owned the Canal. The closure hit the economy of Aden hard, as ships sailed around the Cape of Good Hope. Amid rising tension, British and French forces assembled in the Near East to recover the Suez Canal. On 29 October, Israel launched a surprise attack on Egyptian forces east of the Canal and then, a week later, British and French forces landed in Egypt and regained control of the Canal, before being forced to withdraw in the face of UN disapproval and lack of support from the USA. Politically, the operation was a disastrous humiliation for British interests in the region. Because of fears that the 'Voice of the Arabs' broadcasts accusing Britain and France of colluding with Israel might rebound on Aden from Yemen, in December, 1st Queens Own Cameron Highlanders, returning to Britain from Korea in a troopship that had just called at Aden, was instructed to return to reinforce Aden Garrison. The soldiers were clearly identified by their jungle-green uniforms and by the presence of a piper waking the sleeping garrison from Chapel Hill. In November, 1st Durham Light Infantry also arrived in Aden for a three-month emergency tour.

In the background was the Soviet Union's search for a naval port that could threaten Western oil supplies from the Persian Gulf. The appearance in 1958 of Soviet and Chinese trade missions in Yemen sponsoring capital projects, such as the Soviet Union's development of the port of Hodeida, alarmed the Western allies; however, any influence that Moscow thought that it had with Imam Ahmed disappeared when he invited the US to establish a legation, in return for wheat and engineers to build roads. Nevertheless, Moscow shipped T-34 medium battle tanks, artillery, AK-47 Kalashnikov rifles and machine guns as the Iman modernized his army. Surplus weapons began to appear in the Protectorates in the hands of apolitical tribesmen, giving them prestige or 'face', graded according to the type and number of weapons possessed. If a tribesman wanted a second weapon, perhaps as an investment, he might be asked to prove his commitment by opening fire on patrols, which he usually did at long range because there was no point in inviting retaliation. On 30 September, a combined operation by the retinue of the Amirate of Dhala, who rode a horse, and the APL, whose commander rode a donkey, conducted an operation against the Radfanis; however, the lack of accurate maps and the hostile terrain again proved troublesome. Two weeks later, an ambush on four armoured cars between Dhala and Thumier showed evidence of Soviet weaponry.

When Prime Minister Harold Macmillan came to power after the Suez crisis, the 1957 Defence White Paper attempted to screen military overstretch by stating that Britain would remain east of Suez but that forces would be reduced in favour of increasing the commitment to NATO in Central Europe.

There was, therefore, a need for well-equipped and highly-trained Regulars. Also, in a decision that would halve the size of the Armed Forces, National Service would end in 1960. Several forward-thinking regiments began seeking partners with whom to amalgamate.

On 7 January 1957, the Army took back operational control of the APL when Brigadier D.W. Lister DSO MC took command. The medical officers remained RAF until 1965. As the APL band beat Retreat at Seedaseer Lines on 31 March, Army terminology and organization returned, as did Aden Garrison, with infantry Resident Battalions usually on one-year deployments. The remit remained to defend the border and maintain an internal security presence should the Aden Police require assistance.

When HQ Middle East Land Forces resumed the control of grounds operations, among the British Army units that arrived was the Intelligence Corps to provide counter-intelligence. The Corps was reformed in July 1940 from soldiers who generally conformed to the requirements of the 1922 *Manual of Military Intelligence in the Field*:

> The best sources of supply for the Intelligence Corps will be the professional and literary classes, also public schools, universities, banks and commercial houses with overseas branches or trade connections with foreign countries.

The principle was applied throughout the Second World War and the National Service era. When the Corps was instructed to support British units and the APL in South Arabia, 4 Field Security Section was reformed. It had originally been formed in 1939 to support 3 Division and, after being evacuated from the beaches of Dunkirk, had been posted to the West Indies on port and travel control duties. Section HQ was in the Admiralty Compound in Singapore Lines, while detachments of usually two NCOs were deployed to Beihan, Dhala and Mukhairas, and occasionally in Ataq and Lodar. When the Intelligence Corps introduced the Counter-Intelligence Unit concept in 1958, the Section was absorbed into the Counter-Intelligence Unit, Arabian Peninsula.

Coincidental with Yemen applying to the UN claiming Aden, Yemeni troops closed up to the border. The Yemeni fort at Harib overlooking the western borders of the Amirate of Beihan and also Jebel Manawa opened fire on British armoured cars. The Government Guards covered the border from the fort at Nejd Margab. Operation Whiplash restored control and a camp was established on Jebel Manawa, after which operations focused on the Dhala region.

When a large group of Yemeni soldiers crossed into Upper Yaha and Dhala and attacked Fort Sanah in January 1957, the motive seemed to be a show of strength. After an APL company had driven the Yemenis from their position and help was sought, B Company and the 3-inch mortars and Vickers medium machine guns of Support Company, 1st Queen's Cameron Own Highlanders, the Resident Battalion, cleared a ridge on Jebel Jihaf in a dawn attack, driving the infiltrators back across the border. On 4 January, Major Christopher Grant, the B Company Commander, was with the leading platoon near Al Jua checking his map when the platoon was ambushed. Two soldiers were killed and five wounded, including Grant, when a bullet smashed the binoculars on his chest. The attack was traced to Danaba in Radfan, and 8 Squadron applied Air Control. On the 15th, a 5th APL Company convoy was ambushed on the same road and its commander, Squadron Leader C.R.S. Daly, killed. When these successes encouraged the Azraqi tribe living in south-west Dhala to attack the Government Guard fort at Lazariq and fill in the well, the APL withdrew the garrison. The Azraqis seems to have been content, because 'face' had been retained and they could now plead the difficulties of attacking Dhala from the south-west.

On 22 February and again on 8 March, Yemeni gunners using Soviet artillery shelled the APL fort at Negd Maiser from Harib, and the road between Dhala and Thumier became plagued with roadblocks as Radfani tribesmen raided caravans. A 208 Squadron Meteor was shot down by ground fire in an Air Control operation and its pilot killed, and a helicopter sent to recover the body of the pilot of an 8 Squadron Venom shot down over Radfan was driven off by ground fire. A Twin Pioneer on a casualty-evacuation sortie crashed at Al Milah and was then attacked by dissidents from Al Kusua, until an APL Ferret troop drove them off. The local sheikh was happy to make amends, provided he did not lose too much 'face'. In May, navigation along the Dhala Road was considerably eased when, for the first time, a 15/19th Hussars troop started erecting white-painted milestones. Meanwhile, intelligence emerging from the growing number of dissident casualties seeking medical attention indicated the level of Yemeni subversive penetration, and it became evident that the incursions were not part of a pre-invasion strategy, largely because the Yemenis could not rely upon tribal support in the Protectorates, any more than the British could. Politically, the Amirs of Dhala and Beihan were moving towards the Federation, but as the defence of the border was more important, it followed that APL garrisons should be deployed along it. While this would reduce flexibility and mobility, it played into the hands of rulers keeping the 'security pot' boiling.

A dangerous incursion occurred in May, when 100 insurgents and Yemeni soldiers equipped with a Soviet ZSU-23-4 'Shilka' anti-aircraft gun and 12.7mm machine guns occupied Jebel Dhahat and Jebel Shuqair, about a mile inside the 1934 'status quo' agreement in Beihan State and dominating the villages of Tamara and Ain. A firepower demonstration by 2nd APL Armoured Car Squadron had little effect. Following attacks by Shackletons and Venoms on 2 August and shelling from a 33 Para Light Regiment battery, an assault by 5th APL Company failed because the enemy position was tactically strong. An Aden Airways aircraft landing at Beihan was then hit. Brigadier Lister deprived the Yemenis of water and then, on 18 August, 3rd APL Battalion assaulted the position in a pincer move from the north and south and found that it had been hastily abandoned.

Meanwhile, trouble was brewing around Urqub Pass linking Western and Eastern Area Protectorates. On 5 December, Lister launched Operation Muggah to clear several roadblocks, but failed to tempt the insurgents into ambushes by using the 'tethered goat' strategy of weakly-held camps in tactically unsound positions. An ambush on 7th APL Company was not driven home, convoys were generally ignored and an attempt to block the road was half-hearted; nevertheless, about a third of the APL were tied up in keeping the pass open. At the end of 1957, 8 Squadron had been advised that if Yemeni shells exploded in the Protectorate it could, using artillery phraseology, conduct Counter Battery fire by attacking the gun positions, and that if Yemeni troops crossed the border from a fort, the fort could be attacked. Yemeni pressure on Dhala continued during the New Year, with shelling from three old Turkish 75mm field artillery pieces at Qataba. A Pembroke aircraft taking off from Dhala was hit by ground fire, and 7th APL Company and Government Guards both took casualties. In support was A Company, the Camerons. Yemeni reaction to patrols being sent from Fort Sanah was increased shelling.

On 20 April 1958, a 7th Company patrol checked Jebel Jihaf, where it was thought that Haidera, the brother of the Amir, might be planning something; however, all seemed peaceful. Two days later, a Government Guards patrol and the Political Adviser, Roy Somerset, encountered hostility and sought refuge in the fort at Al Sarir, which was then besieged by insurgents who had seized control of the mountain that day, dominating the APL camp at Dhala and the airstrip below. An APL company reached the fort on the 24th, but did not appreciate the situation. A general strike in Aden, the Queen's Birthday Parade and the tension along the border saw the 1st Buffs reinforced by 1st King's Shropshire Light Infantry, less two companies, from Kenya, and 1st York and Lancasters from England. Three days later, Counter Battery strikes by 8 Squadron Venoms wrecked the gun positions of three anti-aircraft guns that had fired at aircraft. It was raining as C Company, 1st King's Shropshire Light Infantry then diverted the attention of the enemy by openly moving through Dhala and joining a troop of the 13th/18th Hussars in a diversionary left hook, while Shackletons and the 33 Para Light Regiment detachment plastered the summit with high explosive. Meanwhile, 3rd APL Company and A Company, 1st Buffs had used a goat track to climb from the airfield to the escarpment; but as the Buffs crested the summit, they came under sustained fire which killed one and wounded three others. The APL, commanded by Major Boucher-Myers (East Lancashires), supported by Venoms, fought their way up the 2,000ft slopes, slippery with rain, and, after four hours, gained a secure foothold at the top of the pass, which then allowed a Buffs platoon to pass through and seize a peak from which they dominated the enemy and secured a drop zone for parachuted supplies. After regrouping, the advance continued and the fort was relieved just before dark. Even though it was a victory, the fact that a Yemeni force had occupied ground inside Western Aden Protectorate was a serious blow.

David Bushel was serving with C Troop, 33rd Parachute Field Regiment RA, which was then equipped with M-116 75mm Pack Howitzers:

Immediately on arrival, we re-organized and split into three two gun sections. There were no maps, so we used blown up air photos with a grid superimposed. There were no roads so all movements was along wadis, and our guns were stripped down and moved by camel. We were re-supplied by airdrops throughout the campaign as there were no helicopters . . . Our base camp was fired on every night from the surrounding hills. All the locals carried weapons and shooting at us appeared to be the main sport. For some operations we were joined by a section of machine guns and two armoured cars. These were mainly for defence as we moved through the mountains. Movement was a great problem and we often had to move back to the desert then into a different valley to get to the next area of operations. It was impossible to dig in, and we built sangars out of the volcanic rock for protection. It was very hot every day but at night the temperatures dropped dramatically. We only saw about ten minutes of rain during out stay. As the Senior NCO, it was a good command with plenty of action in a very hostile environment. We had no supplies other than food and ammunition, and returned home in the same clothes that we went out in; we also had no pay, but the money was useless . . . therefore we did very well on our return home. [From www.britains-smallwars/Aden]

In order to destabilize insurgency operations, the Governor was permitted to authorize clandestine operations in the following ways:

• Operation Eggshell – laying mines just inside the Yemen border.
• Operation Stirrup – providing arms and ammunition to tribesmen in the border disaffected with the Republican regime.

These were largely controlled by the Political Officers assigned to advise the South Arabian rulers.

On 1 April 1958, Air Headquarters in Aden was converted into the unified HQ British Forces Arabian Gulf, with Air Marshal Sir Charles Elworthy appointed Commander-in-Chief and a major general appointed to command ground operations. When a grenade thrown into Seedaseer Lines killed the British officer commanding the APL MT Section, newspapers in England began to report on Aden. Although the APL experienced higher than average desertion problems as firefights along the border became common and casualty lists rose, it was learning from the Army by developing night-fighting techniques and greater mobility. In early May, 3rd Company was ambushed near Dhala by Yemeni soldiers, but it counter-attacked and forced the enemy to withdraw from its position at the last moment. When another 8 Squadron Venom was shot down in Beihan by anti-aircraft artillery in Yemen, Fort Harib was subjected to Counter Battery.

In August, the West Yorkshire and East Yorkshire Regiments returned to Aden as 1st Prince of Wales's Own Regiment of Yorkshire (PWO) and relieved 1st Royal Lincolns, who returned to England in a troopship after an unscheduled three-month tour in Aden. The two regiments had amalgamated in Dover in April and had been warned for deployment to the Cyprus Emergency until their destination was changed to Aden. The advance guard flew out in a Transport Command aircraft via Malta, Kano and Entebbe, while the remainder of the Battalion boarded HM Troopships *Devonshire* and *Nevada*, the first arriving after eighteen days in August and the second after twelve days in September. Activities during the voyage were typical – weapon training, education, physical fitness, evening entertainment of films and the inevitable 'sod's operas', with runs ashore at Gibraltar. The Medium Machine Gun Platoon on the *Devonshire* found a drill purpose Vickers machine gun, to 'everyone's delight', apparently. The .303 Vickers Mark 1 medium machine gun was introduced into service in 1912 and was synonymous with reliability. Crewed by three men, the Number One, the commander, kept the gun on a steady platform by firing four-second bursts while counting 'One banana, two bananas, three bananas, four bananas – Stop!' The Number Two placed 250-round ammunition belts on to the feed tray and prevented jams. A feature of the weapon was that its barrel was kept cool with water fed from a condenser. The Number Three kept the condenser topped up and ensured the Number Two was supplied with ammunition. When broken down for manpacking, the gun was heavy and awkward.

While the heat of the Red Sea was exceeded by the oven of Aden, the voyage allowed troops to acclimatize and work up a tan, which was seen as the best defence against sun and heat. The Battalion moved into the dusty and uncomfortable Khormaksar Transit Camp, which impressed virtually no one. Training continued on the ranges, with fieldcraft and live firing exercises in the desert at Bir Fuqum. In spite of the risk of sharks, swimming and fishing were popular off-duty pastimes. B Company moved into the half-built camp at Gold Mohur, west of RAF Khormaksar, and helped Royal Engineers complete it. Jebel Shamsan was used to develop mountain warfare tactics, in particular the use of picquets. In 1735, *A Compleat System of Military Discipline* prescribed:

The Picket Guard is a Body of Men always to be ready, lying with their Arms in their Hands, to turn out in case of an Alarm; but are not commanded by the next Officer on Detail, but such as are appointed by the Picket; but must march either faster or slower, to sustain Out-posts, Foraging, Escourts, or any other Service; and it shall be allowed them in their Tour of Duty.

B Company took over from 1st York and Lancasters at An Nu'um, where the National Service drivers experienced the hazards of driving in sand. The camp perimeter and dug-outs were buttressed by 10,000 sandbags. Initially, showers were cold, much to the distress of the officers, until Private Bedford, a joiner, Private Riley, a plumber, and Private Hannam, a bricklayer, built hot showers, using a stove to heat water in an overhead tank. Operations were mainly confined to three-day patrols to Government Guard forts, where the traditional welcome was a cup of hot, sweet tea. The only action came when a Tribal Guard attracted the attention of 5 Platoon by firing a shot and asking for a lift. Mobile platoons in lorries supported by a machine-gun or mortar section and an APL interpreter patrolled the border and checked tracks for mines. When 7 Platoon undertook an 18-mile foot patrol from Wadi Dah to the APL fort at Kirsch, a camel was hired to carry the radio and heavy weapons; and although their arrival was unexpected, the APL commander turned out the guard and invited Second Lieutenant Medd, the Platoon Commander, to inspect it. In early October, Lieutenant Bower and an advance guard from C Company deployed to Nobat Dakin to build a camp on an escarpment from equipment dumped beside a desert track. In between sporadic sniping, tents were erected inside a perimeter of stone *sangars* protected by machine guns and mortars. An airstrip capable of handling Twin Pioneers and helicopters was built alongside the camp. Fresh water was collected from Sheikh Othman, which meant an armed convoy driving along a desert track and a bumpy road that passed through several villages and the town of Lahej, with its market stalls and wandering goats, chickens, dogs and children cluttering the road.

D Company deployed to Lodar in the border State of Audhali to refurbish the former Second World War camp at Mukeiras for two companies of 1st Kings Own Shropshire Light Infantry due to arrive in Aden in May 1958. The camp was about three miles from the border and accessible by the 3,250ft Thirra Pass, which reached the escarpment above the desert. Despite the heat, there was no humidity and the nights were sufficiently cold for the issue of two blankets – sleeping bags were a distant dream for most National Servicemen. The RAF delivered fresh food, mail and other essentials, and gazelle meat supplemented dull 'compo' rations. Patrol routes were sought down the escarpment. In October, D Company returned to Aden to help the police during several strikes. Support Company provided a Wombat anti-tank section, a machine-gun section and a mortar section.

In November, the Battalion moved into seven rows of single-storey, blue wooden huts that had been built to accommodate the BP refinery construction teams at Little Aden and were being leased from the company. The bare terrain was broken by tree-lined patios beside the Officers' and Sergeants' Mess and a much valued small garden and lawn. Across the road was the Armoured Car Squadron of Saladin Armoured Cars, Saracen Armoured Personnel Carriers and Ferret Scout Cars. Most welcome was air conditioning and the ability to keep weapons free of dust, which had not been possible at Khormaksar Transit Camp. After Christmas, the Battalion accepted new National Servicemen taking the places of those due for discharge. B Company rotated with C Company at Nobat Dakin, and then on 12 January 1959, C Company deployed to reinforce Mukeiras, but not without incident. Assuming tide tables supplied by Battalion HQ were correct, at about 1 pm the Company left BP Camp at low tide and drove along the beach toward Sheikh Othman. All went well until dawn rushed over the eastern horizon and it became evident that the tidal information was incorrect. The *XIV/XV Regimental Journal*, April 1959, records:

Naturally enough, the Battalion recovery 3-tonner was the first to bog in on the soft sand; it was followed by Cpl Wilson's 3-tonner, which tried to overtake on the seaward side. The last two 3-tonners stopped in sympathy. The recovery 3-tonner, under Sgt Devine, tried to winch itself out until, eventually, the REME Scammel caught up and pulled the two bogged 3-tonners.

The Company reached Lodar and, after staying overnight with the APL, climbed the Thirra Pass to Mukeiras early one morning, meeting D Company on the way down. On the 23rd, 8 Platoon and the Vickers section occupied 'Hoare Hill' to observe Yemeni activity, but low cloud sometimes reduced visibility to 100 yards. Next day, 7 Platoon made the observation post (OP) more permanent by pitching tents on the reverse slopes and building a perimeter *sangar*. Next night, the platoon was attacked, and although things quietened down in the afternoon, an Aden Airways Dakota and a Beverley were both hit by ground fire from Bheida. On 3 February, 9 Platoon, its support sections and an APL Ferret troop provided ground forces when a Shackleton and eight Hawker Hunters retaliated for a Yemeni attack on the Government Guards fort at Merta'a. When the fighting escalated, C Company laid several ambushes in the chill of the night. In August, with the prospect of a posting to Gibraltar, the Battalion handed over to 1st Warwicks.

Many of the British in Aden were National Servicemen. The Labour Government that ousted Winston Churchill in 1945 had not initially been convinced of the need for conscription; however, a combination of the need to discharge Hostilities Only servicemen, the loss of the Indian Army in 1947, Britain's strategic commitment in West Germany and operations in the Far East and the Near East led to the 1947 National Service Act. Over the next thirteen years, National Servicemen, backed up by a hardcore of Regulars, many of whom had fought in the Second World War, fought Communist terrorists in the Malayan jungles, Arab nationalists in Egypt, the Mau Mau in the forests of Kenya and Greek-Cypriot terrorists in Cyprus. Some survived brutal prison camps as prisoners of Communist North Koreans and Chinese determined to subvert them, while others were involved in nuclear weapon testing in the South Pacific. All had survived the rigours of the Second World War as children, some experiencing close family members killed in action and in air raids. Most had had an interrupted education and had experienced years of rationing until the mid-1950s, when wartime austerity gave way to the excitement of Elvis Presley, Bill Haley and the 'Teddy Boy' fashions of sharp suits and winklepicker shoes. Men aged up to 26 and usually resident in UK were committed to two years' full time military service, followed by three and a half years in the Reserve. Exempted occupations included clergy, merchant seamen and some agricultural workers, and deferments could be given to, among others, apprentices, undergraduates and those studying for professional articles. Northern Ireland was excluded, because of the fear of Catholic dissent, as were the Channel Islands, still recovering from German occupation. The Army accepted 72 per cent of the recruits, the Royal Navy about 2 per cent and the the RAF the remainder. Those with existing skills increased their chances of advancement; a bank clerk, for example, could be sent to the Royal Army Pay Corps (RAPC). Army basic training was usually in dilapidated camps or eighteenth and nineteenth century depots and barracks. Although some had been evacuated to Canada, the USA or the British countryside during the war, for most this was their first time away from home. Many were unhappy at sleeping in large cold dormitories with strangers from all parts of the UK, and eating food that lacked the quality of Mother's ('Take it or leave it, son!'). Royal Navy and RAF accommodation was usually better and haircuts less brutal than in the Army. As military training progressed, however, most recruits adapted to Service life and moulded into their units. Few regarded as bullying or a breach of their human rights the rantings by corporals, sergeants and sergeant majors and the insistence on tradition; they simply accepted these as a feature of life in uniform. Most National Service officers had gained military experience in public and grammar school cadet forces. Other ranks talent-spotted for commissions were assembled into platoons to prepare for the three-day commissioning War Office Selection Board, known as 'WOSBee'. Those selected for three-year Army Short Service Commissions attended either Eaton Hall (Chester) or Mons (Aldershot) Officer Cadet Training Unit and could apply to convert into Regular commissions. Regular Army officers graduated from the Royal Military College at Sandhurst after two years.

CHAPTER SIX

The Mercenary Operations in Yemen

In spite of the persistent 'Voice of the Arabs' broadcasting in the 1950s the vitriolic aspirations of Nasserism, the British were determined that the Protectorates and Aden State should adopt the principle of federation, particularly as the UN Declaration on the Granting of Independence to Colonial Countries and Peoples was due to be adopted by member states (which it was in December 1960). Since Egypt rejected federation as contrary to Arab nationalism, the Protectorate rulers thus found themselves in the invidious political position of supporting independence but having to accept the British military presence in South Arabia.

Tension on the border decreased, although the little intelligence emerging from Yemen suggested that independently-minded leaders, such as 'Sam', could escalate it. Attacks on the Dhala Road by Radfan tribesmen continued, and Royal Engineers building a road to the company base at Mukeiras lost a sapper killed in 1959. When the road was completed in 1960, villagers soon realized its economic benefits.

Aden in 1960 was tense. The Aden TUC had developed close links with the militant TUC in Britain and was opposing a franchise that gave votes only to Adenis, British and British-protected subjects who had lived in the colony for seven years within the previous ten. The disenfranchising of Arabs, Indians, Somalis and Yemenis was criticized by Egypt. The port and BP oil refinery were badly affected by strikes because a high percentage of employees were Yemeni.

The first major manifestation of federation was on 11 February 1959, when the states of Beihan, Audhali, Fadhli, Lower Yafa, Dhala and Upper Aulaqi merged into the autonomous Federation of Arab Amirates of the South, followed a year later by the ten states of Dathina, Aqrabi and Lower Aulaqi from the Western Aden Protectorate. Significantly, the three states in Eastern Aden Protectorate did not, and would not, join. Aden did not join because its elite had no wish to share its growing wealth with rulers that they regarded as impoverished and autocratic. Conversely, the rulers regarded the Adenis as soft. The Federation was guaranteed by a British defence treaty and subsidies financing social improvements; nevertheless, by any stretch of the imagination, it faced considerable obstacles, in particular from Yemen, who regarded it as a hindrance to her claims to all South Arabia, and from Egypt, who saw her regional ambitions thwarted by a strong political base in South Arabia. The UN accused Great Britain of colonialism. On the same day, the foundations were laid of the new capital in the dusty hamlet of Al Ittihad overlooking the port of Aden. The Government Guards were reformed into Federal National Guard 1 (FNG 1) and the Tribal Guards into FNG 2, both controlled by HQ Federal National Guard in Champion Lines, Aden. In reality, FNG 2 still conformed to the requirements of local rulers. Hussan al-Bayoomi was appointed Ministerial Adviser on Security to the High Commissioner.

In March 1960, Middle East Command was reformed thus:

• The new Near East Command, controlling operations from Cyprus in the eastern Mediterranean and North Africa.
• Middle East Command, assuming the responsibilities of British Forces in the Arabian Peninsula, the Persian Gulf, South Arabia and down the east coast of Africa to Swaziland. The discovery of oil in the Gulf became of strategic importance.

The Command was midway between Far East Command in Singapore, with its commitment to the South East Asia Treaty Organisation, and Near East Command on the southern flank of NATO. Command HQ moved into the HQ Aden Garrison building on 'Command Hill' at Steamer Point. On the top floor were the Commander-in-Chief, the three Service commanders and the Chief of Staff. The level down housed Brigadier General Staff and Senior Air Staff Officer, naval staff and G Plans. Technical staff, Administration and Supply, Political Advisers and representatives from the Secret Intelligence Service and Security Services were closeted in a cluster of huts at ground level. Flag Officer, Middle East was based at the shore-based HMS *Sheba* in the naval dockyard. The High Commission was half a mile away. Under command of HQ Middle East Land Forces were HQ Aden Garrison and the APL and HQ 24 Infantry Brigade in East Africa, with a capability to deploy quickly to any regional crisis affecting British interests. The arrival of Command HQ saw an immediate increase in the number of Service personnel and civilian components and their families in Aden, many accommodated in married quarters alongside the dual carriageway of Ma'alla Straight, where they contributed significantly to local employment. They were also a protective security problem. RAF Khormaksar was fast becoming the RAF's busiest station supporting operations in Saudi Arabia and as a staging post for Singapore and Hong Kong. The thirty-two Hawker Hunter (Fighter Ground Attack) Mark 9s of 8 and 208 Squadrons were equipped with weapon fits that included four 30mm Aden cannons and underwing pylons capable of carrying a weapons load of two 450lb bombs or twenty-four 3-inch rockets of Second World War vintage.

The decrease in border tension permitted the British to reduce the number of battalions to two: an infantry battalion rotating about every six months as the Resident Internal Security Battalion based at Waterloo Lines, and 45 Commando. The Commando disembarked from the troopship *Dunera* on 23 April 1960 and took over BP Camp from 1st Royal Warwicks. It was still using the wartime Army commando structure of five 65-strong Troops. X Troop, which had arrived with the advance guard five days earlier on the *Empire Skua*, had deployed to the company base at Dhala. They found the area quiet, with only occasional sniping. Patrols using the old Turkish track to the summit of Jebel Jifaf visited to the Government Guards forts at Qarnah and Saria.

On 30 November 1961, the APL reformed into the Federal Regular Army (FRA), and a week later Brigadier James Lunt OBE took command. Commissioned into the Duke of Wellington's Regiment in 1937, he took part in the epic retreat from Rangoon to India after the Japanese invaded Burma in 1942, and weighed just eight stone when he crossed the border. After serving in the Canal Zone with 16/5th Lancers, he was seconded to the Arab Legion in Jordan before being promoted to command the FRA. Lunt found his chain of command and accountability confusing. As Commander FRA, he was also the Federal Chief of Staff reporting to the Minister of Defence; but as a British officer, he also reported to Commander Middle East Land Forces and had ill-defined responsibilities to the Governor. The consequence was a conflict of priorities. With HQ FRA still at Seedaseer Lines, he was expected to increase the FRA establishment to 4,500 Arab soldiers and 400 seconded British officers and NCOs divided into four battalions, the Armoured Car Squadron, the Motor Transport Company, the Supply Platoon, workshops, the ceremonial Camel Troop and the Training and Depot Battalion at Lake Lines. Three battalions were on the border and the fourth was in reserve in Aden.

Artillery support was provided by a British battery of the field artillery regiment with 24th Brigade in Kenya. In September 1961, 3rd Royal Horse Artillery (RHA) had sailed to Kenya on the last voyage of a British troopship and rotated its batteries to support operations in South Arabia in January 1962. The Italian 105mm Oto Melara Pack Howitzer, which had a useful anti-tank capability and a maximum range of 11,560 yards, had replaced the M-116 Pack Howitzer. It could be dismantled into thirteen components that could either be man-packed or placed on eleven mules; it could also be dropped by parachute complete.

The viability of the new Middle East Command structure was tested in mid-1961. In 1899, Great Britain had agreed with the ruling al-Sabah dynasty to take responsibility for Kuwaiti foreign and defence affairs. This treaty was rejected in 1932 by Iraq on the grounds that Kuwait had been part of its territory for centuries. In June of that year, Kuwait assumed responsibility for its own foreign affairs and was immediately challenged in July by President Kassem of Iraq. Kuwait appealed for military assistance and HQ Middle Eastern Command swiftly assembled a brigade-sized task force controlled by HQ 24th Infantry Brigade, which occupied Mutla Ridge, several miles south of the border, where the heat and lack of water took its toll, until the Iraqi threat dissipated in October.

In January 1962, the Amir of Dhala took advantage of squabbles among Radfan tribes after several poor harvests to support a proposal to develop a route through Wadi Rabwa and Wadi Taym and gain access to the fertile plain of the Danaba Basin and beyond; in so doing, he could improve the local economy by selling Aden grain and other agricultural products. His secondary motive was to exert better control of the tribes, who, historically, valued their independence. Although there were objections, by the beginning of June, most Radfani rulers recognized the value of the proposals. In May, Britain concluded in the Defence White Paper *The Next Five Years* that Aden Base would form part of its global strategy east of Suez, along with Singapore, In September, the Aden Legislative Council agreed by a narrow margin to join with the Federation.

Then on 19 September, the autocratic Yemeni ruler, Iman Ahmed, died of natural causes and was succeeded by his liberal-minded son, al-Badr. But within the week, he was overthrown by several Nasserist, Ba'athist and socialist officers led by Colonel Abdullah al-Sallal, the commander of the palace guard. Al-Sallal came from humble beginnings and had been imprisoned on several occasions, convicted of sedition in promoting Nasserism. On one occasion, al-Badr had secured his early release and arranged for him to be appointed the Harbourmaster at Hodeida. It was here that al-Badr had met with Soviet and Egyptian agents modernizing the Yemen Army, and it was through these contacts that the isolationist strategy promoted by Iman Ahmed was undermined. Al-Sallal joined Yemen to the United Arab

Republic federation of Egypt and Syria to form the United Arab State, and announced that al-Badr was dead.

This coup d'état took place in a period of significant international tension that included the Cuban Missile Crisis, which caused a tremor in the Middle East. In Aden, the leader of the Aden TUC, Abdulla al Asnag, had formed the People's Socialist Party from pro-Yemeni activists and declared that Aden should unite with Yemen. Amid vitriolic propaganda bombarding Aden, the Federation demanded that Britain seal the border and counter the 'Voice of the Arabs' broadcast from Radio Sana'a.

Two days after the coup, Amir Mohammed Hussein, an uncle of Iman al-Badr and a former representative of Yemen at the UN, crossed the border from Beihan and, by mid-October, was leading a Royalist force against the new republic. When reports then emerged that al-Badr was not dead, King Hussein of Jordan met Lieutenant Colonel Neil McLean DSO MP in London and asked him to assess Royalist resistance. A former Royal Scots Greys officer who had developed a taste for unconventional warfare while fighting in Abyssinia, he had served with the Special Operations Executive (SOE) in Albania during the Second World War and now specialized in fact-finding political missions, eventually at the expense of his constituency duties. McLean infiltrated into Yemen from Beihan with two Land Rovers in mid-October and arrived in Saudi Arabia two days later. Returning to London, he reported that the Royalists were being commanded by Hassan and were split into six corps operating from the Jebel Qara region in north-east Yemen; and that while Egyptian aircraft were a hazard, the Royalists were receiving arms and ammunition from the Saudis. Although his observations challenged Joint Intelligence Committee assessments, Prime Minister Macmillan and his successor, Alec Douglas-Home, refused to sanction further clandestine activity beyond the immediate vicinity of the Federal border. Meanwhile, regional hereditary rulers, in particular Crown Prince Faisal of Saudi Arabia, were convinced that while Nasser preached Arab nationalism, he was nothing but a front for the expansionist aims of Moscow.

Loitering in the Westminster background in London was the Aden Group, a descendant of the Suez Group, pressing for more to be done to enhance the security of the Federation of South Arabia and British oil interests in the Persian Gulf. During and after the Suez Crisis in 1956, several senior Conservative Party parliamentarians lobbied key decision makers in Eden's and Macmillan's Cabinets and had been sufficiently influential to undermine the Foreign Office's intention to recognize the Yemen Arab Republic in 1959. Among them was the Rt Hon Julian Amery, son-in-law to Macmillan, a former war correspondent who had also served with the SOE in Albania. The

Aden Group also believed that since the Soviet Union was using Nasser as a front, a failure to support the Royalists was an opportunity missed to preserve British trading links in the Middle East; and that the Yemen civil war should be used as a platform to avenge the humiliation of Suez.

On 9 November, President Sallal declared his stance on Aden at a parade of Yemeni National Guard recruits:

> I call on our brothers in the occupied south to be ready for a revolution and joining battle, we shall wage against colonialism . . . They must follow the example of their brothers in the north . . . Britain's ageing and ailing empire . . . We have been patient too long towards Britain's plotting against us.

It was a significant moment in the history of the Middle East, because London was now forced to choose between recognizing a revolutionary government and supporting autocracy. Four days later, the House of Commons rejected recognition of the Yemen Arab State, thereby challenging Nasserism in South Arabia. In March 1963, London was ordered to close its consulate in Taiz.

On 18 January 1963, Aden State joined the Federation, its prosperity and status as the seat of government recognized by the allocation of 24 members in the Legislative Council, as opposed to six representatives from each of the other states. While there were tensions between historic rivals, Hassan al-Bayoumi was appointed Chief Minister, although he died of a heart attack four months later. Politics hardened as young radicals took over from the older politicians.

Meanwhile, Brigadier Lunt was concerned that the FRA strength was at its lowest because soldiers were failing to re-enlist, and because of desertion and Yemeni subversion. On 4 January, soldiers had received letters inviting them to be part of the liberation and 'occupation of the south'. The Amir of Beihan was collecting good intelligence that allowed him to keep a firm grip on internal security in his Amirate and sending examples of booby traps found in Yemen to be evaluated. The same control could not be said to be present in the Amirate of Dhala, where dissident tribesmen had responded to a clandestine call to arms. A patrol led by Lieutenant Colonel H.J. Newtown (Green Jackets), the 3rd FRA Commanding Officer, was ambushed north of Dhala, and a convoy was attacked two days later in the same area. Ambushes, mines and sniping on the 15-mile stretch of the Dhala Road between Al Milah and Milestone 27 became regular, and the Kuraybah Pass was infested by gangs from Dhala and Yemen. The failure to punish those responsible degraded the credibility of the Amir.

In early 1963, HQ Middle East Command faced a significant military threat when a 15,000-strong Egyptian expeditionary force supported by Egyptian and Soviet aircraft launched the Ramadan Offensive to isolate Royalists in the eastern desert of Yemen from the Zaidi strongholds in the northern mountains. The nature of the terrain and the need to secure long lines of communications saw the army rise to 70,000 men, but it staggered when its officers were undermined by one of Nasser's Stalinist purges. The brigade that eventually captured Marib after severe fighting then advanced toward Harib opposite the State of Beihan across the 2-mile wide Wadi Ayn. Border clashes were now inevitable. Shots were exchanged between republican forces and the FRA on 5th February, followed by two 8 Squadron Hunters buzzing Harib at low level. Their time over target was limited because the airstrip at Beihan was too short to double as a forward operating base and would remain so until 1966. Three days later, fire was directed at Yemeni infantry waving a tricolour who crossed the border, possibly to attract FRA deserters. An incursion on the 25th at Wadi Ablan was repelled. When an Egyptian aircraft crossed the border, the Amir of Behan and his Political Officer, Kennedy Trevaskis, asked the Federal Government for reinforcements. An anti-aircraft battery equipped with Bofors 40/70mm was transferred from Hong Kong to the border. Harib surrendered in early March.

Early one Sunday morning in July, Yemeni infantry supported by artillery and mortars occupied an empty Federal settlement overlooking Wadi Manawa. On Jebel Manawa was the 3rd FRA Tactical HQ and about two miles to its south-west was Centre Section, J Battery with two Pack Howitzers. Leaving its HQ at Seedaseer Lines, the Battery had divided into three two-gun detachments of Right, Centre and Left Sections. Centre Section had exchanged a bottle of whisky for two sturdy Second World War Matador trucks from the anti-aircraft battery before it returned to Hong Kong. HQ Middle East Land Forces instructed that the incursion be destroyed, which was achieved after six hours of shelling and the destruction of a Yemeni gun and two mortars. During the action, as ammunition began to run low, the Battery Quartermaster Sergeant interrupted a day on the beach to arrange a re-supply, but found that the RAF ammunition compound was closed for the weekend. It would not be the only time, by any means, that those engaged in operations along the border would accuse those back in Aden of failing to understand what was happening on the border. During these clashes, three Centurions were landed from Amphibious Warfare Squadron Landing Craft Tanks at Zingibar and driven to Ataq, then through the mountains to the border. They were accompanied by a company of Gurkhas. The Amphibious Warfare Squadron patrolled the Middle East, South East Asia and East Africa with tanks and infantry, conducting exercises and supporting British troops.

When Governor Sir Charles Johnston demanded retaliation, two options were considered: extending covert operations to stimulate a guerrilla campaign along the border, and conducting psychological operations. When a Joint Intelligence Committee paper entitled *Range of Possible Courses of Action Open to Us* recommended Operations Bangle and Rancour as additions to the existing clandestine operations, the Foreign Office vetoed them on the grounds that such operations could entrench the Egyptian position in Yemen and could lead to war:

 • Operation Bangle: sabotage and subversion in the frontier areas and the assassination of Egyptian military officers orchestrating the attacks against Aden
 • Operation Rancour: counter Egyptian subversion by promoting the Royalist cause within 20 miles north, political officers distributing arms and ammunition north of the border to disrupt republican lines of communication.

As always, the success of covert operations was not infrequently as good as the next delivery or payment. It was perhaps inevitable that when an Egyptian newspaper alleged evidence of clandestine operations in the form of a crashed aircraft, it produced photographs showing a Tempest shot down in 1947. Restrictions were also placed on Imagery Intelligence, even though the Chiefs of Staff were pleading that Signals Intelligence was unlikely to produce answers because Royalist forces lacked military radios. It all meant that Federal and British forces were on the defensive. Major General Walker was facing the same problem in Borneo with the Indonesian insurgency.

Meanwhile, the governing Conservative Party was rocked by the defection of the Soviet spy, Kim Philby in March, and by sex and spy scandals. In April, Amery, Colonel David Stirling, the founder of the SAS, and Colonel Brian Franks, the SAS Colonel Commandant, met Neil McLean at White's Club in London to discuss Yemen. McLean had just returned from his third visit, confirmed solid Saudi and Jordanian support for the Royalist cause and, although he was unable to provide a detailed assessment of Royalist forces, suggested they could do 'with a little bit of help'. The meeting agreed that this should be intervention by a private military organisation providing advisers and organizing supply drops. While legal and moral controversy usually surrounds clandestine operations, the Second World War had again shown that their use as a foreign policy tool could be justified; if constitutional force could not be used, the ancient profession of mercenary could. Mercenaries usually fall into one of five categories:

• Foreign nationals who soldier with regular armed forces, notably the French and Spanish Foreign Legions.
• Members of armed forces, or former members, hired out by a government as part of a contract, for example the Papal Swiss Guard.
• Freelance contractors engaged by governments, rebel movements and multinational organisations.
• Volunteers who fight in foreign wars for personal and ideological reasons, for instance the Spanish Civil War International Brigades.
• 'Deniable' intervention forces.

During the 1950s and 1960s, Africa was a mercenary battleground. When Belgium was bullied by anti-colonial rhetoric into giving the Congo its independence, the mineral-rich province of Katanga declared independence and hired the 200-strong *Compagnie Internationale*. The Congo appealed for UN protection, and within two years UN forces had overrun Katanga and expelled the mercenaries.

At the behest of Prime Minister Macmillan, the SIS formed a cell of experienced Arab hands to support the proposal, and Stirling agreed to use his Television International Enterprises offices in London as a front for the project. The recently retired Commanding Officer of 21 SAS (V), Lieutenant Colonel Jim Johnson, organized recruitment for a force that became known as the British Mercenary Organisation. It was based on the Second World War Operation Jedburgh: three-uniformed-man teams inserted to provide resistance forces with advice and organize supply drops. It was decided to attach a team of a commander, a radio operator and a medic to each of Royalist corps HQs. Since serving soldiers were not permitted to enlist, any selected took extended voluntary leave. The project was also seen as an opportunity to sell arms to the Saudis. An early applicant was Major Johnny Cooper, who had been Stirling's navigator and gunner.

Flight Lieutenant Tony Boyle, ADC to Governor Johnston, managed the reception of the teams in Aden by arranging for the Aden Airways Dakota taking the mercenaries to Beihan to be parked near the twice-weekly Transport Command Comet, so that the mercenaries and their equipment could be transferred without attracting undue attention (the People's Socialist Party had a cell at the civil airport). A forward operating base at Negub linking the teams to London was manned by Second World War SAS radio operators. When Johnson needed a conducting officer in Aden to manage the infiltration, he contacted Captain Peter de la Billière, an SAS officer then serving in G Operations at HQ Middle East Command. In between writing Intelligence Summaries, he had run combat survival courses that included an interrogation phase organized by the Joint Services Interrogation Wing. In his book, *Looking for Trouble*, he describes himself as a secret agent – in fact, he was more travel agent. The French Deuxième Bureau was also keen to undermine Nasser's support for the National Liberation Front in Algeria and avenge Suez, and by the summer, about twenty-five French mercenaries had been talent-spotted, including Robert Denard, a soldier of fortune who had fought in the Algerian War and the Katanga secession. The French had raised an SAS regiment during the Second World.

Another member of the SOE in Albania, Colonel David Smiley, a former Royal Horse Guards commanding officer, was recruited to control operations in Yemen. After the war, he had been involved in developing proposals for the SAS, then being reformed as a Territorial Army unit, to adopt the SOE role, and had also been involved in the failed Operation Valuable venture to infiltrate exiles into Albania. In 1958, Smiley commanded the Sultan of Muscat and Oman's Armed Forces and took part in the campaign against Saudi Arabia in which most fighting was confined to the general vicinity of the Jebel Akhdar (the Green Mountain) in northern Oman. In April 1961, he turned down command of the three SAS Regiments because it did not come with promotion to brigadier. He had penned several appreciations of the Royalist position for the Aden Group and suggested that since they lacked artillery and tanks and were exposed to air interdiction, they should conduct a war of attrition by attacking republican lines of communication. In preparation for his first visit, Smiley arranged journalistic credentials as Special Correspondent for *Household Brigade Magazine*, until Amery arranged a press card accredited to the *Daily Telegraph*.

The first group, of three SAS on extended leave and four Frenchmen, were selected for an operation to destroy Egyptian aircraft at Sana'a military air base; but when Commonwealth Secretary Duncan Sandys heard about the raid, on the day before Cooper and his team were due to leave, he instructed their departure be cancelled. Nothing ventured, nothing gained, Johnson arranged for the team to fly to Libya and thence to Aden, where they pioneered insertion by crossing from Beihan State on camels, not dismounting for ten hours in case observant Yemeni patrols sighted foot- or boot-prints larger than those of the average Arab.

Assisted by the British Mercenary Organisation, the Royalists started achieving successful results by ambushing Egyptian convoys and patrols. Cooper spent a month instructing on the use the Bren gun and then ambushed an Egyptian armoured column with devastating results. A month after their insertion, the first group exfiltrated through Beihan. As the number of advisers increased to 48 (about 30 French and Belgians and 16 British), the

Aden Group collected more intelligence about the civil war than the SIS and the War Office together. When Cooper sent a captured Soviet military radio to the SIS office in Aden, he was dismayed when it was returned to him inside Yemen four months later. To be fair, the SIS was constrained by Foreign Office principles that clandestine operations in Yemen should be restricted to the border. The enthusiasm of the Deuxième Bureau also turned sour when Paris instructed the French authorities in Djibouti to impound the first aircraft contracted to fly a weapons consignment to Aden – an indication that President Charles de Gaulle wanted, after the debacle in Algeria, to take a conciliatory approach with Arab governments. By September 1963, the British Mercenary Organisation had become primarily a British operation and for the next five years was run by Smiley and McLean.

By 1963, the last National Serviceman had been discharged and the Armed Forces became a Regular force with the minimum length of service for officers set at three years and other ranks at six. The Army had been reduced from 385,000 men to 180,000, and although the 44,000 infantry made up a quarter of the strength, the number of infantry battalions had been reduced from 75 to 64, principally through mergers, for instance, 1st Suffolks amalgamating with 1st Norfolks to form 1st East Anglians. Twenty-one battalions were committed to West Germany and Berlin. The thirty armoured regiments fell to twenty-three, with the Royal Tank Regiments merging from eight into five; fourteen regiments were in West Germany. The Royal Artillery was halved to thirty-four regiments that included nuclear, field, parachute and commando batteries. The reductions allowed the four divisions with the British Army of the Rhine to be reduced from four to three. With just twenty-three infantry battalions available to provide home defence and overseas garrisons, a larger Army Strategic Reserve of five brigades was created, although Major General Walter Walker in Borneo had insisted that the 17th Gurkha Infantry Division was the Far East Strategic Reserve, and 3rd Commando Brigade was essentially independent. Since the Reserve was expected to be a quick-reaction force, troopships were phased out in favour of RAF Transport Command and commercial airliners. Battalions rotated as the Spearhead Battalion, which expected to be on immediate notice of deployment. Logistic and administrative tails were reduced in size, with locally-employed civilians in depots and bases, thereby releasing soldiers for operations. The Territorial Army establishment stood at 210,000, most of whom were National Servicemen drafted in for three and half years Reserve service.

The Intelligence Corps profited from the reorganization. Nearly disbanded in 1945 because the War Office saw no need for operational intelligence, the Cold War reprieved it to fulfil its original role of counter-intelligence, of addressing overt and covert threats from espionage, sabotage, subversion and, later terrorism, by hostile intelligence services and domestic subversive organizations against the Army. In the North Atlantic Treaty Organisation's definition:

> Intelligence is the product resulting from the collection, processing, integration, analysis, evaluation and interpretation of information concerning foreign nations, hostile or potentially hostile forces or elements, or areas of actual or potential operations.

The availability of intelligence depends on the protective security measures surrounding the target. Fundamental to the product is the Intelligence Cycle, a never-ending sequence of four mutually supporting processes:

- Direction. Selecting the Essential Elements of Intelligence and maintaining a continuous check on productivity.
- Collection. The exploitation of agencies and sources. Agencies can be described as formed bodies, such as security and intelligence services and allied forces. Sources include prisoners of war, refugees and border crossers, photography and informers.
- Processing. The fusion of information into evaluated intelligence and grading it according to the reliability of the source and co-lateral of other information.
- Dissemination. The timely distribution of intelligence, in an appropriate form, without bias and not tailored to please the decision-maker. Methods include verbal briefings and Intelligence Summaries and Intelligence Reports.

In January 1957, the Army Council agreed that the Corps should have a cohort of Regular officers because:

> For an efficient Intelligence system, it is essential to have a nucleus of officers with a sound military background who are experienced in knowing what information is required, and how to get it, to assess it and to present the results.

In December 1959, a fundamental shift in the employment of the Corps saw it take over Operational Intelligence from All Arms intelligence clerks and then supply intelligence units to brigade headquarters upwards to the War Office with the aim of providing accurate information to allow commanders to fight the enemy. Brigade intelligence platoons supplied Interrogation,

Imagery Intelligence, Document Exploitation and Counter-Intelligence. The mysteries of Signals Intelligence were rarely seen at tactical level. The 3rd (Strategic Reserve) Division at Colchester was supported by 4 Intelligence and Security Platoon and followed by its six Brigades, including 1 Intelligence and Security Platoon supporting 24th Infantry Brigades, then in Kenya. Platoons (TA) supported the Home Commands. The Royal Marines HQ 3rd Commando Brigade in Borneo also had an Intelligence and Security Platoon provided by the Intelligence Corps. The experiment was reassessed in 1960 for several reasons, not least of which were that the platoons were not under command of an Intelligence Corps officer of field rank, they were frequently seen as a general duties resource and career development was difficult to organize because operational and exercise commitments took priority. This led to the formation of Intelligence and Security Groups of intelligence and security companies. For instance, the Counter-Intelligence Company, Arabian Peninsula (converted into the Counter-Intelligence Company) provided protective security advice and investigatory support to defend information, assets and resources from compromise by hostile intelligence services. Regiments and battalions continued to raise intelligence sections, which were trained at Maresfield and, after 1966, at Templer Barracks, Ashford.

In May, Lieutenant General Charles Harington was appointed to command HQ Middle East Command. Commissioned into the Cheshire Regiment in 1930, he had won the MC commanding the machine-gun company of the 2nd Battalion during the retreat to Dunkirk, and after re-invigorating the 1st Manchesters in time for the fighting in Normandy, was awarded the DSO. He held then several senior staff appointments and had commanded 1st Para and also 49th Infantry Brigade between 1955 and 1956 during the Mau Mau uprising in Kenya. He commanded 3rd Division in 1959 and was appointed Commandant, Staff College, Camberley in 1961. This was followed, in August, by the appointment as High Commissioner of Sir Kennedy Trevaskis on the retirement of Sir Charles Johnston. A career diplomat and Arabist, Trevaskis recognized the political and military threat posed by Yemen. He had been political officer to the Amir of Dhala and also Deputy High Commissioner, and had been knighted for his contribution to the establishment of the Federation.

On Saturday, 22 June, border tension increased when an HQ Aden Garrison Adventure Training expedition of forty-five all ranks strayed over the border in six vehicles not far from the FNG fort at Tot Al Bahr and was ambushed by tribesmen. Lance Corporal R. Jeffrey (Royal Marines), Signalman R.B. Leech, (Royal Signals) and Corporal L. Dean and Driver

R.A. Morley (both RASC) were killed, and twenty-one, including four Servicewomen and the two wounded, were captured and taken to the Yemeni fort at Makak. Of the eighteen who escaped the ambush, a Royal Signalman reached an FNG fort and raised the alarm. Immediately, 45 Commando was instructed to send a company to the border and establish a firm base 2,000 yards south of the incident; but because it was a Sunday, and in a scenario reminiscent of the British assembly of a force to deal with Brunei Revolt in December 1962, Royal Marines from X Company, aircrew and drivers were gathered from beaches and bars and rushed to the border the next day in a combination of Beaver aircraft, Belvedere helicopters and land vehicles. Y Company was placed on stand-by for a move by air from RAF Khormaksar. As diplomacy gathered pace, Surgeon Lieutenant Alistair Thom, the Commando Medical Officer, visited the prisoners, and on his second visit spent the night sleeping with them under the tarpaulins of their lorries. He left the next day with two suffering from heatstroke and witnessed the remainder being taken to Taiz under the armed escort of Egyptian soldiers. In the meantime, the bodies of the four killed were handed to the British, along with the four Servicewomen. The prisoners were released ten days later.

During the month, Nasser convinced Qahtan Mohammad al-Sha'abi to form the National Liberation Front for the Liberation of Occupied South Yemen. An agricultural engineer born in Lahej, while living in Sheikh Othman he had supported the principles of the South Arabian League of an independent and united state of South Arabia then being promoted by the Al Jifri family in Lahej in 1951. When the League came to the notice of British counter-intelligence in 1958, Sha'abi was one of several radicals who fled first to Yemen and then Cairo, where he joined several revolutionary Yemenis and Adenis rejuvenating the League. The arrival of Egyptian intelligence officers in Taiz saw the foundation of its military wing, the National Liberation Army, being formally announced on 28 July:

Our aspiration in Occupied Yemeni South has now entered a phase which demands a fundamental change in the methods of the struggle to win complete independence and overcome imperialism. The weakest point is the lack of co-ordination in the struggle in Yemeni South as a whole. The major reason for this is the lack of common command in Aden and the Amirates. Another reason lies in the circumstance that the majority of political organisations limit their activity to Aden.

'National Liberation Front' was a common revolutionary movement title. A National Liberation Front had operated with considerable effectiveness in Occupied Greece. The National Front for the Liberation of South Vietnam was formed in 1960, and the National Liberation Front in Algeria had won independence from France. In Uruguay, the Tupamaro National Liberation Front was about to launch a long guerrilla campaign, while in Central America, Nicaragua's Sandinista National Liberation Front led the opposition to the Somoza dynastic dictatorship. As with all effective resistance groups, a key principle was the organizational secrecy of cut-out cells, in which only leaders knew the identities of the next senior level and the objectives. The NLF lacked public figures of international note, and its philosophy favoured violence against British and Federation interests in order to instal a socialist state throughout South Arabia.

CHAPTER SEVEN

Operation Nutcracker

The international reaction after the retaliatory attack on Fort Harib led London to review its position in South Arabia. While the Chiefs of Staff advocated expanding the existing covert activities, the Joint Intelligence Committee still believed that such proposals would entrench the Egyptian presence and could spread the Yemen Civil War throughout South Arabia.

Sixty miles from Aden and thirty miles from the Yemen border lie the grim volcanic mountains of Radfan stretching from horizon to horizon and sitting astride the ancient pilgrim and trading route to Mecca that slices through the Kuraybah Pass until it reaches the fertile Dhala plateau at 6,000 feet. The moonscape of steep jebels (hills) is divided by *wadis* littered with boulders that had fallen from the cliffs or been swept along by flash floods, known in South Arabia as *seils*. The evaporation of surface water hardens rock, and thus heavy rain cascades down the sides of jebels into narrow, steep-sided and interconnected wadis, generating sometimes a 6ft wall of water, which bursts into the dry desert plains, leaving pools of stale water infested with bilharzia, a collective term for several parasitic diseases that can cause blindness. Scrub and camel thorn are the main vegetation, although rain collecting just below the surface creates fertile soil. Fiercely independent families tending agricultural terraces occupy clusters of stone huts resembling small forts clinging to the mountainsides, their only loyalty being to their sheikh. Attempts at conciliation were treated with contempt. Brigadier Lunt wrote of the area:

> Its inhabitants dwell close-cooped in their stinking hovels, the accumulated manure of generations rotting beneath their noses and their animals stabled immediately beneath their living quarters. Riddled with disease, suspicious of every foreigner, their withered and stunted physique bears witness to their under-nourishment. Instead of growing food in their fields, they choose instead to

cultivate qat, which they chew from noon until sundown, by which time their minds are sufficiently stupefied to commit any crime.

Stone *sangars* (temporary fortifications) cover likely approaches to these communities. Radfan was not well known to the British until after Aden had become a colony in 1937.

A feature of successful resistance movements is their selection of a sympathetic population and advantageous terrain. The mountains surrounding Jebel Radfan were ideal: isolated, rarely patrolled and inhabited by tribes holding grievances against the authorities and enjoying a scrap. The men were generally competent shots and knew when something in their bailiwick was out of place. Their isolation meant they were susceptible to subversion by wily Egyptian intelligence officers offering weapons and also cheap transistor radios so they could listen to the 'Voice of the Arabs'. Using Qataba as his forward headquarters, Qahtan al-Sha'abi targeted the Qataibi in Wadi Misrah; along with activists from the Aden TUC, he sent cadres to an isolated training camp near Taiz run by the Yemen National Guard, where they learnt guerrilla warfare developed in Algeria and Cuba and returned home with new weapons. Although formed into 'liberation battalions', most were suspicious of the Yemeni and Egyptian officers advising battalion commanders and preferred to follow their own leaders. In short, insurgency was being developed in the Radfan.

For centuries, the Qataibi had supplemented their earnings by levying 'customs surcharges' and by raiding caravans, traders and pilgrims slowly winding their way along Dhala Road. They were meant to halve the levy with the Amir, but this was generally ignored unless the Amir had a character strong enough to insist. Government traffic was not usually attacked. Before Federation, individual states all raised dues, and consequently travelling from Aden to Yemen could be expensive. When the Federation agreed a single level of Customs dues, while it was recognized that this would be socially beneficial, little attempt was made to convince tribes in the hinterlands of its value. Consequently, the tribes were aggrieved, and Sheikh Said Hassan Ali, the principal Qataibi leader, declared that he was being oppressed by the Amir and, demanding independence, assembled the five main Radfani tribes into a loose federation calling themselves the 'The Wolves of Radfan'. From a total population of about 40,000 people, their estimated fighting strength was about 7,000. They became known as 'dissidents', which can be defined as people who oppose official policy. Peter Hinchcliffe, the Political Officer based at Thumier, wrote;

The Dhala area had always been turbulent, and movement of convoys to it required a two-day operation with armoured car and infantry escorts and the hills along the route secured by picquets. For those of a romantic turn of mind, service in the Aden hinterland held echoes of the great days of Empire, the years of skirmish and ambush on the North West Frontier of India; the burning sun, the craggy, scrub-covered hills, the wild tribesmen, each with his rifle, the wheeling hawks, the stone villages with every house built like a miniature fortress – all this provided a backcloth of a type familiar to generations of British soldiers.

At the end of September 1963, 4th Royal Tank Regiment arrived in the Middle East from Edinburgh and deployed C Squadron to Sharjah, while A and B Squadrons supported FRA operations in Dhala and Beihen. Regimental HQ was in Little Aden. The Regiment was so spread so wide that Morse code was used to communicate and the weekly pay parade was conducted by the Paymaster being flown to the Troop locations. One Troop (7) of two Saladin Armoured Cars, two Ferret Scout Cars and a 1-ton Morris water bowser spent four months patrolling Wadi Manawa. Apart from mines laid by insurgents, the main problems were lack of water and the heat, so fierce that vehicles became unbearably hot to touch. Re-supply of rations, ammunition and other essentials meant a weekly seven-hour round trip to Beihen. The newly formed Air Troop flew Austers. One pilot, Lieutenant Edward Hardman, lost an eye when a bird strike fractured his canopy.

On 14 October, the NLF announced the unarmed struggle was not working and, pledging a campaign of violence to attain a revolutionary victory and shifting its political stance, gained international support from China and Algeria. Encouraged by NLF insurgents, Radfani dissidents placed British Mark VII mines left behind when the British closed their Base Ordnance depot at Tel-el-Kebir in Egypt in 1954, on the Dhala Road. The Government Guard fort at Thumier was attacked. Brigadier Lunt was reorganizing the FRA to be less reliant on seconded British officers and NCOs; indeed, by July 1963, 1st, 3rd, 4th and 5th FRA were commanded by experienced Arabs, including one who had been awarded an MC and another an MBE. Desertion, however, remained a concern.

Meanwhile, Nasser had generated dissent between the People's Socialist Party and the NLF. During the morning of 10 December, High Commissioner Trevaskis arrived at Khormaksar Airport en route to London with a delegation of Federal politicians and Colonial Office officials to attend a constitutional conference to discuss ceding the sovereignty of Aden to the Federation, in exchange for British retention of its military base. The delegation was chatting on the tarmac, waiting to board the Comet airliner, when a member of the Aden Airways cell of the People's Socialist Party threw a grenade. It hit a wall, and stone and steel splinters killed a woman and injured 48 others. Trevaskis was shielded by his aide, George Henderson, who was also killed and posthumously awarded a bar to his George Medal. The conference was cancelled and the Federal Government immediately imposed a State of Emergency, closing the border with Yemen and detaining fifty-seven suspects from the People's Socialist Party (PSP). Subversive psychological warfare rhetoric from the 'Voice of the Arabs' condemning the detentions implied that those who supported the 'colonialists' rather than their 'Arab brothers' would be punished after the British left. Dissent fermenting in the backstreets of Aden appeared to be directed towards immigrants. A delegation of British Labour politicians, then in Opposition, arrived in Aden to lobby for the detainees, a worrying initiative since Labour was expected to win the next General Election, probably within the year. A state of emergency is defined in the *Cambridge Advanced Learning Dictionary and Thesaurus* as 'a temporary system of rules to deal with an extremely dangerous or difficult situation'. In a state of emergency, several executive, administrative and legislative powers and functions are suspended in order to give the executive the opportunity to address the crisis. Normal rights, such as freedom of movement, might be suspended, and other measures could include arbitrary arrest and detention of individuals suspected of committing offences against the state, searches without warrant and seizure of property.

A week later in London, Colonel Smiley briefed the new Prime Minister, Alec Douglas-Home, that since British Mercenary Operations had arrived in Yemen, Royalist forces had inflicted 10,000 casualties on the Egyptian Army and encouraged support for Al-Badr. He was supported by the SIS Station Chief in Aden, the former Intelligence Corps officer, John Da Silva. When the Allies were preparing to invade Sicily in 1943, Da Silva had, as a passenger in an RAF Beaufighter which took off from Malta, reconnoitred a proposal to seize the Primosole Bridge near Catania. His conclusions that glider operations would be restricted by trees and field walls and the parachute drop zone (DZ) on high ground would be confined to a brigade proved correct.

At a conference held at HQ Middle East Command in late December to review the insurgency in Radfan and the security of the Dhala Road, several factors emerged. Political officers were reporting that Egyptian, Yemeni and NLF agents had crossed the border intent on stirring up trouble. Twelve Qataibi villages were involved in attacking the Dhala Road and something needed to be done to bring them to heel and to reinforce the credibility of the

Federation and reputation the Amir of Dhala, which were at risk of nationalist criticism. But the options were limited. For decades, the authorities had played off one community against another, but now they were facing organized opposition, and therefore a psychological warfare programme to regain hearts and minds would be hampered. Air Control was fast becoming politically unacceptable. A punitive military response seemed the only option, with the aim of regaining the initiative and signalling to the Radfan tribes, and their provocateurs in Yemen, that challenges to the Federation would be met. While High Commissioner Trevaskis supported the concept, Brigadier Lunt was not convinced that a counter-insurgency operation would resolve the historical opposition from the tribes and suggested instead that a bag of gold would heal their resentment. He was critical that no plans were on the table to enhance the reputation of the Amir and address Yemeni subversion with a psychological operation. Intelligence was limited, largely because opportunities to cultivate Human Intelligence sources within Radfan had not been exploited, except by a few journalists, notably from *Paris Match* and *Life*. While Lieutenant General Harington supported Lunt, Major General John Cubbon, Commander Middle East Land Forces, and Air Vice Marshal James Johnson both thought that a military response was preferable. Johnson was Air Officer Commanding Middle East Air Force and well known as 'Johnnie' Johnson, the highest-scoring Allied fighter pilot of the Second World War with 34 confirmed kills and seven shared victories.

After Christmas, the Federal Government instructed the FRA:

> To carry out a demonstration in force in the area of Radfan, with a view to compelling the withdrawal from the area of twelve named dissidents, and convincing the tribesmen that the Government had the ability and the will to enter Radfan as and when it felt inclined.

Political opinion indicated that opposition would be limited. Unlike the British Armed Forces, who were allocated a name for an operation by the relevant Service ministry, Lunt could choose and so named this Operation Nutcracker, perhaps to express his frustration. The military objectives were:

• Revive the plan to open access to the Danaba Basin by dominating Wadi Rabwa.
• Convert an existing camel track through Wadi Rabwa to be fit for Land Rovers to facilitate entering Wadi Taym.
• Conduct a show of force in Wadi Misrah, the main stronghold of the Quteibi.

Wadi Rabwa and Wadi Taym formed part of the main trade route to Upper and Lower Yaha. The standard mountain warfare tactic of picquets seizing high ground to protect the advance of the main body was fundamental. Water would have to be delivered. Leaving 1st FRA on internal security duties, Brigadier Lunt decided to use:

- 2nd, 3rd and 4th FRA.
- The Armoured Car Squadron.
- The FRA Signal Squadron commanded by Major John Agar. His principal task was to train Arab signallers as part of the Arabization process. He found them to be adept, because communication failures meant loss of respect. When the reliable C-42 Very High Frequency sets were later introduced, Agar recalled that if the operator succeeded, he took the credit, but if he failed, then Allah was to blame. Because of the communication problems associated with high ground, High Frequency radios were used.

The British provided:

- 1st Troop, B Squadron, 16/5th Lancers commanded by Brigadier Lunt's son. Robin. The tanks were Mark 10 Centurions fitted with 105mm main armament. The Squadron was deployed with Landing Craft Tank of the Amphibious Warfare Squadron. The tanks were to be driven to Thumier.
- Two sections, J Battery, 3 RHA.
- 12 Field Squadron RE. It had arrived in Aden in October 1963 on a one-year tour and had been working on sapper tasks on the Dhala Road.
- An RAF Air Staff Officer to control air operations.

Brigadier Lunt's plan was as follows:

- 2nd FRA to dominate the entrance to Wadi Misrah with picquets.
- 3rd FRA to advance from Thumier along the Dhala Road, enter Wadi Rabwa and then swing south-east on to the northern slopes of Bakri Ridge.

For the first time in South Arabia, the British would use helicopters in the assault role. The Fleet Air Arm had pioneered helicopter assault operations when 846 Naval Air Squadron (NAS) landed 45 Commando during

Operation Musketeer at Suez. Six Wessex HAS-1s with their anti-submarine warfare equipment removed were provided by 816 NAS. Although the RAF were less experienced, 66 Squadron in Borneo was pioneering the use of Belvedere helicopters. Since March 1963, 26 Squadron had been based at RAF Khormaksar and was also equipped with Belvederes. The Belvedere was a twin-engined, short-range tactical aircraft operated by two crew and able to carry eighteen fully armed troops 460 miles at a cruising speed of 138mph. There were two concerns: marksmen on mountain crags would have plenty of time to shoot at helicopters; and there were anxieties about the aircraft's capability to perform at 4,000ft in high temperatures. Although unfamiliar with helicopter operations, Lunt decided to use them to land picquets. In support were 8, 43 and 208 Squadrons with Hawker Hunters FGA 9s. 43 Squadron had arrived from RAF Nicosia in March 1961 while 208 Squadron had been at Khormaksar since 1961. Four 37 Squadron Shackleton Maritime Reconnaissance 2s were available to support night operations with 4.5in flares.

Phase One commenced when the FRA moved into the assembly area at Thumier. After the usual New Year's Party in Aden, HQ J Battery drove to Thumier where it was joined by Left and Right Sections supporting the FRA at Dhala, giving four guns. It is inconceivable that this increased military activity at Thumier went unnoticed.

H-Hour at first light on 4 January was delayed by low cloud and mist, and it was not until 10 am that the first Belvedere dropped No. 1 Picquet of sixteen FRA commanded by an Arab lieutenant on to the northern ridge covering Rabwa Pass. As the second helicopter was about to deliver No. 2 Picquet, it was hit by ground fire, but the troops succeeded in landing. A third picquet was also landed. It had not been intended that the Belvederes should be exposed to fire, which was, at first sight, extraordinary, considering they were delivering the advance guard of a force about to enter enemy territory in which there were armed men. Brigadier Lunt recalled:

> The pilot called up Force Headquarters six miles away and reported that he had been shot up and holed; he had landed his picqet but was returning. The British Air Staff Officer then recalled all the helicopters to base. I looked over my shoulder and saw all six helicopters turning round and disappearing, and there we were stuck in the Rabwa Pass, with only two picqets established, and we had to stay until the British Air Staff Officer obtained permission from the Air Officer Commanding for the helicopters to complete their mission. This naturally took some time, and I could not wait. We

were being very heavily fired on at the time, and there was no alternative but to send up picquets on their feet. This is obviously a difficult situation for a commander who is carrying out an operation. If he has not got full control over all the resources on which his plan is based he is not a free agent.

By 'all', he meant all helicopters. Furious that his plan was in jeopardy, Lunt had no alternative but wait as the matter was referred to Air Vice Marshal Johnson, who listened to both arguments and then ordered helicopter operations should continue. In Borneo, Major General Walker had overcome the RAF preference for controlling helicopter operations by devolving them to brigade, battalion, and even company commanders.

No. 1 Picquet fought a steady withdrawal against at least fifty dissidents and reached Thumier at about 1 am the following morning. No. 2 Picquet was forced from its positions and reached safety with three casualties, while the third picquet defended its position until relieved by a company the following dawn. Meanwhile, the dissidents had been distracted sufficiently to allow 3rd FRA to reach the head of Wadi Rabwa. Captain Tim Thompson, commanding Left Section, was the Forward Observation Officer attached to the leading FRA company:

> We saw the picquets being dropped by Belvedere helicopter on either side of the wadi until they came under fire and the two Belvederes were withdrawn; thereafter the move up the wadi became very slow as picquets had to climb up the steep sides during which one of my two signallers became exhausted and I had to send him back. On reaching the top, the company came under fire and it grew dark. I attempted to engage the enemy but was prevented by crest clearance and the danger of hitting the ridge on which the company was deployed. Gunner Knott and I spent a very uncomfortable night on the rocks without any re-supply of food and water but a welcome brew of tea was produced at first light.

With the entrance of the *wadi* under the control of 3rd FRA by dusk, a Belvedere flew two guns to the head of Wadi Rabwa, followed a few days later by the second section. The gun position was opposite a high feature that became known as 'Cap Badge' and which presented several problems when the guns were required to fire over its crest. The Gun Position Officer was Captain Mike Bembridge, who was usually the Battery Adjutant. Captain Thompson and Lieutenant Briggs and their signallers established an

OP in a *sangar* on Jebel Meyun overlooking Danaba Basin. Taking turns to man it, they were hampered by maps drawn in black and white to a scale of 1:100,000 and lacking contours, until Briggs sketched a panorama to help identify targets, although it also lacked contours. Supplying the OP was laborious. Bembridge recalled:

> For the most part, re-supply to OPs and rotation of OP parties was on foot. We were on compo for approximately a month until the Battery Captain, Captain Peter Cook, managed to get some kerosene fridges so that we could have some fresh rations. Some guns were in the direct fire role at night for self protection. There was certainly quite a lot of activity because I remember distinctly feeling bright and breezy one morning to hear I had slept through the guns firing. Being in an OP was interesting as one really lived amongst the Arab soldiers. They made very good chuppattis which with compo apricot jam made an enjoyable snack. One certainly got used to tea made with evaporated milk as there was no such thing as fresh milk . . . Water was kept cool with chaguls, goatskin bags that kept water cool but allowed a steady drip from the outside as it evaporated. PT shorts and bare buff was the usual working dress.

Then 4th FRA pushed through 3rd FRA and advanced along the farmed terraces of Bakri Ridge until it dominated Wadi Dhubsan. It was supported by two Pack Howitzers flown in by Belvederes with sufficient skill that the guns were landed facing the enemy. Dissident snipers keeping everyone alert were either killed or slowly winkled from their positions by rocket-firing Hunters. In Wadi Rabwa, 12 Field Squadron and local labour, some of whom had probably earlier been shooting at the FRA, were building a sand and gravel road. When dissidents attacked them, the RAF dropped leaflets advising them either to hand over the ringleaders or banish them to Yemen or face the consequences. A fort built to control the entry into the *wadi* became known as 'Hinchcliffe's Folly', after Peter Hinchcliffe.

Throughout the operations, the RAF played an important part. Under Operation Ranji, the RAF had two Hunters and a Shackleton on 30 minutes Air Defence readiness to respond to Yemeni incursions and provide convoy escorts. In fighter ground attacks 8 and 203 Squadrons expended 11,000 rounds of 30mm cannon ammunition. Hunters and Shackletons conducted air photographic recces and provided air cover for ground operations, such as convoys. Shackletons, Hunters and Venoms dropped leaflets warning people to 'leave this area because it has been harbouring bad men', while

Shackletons conducted coastal patrols to monitor Soviet merchant shipping suspected of arms smuggling. Leaflets were pushed into the flaps of the fighters. Flight Lieutenant Swain was killed when his Hunter crashed into a hill during a leaflet drop. Scottish Aviation Twin Pioneer 'Voice' Aircraft of 78 Squadron also delivered leaflets. Versatile aircraft that could carry a 1,000lb bomb load, ground attack firing rockets, and grenades, these carried two fixed Browning machine guns in the front and coaxial Bren Gun firing through the rear entry door; they could be used for troop transport and casualty evacuation and could be fitted with large amplifiers and loudspeakers for 'Sky Shout' propaganda missions.

When the Royal Engineers opened the road on 31 January, Brigadier Lunt drove Lieutenant General Harington from Thumier through Wadi Rabwa to Wadi Taym in a Land Rover.

Under the title of Operation Rustum, the next phases saw the FRA advance into the Wadi Taym and Danaba Basin against limited opposition. Meanwhile, the FRA and a section of guns entered the lower reaches of Wadi Misrah. A platoon was ambushed near Dhanaba on 2 March, and it then emerged that an FNG officer on leave in the village had known about the ambush, but had not warned the 4th FRA platoon commander. This highlighted a persistent security issue, that Arab commitment was defined first by tribal loyalties, and only then, perhaps, by loyalty to the Federation. The officer was arrested and arrangements made that next day a board of inquiry would convene in the village to investigate his conduct. When an FRA company was instructed to escort the board to the village, Captain Bembridge, who was FOO- and FAC-trained, was instructed to join them. At 9.30 am the next day, the company and a support weapon of a section of mortars and three machine guns carried by camels, set off. However, the company commander decided not to deploy the support platoon to cover the approach, and at about 11 am and 1,000 yards short of the village, the column came under heavy fire from some 100 dissidents on high ground. Caught in the open, soldiers dived for cover and most of the camels stampeded. Among several hit was Captain Bembridge, badly wounded in the arm; nevertheless, he and his radio operator, Gunner Doody, had prevented their camel, which carried their radio, from stampeding, and they passed corrections and information to Captain Briggs. The guns fired 230 rounds. Bembridge also controlled Hunter strikes that enabled the company to withdraw into shelter and reorganize before it entered the village. Two FRA had been killed. Bembridge was flown by helicopter to BMH Aden during the evening to be stabilized and then flown to UK for further treatment and rehabilitation at Headley Court. A member of the board, Colonel J.B. Chaplin DSO OBE,

Permanent Secretary at the Federal Ministry of Defence, took photographs of Bembridge during the fighting. The citation for his Military Cross reads:

> Despite his wound and heavy loss of blood, this young officer behaved most gallantly, and continued to direct artillery fire and aircraft onto targets for two and three quarter hours without concern for his own safety. He frequently exposed himself to enemy fire in order to perform his task.

Operation Nutcracker cost the FRA five killed, including a company commander, and twelve wounded, but Brigadier Lunt had proved that his Arab soldiers were capable of sustained operations. Having driven about twenty miles, the 16/5th Lancer Centurion troop was not required and returned to Aden. The naval and RAF helicopter pilots re-learnt that dust, like snow, obscures vision at low level. And everyone experienced the damage that dust and sand does to the moving parts of weapons, vehicles and radio sets. The gunners continued to shell the Danaba Basin for the next ten days. Meanwhile, 1st FRA was having a little difficulty in maintaining internal security in the Federation; and because the FRA lacked the strength to keep a military force in Radfan and also defend the border, Brigadier Lunt had no alternative but to withdraw in March, leaving the RAF to apply Air Control.

But no sooner had the FRA withdrawn than the wily Qataiba destroyed the road, flattened Hinchcliffe's Folly and ambushed the Dhala Road. The 'Voice of the Arabs' quickly claimed that the 'Wolves of Radfan' had driven out the 'imperialist forces' in the first battle for 'the liberation of the Occupied South Yemen'. Encouraged by this rhetoric, dissident activity increased in the Federation and Yemeni aircraft raided the border, attacking a frontier post and shooting up grazing camels and livestock nearby. The most serious attack was on 13 March, when an armed helicopter and two MiG fighters bombed and machine-gunned Bulaq, a village near Beihan, an act which infuriated the strongly loyalist Amir Hussein of Beihan. A firm believer in retaliation and a man whose support for the Federal structure was deemed crucial, he complained that he had been let down and that the defence treaty with the British had little value. Six days later, the Federal Government sought protection from air incursions by invoking the treaty. Wary of international accusations of 'colonial aggression', London issued a strong protest to Sana'a on the 26th, but when this was ignored with a further air incursion next day, London had no political choice but to retaliate. After Fort Harib had been selected as the target, two Hawker Hunters from 8 Squadron and 1417 Flight delivered warning leaflets and then a force of eight Hunters from 8 and 43 Squadrons destroyed the fort with 54 rockets and 2,895 rounds of 30mm ammunition. Post-sortie photographs showed that several anti-aircraft guns and vehicles had also been wrecked. Inevitably, when Yemen complained to the UN about 'an act of aggression', the UN showed its colours by passing a Resolution instructing Yemen and Great Britain to keep the peace. It was a hollow gesture, and although no further incursions were made by Yemeni aircraft, a torrent of international criticism of 'blatant imperialism' was hurled on London at the UN, by the Arab League and by vitriolic elements of the British press – in spite of provocation by Egypt and Yemen. Yemeni and Egyptian propaganda continued to incite tribes in Radfan to stir up every kind of trouble, and attacks on the Dhala Road intensified as dissidents, reported to be 500 strong, and 200 uniformed Egyptian-trained insurgents, escalated opposition to the Federation. While the FNG did well to contain the spread of subversion, the fact remained that the political initiative was being eroded, a clear signal being a drop in the collection of intelligence.

CHAPTER EIGHT

'RadForce'

After some opposition from the Defence and Internal Security ministers, and since Operation Nutcracker had not wholly achieved its political aim, the Federal Government concluded that a second operation should be launched to defeat the insurgency and that, within the terms of the defence treaty, British forces should take the lead. However, there were misgivings that the escalation of a British operation could be counter-productive, both in Great Britain and in the Federation.

Overall command of the operation was handed to Major General Cubbon and HQ Middle East Land Forces. However, there was a problem in that HQ 24th Brigade was providing military support to emerging countries in East Africa and there was no other available Brigade HQ. Units of 3rd Division, the Strategic Reserve, had been sent to Cyprus, where the Government of Archbishop Makarios was coping with yet another period of inter-factional tension among Greek-Cypriot nationalists. The despatch of HQ 51st Infantry Brigade to Borneo meant that HQ 5th Infantry Brigade with the British Army of the Rhine had returned to UK to fill the gap. No troops could be released from West Germany without the permission of Supreme Headquarters, Allied Expeditionary Force, Europe, and that was most unlikely to be granted.

On 14 April, Cubbon instructed the new Aden Garrison commander, Brigadier Louis Hargroves, to 'end the operations of dissidents in the defined area' and gave him three days to submit his plan and eleven days to begin operations. Villages were not to be attacked until leaflets had been delivered warning inhabitants to vacate with their animals within a given period, and no fire was to be directed at areas likely to contain women and children. Troops could retaliate if they came under fire. But Hargroves was responsible only for internal security in Aden and the administration of the Garrison. He had no operational commitments and did not have a Brigade HQ; indeed, he had been occupied with planning the Queen's Birthday Parade, which he was to command. Although not regarded as a top-drawer brigadier, Hargroves was an experienced soldier who had been commissioned into the South

Staffordshires in 1938 and had landed with the glider-borne 2nd Battalion in the invasion of Sicily in 1943. He commanded the 1st Battalion in West Germany between 1959 and 1961 and had been responsible for military training at Sandhurst until posted as Commander, Aden Garrison in January 1964. Hargroves named his force Radfan Force, usually shortened to 'RadForce', and assembled an ad hoc Brigade HQ of himself and three others, including Major Clive Brennan (Royal Inniskilling Fusiliers), who moved from HQ Middle East Land Forces to become Brigade Major, and Major Tony Stagg, who commanded J Battery, as Commander Royal Artillery and Deputy Commander. He turned up at the first planning meeting in his ceremonial white uniform, complete with sword. The Force Signals Squadron was provided by 254 Signals Squadron and with the RAF they constructed a radio connecting Aden with Brigade HQ. The Aden Internal Security Battalion, 1st East Anglians, loaned their Intelligence Section, with the Intelligence Officer appointed the Force Intelligence Officer. Also attached was James Nash, a tough and the unconventional Radfan Political Officer, who had been associated with Operation Rancour and was a target of the dissidents. Logistic problems were formidable, but these were eased when 1 East Anglians provided a composite company commanded by Major John Churchill MC, who established a logistic headquarters with HQ RadForce. On the 16th, he asked the Battalion Quartermaster to source enough material to build a 1,000-man tented camp at Thumier. It was estimated that the front line troops would need 2,200 gallons of water per day, although the total requirement for RadForce was 6,000 gallons. Fortunately, a well was available at Thumier.

Brigadier Hargroves discussed Operation Nutcracker with FRA officers and knew from his experience of the North West frontier in India that seizing high ground is crucial. Fighting an unsophisticated enemy on ground of their choosing usually relies on Human Intelligence as the principal intelligence lever, in which defectors, bazaar gossip, information collected during the fighting and interrogation are all factors. However, little new intelligence had emerged from Operation Nutcracker, except for the figures of 500 dissidents and 200 insurgents, all probably believing that they had just scored a victory and therefore with morale high. Without an accurate picture of enemy locations, Hargroves decided to disrupt their operations by a strategy of denying and restricting their activities and damaging their prestige by forcing them into a battle they could not win. Wadi Dhubsan south-east of Bakri Ridge and the village of Danaba in the fertile Danaba Basin were identified as principal enemy strongholds. He also focused on Wadi Taym, a fertile valley measuring about nine miles east to west and about three north to south, with a decent water supply and farmed from several hamlets. It was also part of the main caravan route to Dhala from Upper Yaha and its border with Yemen. The neutrality of Upper Yaha, which had not joined the Federation, was not to be risked by encroaching into Wadi Bana. The two plains were dominated by mountains. To the south, a ridge and an escarpment were nicknamed 'Rice Bowl'. To the east was Cap Badge, whose seizure would offer domination of Wadi Rabwa and other parts of Radfan.

Hargroves discussed his plan with Major General Cubbon on 17 April. In Phase One, he proposed to use the helicopter assault experience gained by 45 Commando at Suez to seize Rice Bowl, thereby dominating Danaba Basin and Wadi Taym and cutting infiltration routes from Yemen. The objectives were to be seized by daybreak. Cubbon agreed, but as the plan was developed and training began with four RAF Belvederes and two 13 Flight Scouts in Little Aden, it soon became apparent the number of helicopters was insufficient and they were too precious for a regimental assault on to an unsecured landing site. When Cubbon instructed him to advance on foot, Hargroves selected Cap Badge as his principal objective. He had two options:

1. A straight punch through Wadi Rabwa used by the FRA during Operation Nutcracker and then across Danaba Basin or from Wadi Taym. But the dissidents had destroyed and mined the road built by the Royal Engineers.

2. A left hook from the north by following Wadi Boram from Milestone 27, then seize two features nicknamed Sand Fly and Coca Cola that dominated the Basin from the west. Air photographs suggested that it would then be possible to construct a road.

Since the 'punch' was the obvious approach, he believed that it would require a major military operation to breach the waiting defence; so he opted for the left hook, which would probably encounter light defence, if any. On the 22nd, a heavily-laden convoy of 75 vehicles carrying the base camp and other assets left Aden for Thumier in a drive that took nine hours, as opposed to the usual five.

Illness had forced Brigadier Lunt to hand command of the FRA to Brigadier M.E.M. MacWilliams (late Queens Surreys); however, MacWilliams would have grave concerns that the FRA should be involved in second operation, and he resigned. Brigadier Hargroves arranged to meet MacWilliams and his Brigade Major, Major John Monk (Royal Inniskilling Fusiliers), at Thumier on 25 April in order to discuss the FRA's role in the operation and conduct a recce. Accompanying MacWilliams was Lieutenant

Colonel Roy Watson (Royal Sussex), who commanded 2nd FRA. He had good knowledge of Radfan and was appointed to control FRA operations from a small Tactical HQ alongside HQ RadForce. Hargroves declined an invitation from Watson to travel with him and used his own Land Rover. Soon after the convoy left the road at Milestone 25, the third Land Rover, driven by Watson, struck a mine that killed Major Michael Linfoot (RAOC), the FRA Deputy Assistant Adjutant and Quartermaster General. Major Monks was seriously wounded and although an artificial kidney machine was flown from Great Britain, he later died. Watson was also badly wounded, and although he recovered, he relinquished command of his Battalion. Lieutenant Colonel D.M. Pontifix MBE (Rifle Brigade) moved from 1st FRA to command the FRA Tactical HQ, and two Arab lieutenant colonels transferred to 1st and 2nd FRA respectively.

The absence of motorable roads and tracks meant that the role of the RAF in providing helicopters to move men and supplies was critical; however, the height of the Radfan and weather conditions during the afternoons meant that loads had to be halved. Up to six Belvederes per day were provided by 26 Squadron. By 29 April, Beverley transport aircraft were using the airstrip at Thumier, which had been upgraded by Royal Engineers.

Meanwhile, Major de la Billière had returned to Aden in order to reconnoitre a desert exercise for A Squadron, which he was now commanding. After hearing about the second Radfan operation, in an interview with Lieutenant General Harington he secured agreement that the squadron could help with deep penetration and intelligence patrols. Such was his enthusiasm that he sent a 'Top Secret Operational. Immediate. Exclusive' signal to Lieutenant Colonel John Woodhouse, then commanding 22 SAS, about his proposal and immediately returned to Hereford. Woodhouse was unimpressed with the priority given to the signal, but agreed, nevertheless, that A Squadron should participate. De la Billière considered the deployment so secret that families were told the squadron was on a quick-recall exercise on Salisbury Plain. After its nine years in the Malayan Emergency, the SAS lacked a foreseeable role, and when it reduced from four squadrons to two, with B and C (Rhodesian) Squadrons being disbanded, a debate emerged between those who believed its primary role was to support the British Army of the Rhine and those who saw it as having a global role. When the Brunei Revolt broke out, Woodhouse, who supported a global role, had successfully lobbied for A Squadron, with its four Troops, to be deployed on information-gathering along the border with Indonesia. On arriving in Aden on 22 April, it was hosted by 1st East Anglians and, arriving in Thumier two days later, began familiarization training with J Battery.

RadForce consisted of a 2,500-man brigade, of whom 1,100 were on the fighting strength, including:

• 45 Commando, which had recently returned from quelling a mutiny in Tanganyika (now Tanzania).
• 1st East Anglians.
• B Company sent by 3rd Parachute Battalion (3rd Para) in Bahrain.
• A Squadron, 22 SAS.
• The FRA Group of 1st and 2nd FRA.
• D Squadron, 4 RTR. After A Squadron had exchanged places with C Squadron in Sharjah, and with the need for a fourth squadron, D Squadron was formed from C Squadron and sent to Aden.
• J Battery, 3rd RHA.
• 2 Troop, 12th Field Squadron RE.
• 13 Flight, Army Air Corps equipped with Scout and Sioux helicopters.
• C Troop, 60 Company RASC. Part of 24th Brigade, it had moved from Kenya in April with long-wheelbase Land Rovers, airportable Bedford lorries, tractors and trailers. Two sections of the Composite Platoon were detached to Thumier to assist with the delivery of supplies from the Base Ordnance Depot in Aden.
• 10 Brigade Group Medical Company RAMC.

The Medical Company was essentially a small field ambulance responsible for triage and casualty evacuation to the RAF Hospital at Steamer Point. In due course, serious casualties evacuated by helicopters and aircraft were stabilized at Khormaksar Beach Hospital before being sent either to Steamer Point or direct to a military hospital in Britain for specialist treatment and rehabilitation. In general, Aden was not an unhealthy place in which to serve, the main illnesses being sandfly fever, prickly heat, dysentery and dehydration. One RTR corporal attempting to resolve his thirst by drinking beer was evacuated with dehydration. The hospitals and Medical Reception Centres also looked after families, including providing maternity services.

By this time, the air supply lift from Thumier was 30,000lbs, about 20,000lbs of which was water, the next heaviest category being ammunition. This equated to about 35 helicopter sorties per day, bearing in mind that flying was very limited during the afternoon. By 1964, RAF Khormaksar had become the busiest station in the RAF, the single runway handling not only military aircraft from other stations in the Middle East, but also those en route to and from the Far East. It was also a busy international civil airport, as well as providing services for the local airline, Aden Airways. As of 1 January, the units based at RAF Khormaksar were:

Unit	Aircraft	No.	Role
8 Squadron	Hunter FGA 9	14	Fighter Ground attack
43 Squadron	Hunter FGA 9	12	Fighter Ground Attack
208 Squadron	Hunter FGA 9	12	Fighter Ground Attack
1417 Flight	Hunter FR 10	4	Photo Reconnaissance
1417 Flight	Hunter T7	1	Trainer
26 Squadron	Belvedere HC1	6	Transport helicopter
37 Squadron	Shackle ton MR2	4	Maritime Reconnaissance
78 Squadron	Twin Pioneer CC1	8	General purpose transport
84 Squadron	Beverley CC1	6	Transport
105 Squadron	Argosy C1	10	Transport
233 Squadron	Valetta C1	6	Transport
SAR Flight	Sycamore HC14	4	Light Helicopter
SAR Flight	Whirlwind HAR 10	1	Helicopter
Comms Flight	Canberra Flight B2	2	Bomber
Comms Flight	Hastings C4	1	Transport
Comms Flight	Valetta C2	1	Transport
Comms Flight	Dakota	1	Transport
Total		**93**	

The RAF operations were under control of the Brigade Air Support Officer.

Brigadier Hargroves and Lieutenant Colonel Paddy Stevens, the 45 Commando Commanding Officer, who had taken part in the D-Day landings, based the plan on the principle of denial. Troops would be restricted to carrying three quarters of a gallon in three water bottles and would rely on air re-supply next day. The plan was as follows:

Night of 29/30 April
3 (Mobility) Troop to secure the para DZ in Wadi Taym. The Troop was commanded by Captain Robin Edwards (Somerset and Cornwall Light Infantry).

Midnight 30 April/1 May
B Company, 3rd Para to seize Cap Badge.

30 April/1May
45 Commando to infiltrate using Wadi Boran.
• Z Company to seize Sand Fly and secure the main supply route.
• X and Y Companies to seize Rice Bowl in a helicopter assault.

1 May
1st and 2nd FRA to seize Coca Cola and Sand Fly.

Wadi Rabwa Diversion
• 1st East Anglians platoon and an Assault Pioneers section commanded by Lieutenant Paul Long.
• 13 Troop, D Squadron, 4 RTR commanded by Lieutenant Jeremy Rawlings.
• A 12th Field Squadron section.
• J Battery on call. The FOO was Lieutenant Richard Mountford.

The political aims of the operation issued to Brigadier Hargroves on 29 April were:

To bring sufficient force to bear down on the Radfan tribes:
(a) To prevent the tribal revolt from spreading.
(b) To reassert our (i.e. Federal) authority.
(c) To stop the attacks on the Dhala Road.

The British troops had two battle-winning weapons that the FRA did not possess. The first was the semi-automatic L1A1 7.62mm Self Loading Rifle (SLR), the British version of the Belgian FAL. With an effective range out to about 600 yards, its maximum rate of fire from its 20-round magazine is 40 rounds per minute. The second was the linked-fed 7.62mm General Purpose Machine Gun (GPMG), developed from the Belgian FN and replaced with the Vickers and Bren gun in Infantry units. A formidable weapon with a range out to 1,800 yards, it can fire 800 rounds per minute from a bipod or on a tripod in the sustained fire role. There was one GPMG in each section. The Royal Marines and the FRA still had Vickers machine guns. The troops were lightly equipped, generally carrying on their (19)58 pattern harnesses two waist ammunition pouches, a bayonet in its frog, three water bottles, two kidney pouches containing food and spare underclothing, socks, washing kit and, for some, a roll of hessian used for camouflage, shade and a blanket. Infantry and artillery radio operators carried A41 radios, spare batteries and a satchel of radio ancillaries. The medics took a satchel of medical equipment.

In preparation for the operation, Brigadier Hargroves ordered several 'shake-down' exercises with particular emphasis on artillery and aircraft coordination. Shackletons began operations to familiarize the dissidents with their presence. On the 26th, the SAS infiltrated into Quatabi territory and from a ridge south of the Danaba Basin known as 'Knife, Fork and Spoon' directed artillery fire on to groups of dissidents. During the return to Thumier, the squadron experienced the difficulties of moving through the terrain. 1st East Anglians conducting several cordon-and-search operations in the vicinity of Thumier also disrupted the usual habits of the tribesmen.

Phase One began after dark on 29 April when two 13 Flight Scouts delivered the nine men of 3 Troop to their landing site about five miles from Wadi Taym; but as they began climbing the 4,000ft Jebel Ashgab, Trooper Nick Warburton, the signaller and transferee from the Royal Engineers, was struck by stomach cramps, apparently originating from a meal eaten before departure. The pace inevitably slowed, and by 2 am Major de la Billière and Captain Edwards had agreed that not only did Warburton need rest, they had miscalculated the going and they would not reach the DZ on time. Shortly before dawn, Edwards divided his Troop between two old *sangars* on the lower northern slopes of Bukri Ridge, intending to remain concealed throughout the day and then drop down the next night to Wadi Rabwa and march the three miles to the DZ. The day in concealment should give Warburton time to recover. But as the sun rose, the Troop saw they were about 1,000 yards above the village of Shab Tem, and they could see about twenty-five men dressed in green uniforms

In circumstances not dissimilar to the disaster that befell the SAS patrol Zero Two Bravo during the Gulf War, at about 11 am a young goatherd appeared, following a flock nibbling at the vegetation below the *sangars*. Edwards had three options: overpower him, let him see them and run the risk of enemy being alerted, or shoot him. The goatherd then spotted the soldiers, and as he shouted to a woman nearby, a shot shattering the desert silence killed him. This alerted the uniformed insurgents and as they began clambering up the slopes towards the *sangars*, Edwards sent a situation report to Major de la Billière. The Troop conserved ammunition by firing only at the enemy in the open, but requesting air support was complicated. The arrangement was that the Troop passed messages to a small SAS Tactical HQ at Thumier, where they were amplified using a transistor radio by Major

Wingate-Gray, the SAS second-in-command, who then passed the message by field telephone to Squadron Leader Roy Bowie, the Brigade Air Support Officer, in another tent. Bowie recalled:

> The SAS never carried ground to air radio equipment so they had to speak to their HQ on their discreet net, who passed the information to us and we passed it on to the aircrew – long-winded but it worked. 208 were the duty squadron on that day and a constant cover was maintained during daylight hours. At one point the SAS leader called to say that some of the opposition were creeping up on them and they could be heard but not seen, 'could the RAF do something about them'. Anthony Mumford was leading the flight and reported that he could see the immediate attackers but they were extremely close, 'about 25 yards' – 'OK Go Ahead' was the response. A brief pause and then a very laconic 'Bloody good shooting'. A few days later, the Minister of Defence (Air), Mr Hugh Fraser, on a visit to Aden told the correspondents, and I quote, 'I think that it is amazing that the troops in the forward area have been calling down RAF fighters to strike dissident strongholds only 25 yards from their own positions. This not only emphasises the skill of the Hunter pilots, but also underlines the confidence of the troops in the pilot's ability to press home their attacks with pinpoint accuracy'. [From the 208 Squadron Association]

Meanwhile, the Rabwa Diversion had made reasonable headway into Wadi Rabwa until it rounded a tight bend and was confronted by a 4-foot high obstacle built of rocks. The leading troops were immediately pinned down by heavy fire. As Lieutenant Long ran to confer with Lieutenant Mountford of J Battery, he was shot in the chest. Lieutenant Rawlins of 4th RTR then moved his Ferret to shield Long, dismounted and lifted the wounded officer on to its back decks, climbed on and ordered his driver, Trooper Jack, to reverse out of danger. Mountford recalled:

> The firefight lasted thirty minutes or so, but as ever it was extremely difficult to spot the enemy tribesmen. As the Saladin armoured cars with their 90mm guns came forward into the action, the enemy melted away, the Saladins clearing the ambush wall by firing at twenty metres range.

By about midday, the diversion had reached Rabwa Pass, and 2,000 yards to the east was the besieged SAS Troop.

J Battery was also supporting the SAS. At about mid-afternoon, soon after the diversion had withdrawn, its gun position in Wadi Rabwa and the protecting infantry platoon was attacked by about 250 enemy, who skirmished to within 200 yards of the position. Lieutenant Mountford ordered the three Pack Howitzers to engage the enemy in the direct fire anti-tank role, while the infantry and gunners not serving the guns poured fire into the enemy, their SLRs and GPMG delivering something of a shock to the dissidents, who then sniped from rocks.

Throughout the day, the aircraft and guns supported 3 Troop, the Pack Howitzers firing at high angle. Although the ground crews at RAF Khormaksar quickly 'bombed up' the aircraft in between strikes, fuel limitation meant time over target was restricted to about twenty minutes; nevertheless, the Hunters carried out eighteen sorties, fired 127 rockets and expended 7,131 rounds of 30mm ammunition. As the airstrikes became less effective in the late evening, the attackers became more confident, but the Troop, which had several wounded, continued to inflict casualties. An attempt to storm Edwards' *sangar* was beaten off. By about 6 pm, as dusk darkened the slopes and the Hunters were forced to withdraw, the enemy became yet more confident and approached the *sangars*, dodging from rock to rock. Edwards decided to abort his mission and return to Thumier, ordering his men to lighten their loads to water, ammunition and emergency rations and to wreck everything else. Breaking close contact with an enemy is always difficult. Edwards planned that his *sangar* would break out first, covered by Sergeant Reg Linham from the other group; then he would cover the sergeant until all contact had been broken. But as they broke out, Edwards' group came under heavy fire, which killed Warburton, wrecked his radio and wounded Edwards in the stomach.

As the afternoon shadows stretched across the battlefield and it became clear that Edwards was not going to reach the DZ on time, plans were drawn up for Captain Ray England and half his 1 (Mountain) Troop to be parachuted from two 13 Flight Scout helicopters in the pathfinder role to secure the DZ. England and the two pilots selected a route to the DZ from a 653 Squadron Beaver and identified a stone building as a strongpoint. Late in the afternoon, when England was summoned to the SAS Tactical HQ and told that the 13 Flight commanding officer, Lieutenant Colonel Francis Graham-Bell, and his second-in-command would be flying the mission and that the helicopters had to be back at Thumier before last light, he protested that they did not know the plan. Although radio contact from 3 Troop had been lost, Major de la Billière ordered Edwards, in case their radio was still receiving, to break out to the east and join England at the fortified building. Half an hour before last light, the two Scouts took off but the pilots took an incorrect route and, flying too low through the *wadis*, drew ground fire that punctured their fuel tanks. England was furious that the operation had been compromised and, in the belief that Edwards was making his way to the fortified house, he asked that 1 Troop be dropped by parachute from a Twin Pioneer to secure the DZ half an hour before B Company was delivered. However, Major General Cubbon cancelled the drop.

Throughout the night, the SAS worked out plans to rescue 3 Troop, and then, soon after dawn, the survivors were seen and collected by Major de la Billière and a Ferret. After breaking out, the Troop had stuck to the plan and the two groups covered each until they reached a goat track along the upper slopes of Wadi Taym. Corporal Paddy Baker formed the rearguard and ambushed pursuing Quatabis until they eventually gave up. He was awarded the Military Medal. The Troop reached Wadi Rabwa and laid up about a mile short of Thumier until dawn, in case sentries mistook them for dissidents.

During the late afternoon of the previous day, 45 Commando had been driven in trucks to their concentration area at 26th Milestone. As the shadows stole across the mountain slopes, the long column, including Support Company and parts of Recce Troop carrying the 81mm mortars and Vickers machine guns, snaked through the scrub toward Wadi Boran. Z Company then peeled right in the darkness to occupy Sand Fly, leaving X and Y Companies to enter the *wadi*. At about 10.30 pm, a radio message was received from Brigade HQ, but the interference was so bad that it could not be interpreted. X Company, in the lead, then encountered 'The Puddle', a simple obstacle as it appeared in air photographs but which turned out to be a pool with a sheer drop of several feet in front of it. Two Royal Marines had already fallen in. The pace slowed as each man clambered along the near vertical slope of the *wadi* to the other side. At midnight, Tactical HQ had reached the base of Coca Cola. Communications had improved, and Brigadier Hargroves told Lieutenant Colonel Stevens that the parachute drop had been cancelled and that 45 Commando was to consolidate on Coca Cola and Sand Fly and await orders. So far, 45 Commando had infiltrated about three miles into enemy territory against no opposition. Against the starry night was the summit, 1,600ft above them.

As Stevens and his officers examined air photographs and constructed a plan, Major Mike Banks, who commanded X Company, suggested that the heavily-laden Royal Marines would find the climb difficult because, in his experience, soldiers carrying over 40lbs of equipment became exhausted beasts of burden as opposed to soldiers fit to fight. Banks was an expert mountaineer who had fought with 42 Commando in Burma, had commanded the Commando Cliff Assault Wing in Cornwall and had notched several notable climbs in the Himalayas, Greenland and the Alps. There being no alternative, in the shadow of the moon, he and a pathfinder patrol from Recce Troop crossed two *wadis*, negotiated a steep ravine and then pioneered a path up the steep, rocky Coca Cola, belaying manilla ropes so that the marines could haul themselves up. As Marine Brian Downey, of Recce Troop, helping Support Company carry the Vickers machine guns, said, 'It was hard work and difficult, but it had to be done.' Z Company had an easier climb up Sand Fly. Within four hours, 250 Royal Marines had seized both and were overlooking the Danaba Basin and Cap Badge as the sun rose.

After the parachute drop had been cancelled, Brigadier Hargroves ordered that B Company be driven to Thumier for the next phase:

- X and B Companies to capture Cap Badge from the south.
- Y Company to seize Gin Sling and control Danaba Basin and Wadi Taym.

When Major Banks suggested that he examine the feasibility of descending from Coca Cola, crossing Danaba Basin and then scaling Cap Badge, his proposal was rejected in favour of taking the longer route of climbing the south-west ridge. Meanwhile, the FRA Group were dominating Wadi Boran.

On 2 May 1st Kings Own Scottish Borderers (KOSB) returned to Aden from Folkestone, where it had been the Spearhead Battalion. It had been the Internal Security Battalion at Waterloo Lines between 1962 and early 1964 and had rotated with 1st East Anglians. Its arrival allowed the East Anglians to join RadForce, and during the late afternoon of 4 May they relieved 45 Commando on Sand Fly and Coca Cola. As the Royal Marines descended to Wadi Boran to link up with heavily-laden B Company for the five-mile march to the Danaba Basin, Stevens recognized that the four days' exposure to sun and heat with minimal water had tired his men. An additional complication then emerged when the water re-supply and food echelon was found to be 800 yards out of position to the east, which meant an additional round trip of about a mile. These factors affected his timings to the extent that the long column picked its way through the *wadis* in pitch darkness. Y Company, commanded by Captain Gavin Hamiliton-Meikle, navigated the three miles to the southern rim of the Danaba Basin and then seized the 1,000ft Gin Sling by dawn. X Company made quick progress and had scaled the 1,200ft Cap Badge, also by dawn. On the summit they found several recently-used but empty *sangars*. Flickering lights below were the only sign of life.

Meanwhile, B Company skirted around the southern flanks of Gin Sling and advanced toward the village of Al Naqil situated below the eastern cliffs of Cap Badge, but matters were complicated by inaccurate maps, barking dogs and, twice, small parties of dissidents carrying torches – the flickering lights seen by the Royal Marines. As dawn broke, the paras were within half a mile of and below Habil Sabaha, a collection of mud buildings and stone houses on the outskirts of Al Naqil. When Lieutenant Colonel Stevens gave Major Walters the option of withdrawing to Cap Badge or attacking the village, Walters decided to 'kick' his way into the village, but his men were halted by heavy fire from the left flank. J Battery was shelling Habil Sabaha at maximum range over Y Company on Gin Sling. The Vickers machine gunners and mortars on Cap Badge did not have a clear view of targets. Major Peter Walters, the B Company Commander, led a platoon attack on a troublesome small house. A dissident counter-attack aimed at getting behind the Company was itself counter-attacked by a force led by Captain Edward Jewkes, the second in command, who then attacked Habil Sabaha while the bulk of the Company assaulted Al Naqil. But as B Company was regrouping on the eastern fringes of the village, it came under fire from snipers using dead ground that could not be seen from Cap Badge, and Jewkes was killed while tending the badly-wounded Sergeant Baxter lying in the open. Private Davies was also killed and six others wounded. Two Beavers accurately dropped ammunition and water, although one was damaged by ground fire. At midday, 8 Squadron Hawker Hunters attacked a suspected arms dump at the base of an extensive cliff. As 208 Squadron Association reported:

> The problems of firing into a cave at the bottom of a cliff from a 30 degree dive all done at about 5,000 feet above sea level bears some thinking about, but the 8 Sqn team did the job and the resultant explosion and increase in the cave's size was a 'joy to behold'. Initially, the aircraft were firing the HE variety but they appeared to do no damage to the mud forts because the heads were penetrating the mud and detonating on the hard ground within the fort. Someone then came up with the good idea of using our practice rockets equipped with concrete heads and these became 60lb 'supersonic sledgehammers' with devastating effects on the mud walled forts.

It was now crucial to reinforce the paras. Lieutenant Colonel Stevens asked for Z Company to be brought forward from Coca Cola to Cap Badge by Belvederes. It then descended the eastern slopes and by about 3 pm was squeezing the dissidents towards B Company and forcing them to withdraw. Once the Royal Marines had secured the area, the weary paras joined 45

Commando on Cap Badge, from where a Belvedere evacuated the wounded. For B Company it had been a tough time, including the drive from Aden, a ten-hour march and an eleven-hour battle – and only the Company Commander and Company Sergeant Major had seen action before. In recognition of this achievement, the paras renamed Al Naqil 'Pegasus Village'.

A Squadron was also flown into Wadi Taym and patrolled the trade route from Wadi Bana from twin features nicknamed 'Sabrina' after a statuesque actress of the period. When a camel train sprung a dissident ambush near a well, 1 (Mountain) Troop became involved in a three-way ambush. The squadron then descended into the *wadi* and, after Intelligence had suggested two Yemeni officers were supporting the Qatabi, 1 Troop ambushed a track intersection and challenged an old man and woman carrying wood. They both dropped their loads and sprinted down the track, but were both shot dead by the cut-off. Underneath their shaggy robes both were wearing Yemeni uniforms.

By the evening of 5 May, the under-rated Brigadier Hargroves, the Garrison Commander, had successfully completed the objectives of preventing 'tribal dissidence from spreading and stopping attacks on the Dhala Road', but it had cost two killed and ten wounded. He reasserted Federal authority by temporarily moving villagers out of the area between Wadi Taym and the Danaba Basin as a punishment and enforced his decision with patrols and the threat of Air Control. On the 7th, representatives from the Hujari sought terms, but although they claimed that the dissidents had abandoned Wadi Rabwa, their request was rejected on the grounds that there were not enough dissidents in the delegation. The *Evening Standard* reported:

It was revealed on 9 May 1964 that a Shackleton bomber has made seven runs over a target peak near Thumair [sic], dropping a stick of two bombs each time. Before the attack took place, leaflets were dropped warning civilians to stay clear of the area. A week later another Shackleton flew over the area dropping leaflets.

Hargroves had opened up routes from Thumier to Danaba Basin and beyond. Wadi Misrah was found by 4 RTR patrols to be strongly defended, and the dissident heartland on Bakri Ridge had yet to be tested. Although the dissidents had been driven from the north and western area of the Radfan, there was still resistance in rugged mountains to the east and south. The FRA Group moved onto Coca Cola and Sand Fly, 1st East Anglians having relieved 45 Commando. However, no prisoners of value were captured, and consequently intelligence collection remained at a premium. On Cap Badge 45 Commando continued to be niggled by long-range sniping. Shortage of water meant that drinking took priority over washing and shaving. Army Air Corps Scouts and Beavers of 653 Squadron moved to Thumier and again proved their versatility. On 6 May, Belvederes were tasked to lift three Pack Howitzers and 150 shells to Coca Cola, but atmospheric conditions meant that only two guns could be landed, as underslung loads, about 1,300 yards from the gun position. The gunners broke the guns down and carried them to the position, but the ammunition never arrived.

When a 1st FRA patrol in the area of Shab Tem came under fire on 13 May from about 25 rebels, and called down artillery fire, they subsequently found the headless bodies of Captain Edwards and Trooper Warburton buried in a shallow grave, bringing to an end a difficult period for Major General Cubbon. At a press conference ten days earlier, when Cubbon was asked to comment on a Radio Taiz report that the heads of the two SAS had been displayed on stakes, he replied that HQ Middle East Land Forces had reliable information that the report was correct and expressed deepest sympathy to the families. His comments sparked international publicity and were received in Great Britain with shock and anger. Unfortunately, the next of kin had not been previously informed, and there was concern that the SAS had been identified as being in Aden. Since the British Government had no diplomatic representation in Yemen, the US Embassy investigated and replied that there was no evidence to support the allegations. HQ Middle East Land Forces stuck to its claim, with Cubbon suggesting that his report came from a 'usually reliable source'. In the House of Commons, Denis Healey, of the Labour Opposition, criticized Cubbon for releasing such information without first referring to the Secretary of State for War. Prime Minister Douglas-Home gave qualified support to Cubbon. When the bodies were found and it emerged that they had been decapitated, Healey apologized for his treatment of Cubbon. The next day *The Times* leader opined:

> The least the fighting troops can expect is that politicians, as well as the official information services, should treat their affairs with as much respect when something goes wrong, as they do when things go right.

The same charges could equally have been directed at journalism. HQ Middle East Command's public relations policy was to give journalists as much facilities and freedom as possible within operational and security restrictions; however, the demands of self-important reporters and cameras crews became a nightmare for the limited public relations staff and for troops on the ground, few of whom were trained in managing the media. During the 1964 operations in the Radfan, at least 55 correspondents and camera crew turned up, all demanding preferential treatment, even in Thumier, where there were no facilities. Lieutenant Colonel Julian Paget described the reporters as a 'horde'. Balanced against this was the fact that the Aden conflict was fought at a time of growing liberalism, in which the perceived excesses of colonial powers and security forces encountered far more criticism than those of nationalism and revolution. The Rock Hotel in Aden became the journalistic watering hole, as did, later in the decade, the Europa in Belfast.

When it came to writing to the next of kin of the two dead SAS, Major de la Billière had faced a conundrum – how was he going to explain to the families that they had died not on Salisbury Plain, but on a hot, rocky hillside in South Arabia? Fortunately, Lieutenant Colonel Woodhouse injected a dose of realism into SAS sensitivities in a letter to de la Billière, mentioning they were in uniform in Aden and criticizing his decision to cover it up as 'pointless'.

CHAPTER NINE

39 Brigade in Radfan

With the northern parts of Radfan under control and the trading route from the border and Yahya cut, it had been intended that the pacification of Radfan would continue without interruption. However, RadForce was not equipped for such a role, quite apart from increasing tensions in Aden. Offensive operations were therefore scaled down to building of the intelligence picture, in particularly gathering evidence of insurgency.

Major General Cubbon therefore requested a conventional Brigade HQ be given the only headquarters then available, namely HQ 39th Infantry Brigade based at Lisburn in Northern Ireland. It was commanded by Brigadier Cecil 'Monkey' Blacker MC, who had been commissioned into the 5th Inniskilling Dragoon Guards in 1936. He had been evacuated from Dunkirk and, transferring to the 23rd Hussars, had won the Military Cross in Normandy. He had been Military Assistant to the Chief of the Imperial General Staff before being appointed to command 39th Infantry Brigade in 1962.

When Blacker took over from Brigadier Hargroves on 11 May, Cubbon briefed that he was to:

• Demonstrate that British troops could penetrate into any part of the Radfan at any time of their choosing.
• Demonstrate that troops would invade areas of prestige value to the tribes.
• Provoke the dissidents to fight and suffer casualties, and help reduce morale.

Twenty dissidents who had bid farewell to RadForce the previous year by attacking Thumier were beaten off by a King's Own Scottish Borderers picquet.

Intelligence was still limited. So far, no prisoners had been captured and defector and informant information was weak. HQ 39th Brigade did not have an Intelligence Platoon and was loaned 15 (5th Infantry Brigade) Intelligence and Security Platoon, then based in Iserlohn in West Germany. It had five broad tasks:

- Intelligence: study enemy activity from patrol reports, air and ground recce and post operations conclusions.
- Brief and debrief battalion and company operations.
- Technical Intelligence: evaluate captured weapons.
- Security: provide advice to Thumier Base.
- Psychological operations: maintain contact with the local population.

Brigade HQ spent a fortnight acclimatizing and undergoing consolidation. Lieutenant Colonel Brian Watson, the 4th RTR Commanding Officer, was appointed Commander, Royal Armoured Corps with his Regiment, less A Squadron in the Persian Gulf, and 1st Troop, B Squadron, 16/5th Lancers. Second Lieutenant R.M. Smylie, who had four Centurions, an Armoured Recovery Vehicle and a small echelon, recalled:

After three weeks of stand-by, this long awaited order was given. How tremendous it was to have the chance to get rid of Aden and our outlandish camp for a while, and to have the prospect of some action! No hitches occurred on the extremely rough, dusty seventy-mile journey up to Thumier, where there was a camp, much less barbaric than what we had all expected and which included, to everyone's delight, a NAAFI tent selling iced beer in the evenings.

Major Stagg was appointed Commander, Royal Artillery. A valuable reinforcement was two 5.5-inch guns from 170 (Imjin) Battery, 45 Field Regiment, its battle honour having been gained during the Korean War. It arrived on 22 May on the commando-carrier HMS *Bulwark* from Borneo, where the gunners had also been employed as infantry; they were still wearing their jungle green uniforms. Their Leyland lorries were unable to tow the guns in the sandy terrain and were replaced by Matadors. The arrival of a three-gun Troop from 1 Parachute Battery, 7th RHA from Bahrain gave J Battery thirteen guns compared to the twelve with 3rd RHA in Kenya. To support future operations, a three-gun section provided by J and I Batteries moved to near 'Pegasus Village', leaving the remaining three J Battery guns in depth in the Danaba Basin below Cap Badge. Shortage of helicopters meant that gun positions were confined to *wadis* and fields close to roads so that lorries could deliver ammunition.

The infantry consisted of:

• 45 Commando less X Company. It returned to Thumier on 18 May after just nine days rest at BP Camp.
• 1st East Anglians.
• 3rd Para from Bahrain less B Company, which was rested and replaced by X Company. Since the prospects for heavy drop were limited, its 17 Para Heavy Drop Platoon RAOC was converted into infantry. The Battalion was commanded by Lieutenant Colonel Tony Farrar-Hockley, who had been Adjutant of 1 Glosters at the Battle of the Imjin River in April 1951 and had spent three years as a prisoner of war in North Korea.
• 1st KOSB.
• 1st Royal Scots, which arrived for a year in May 1964.
• 2nd FRA.

Meanwhile, on 11 May, Royal Engineers had opened a firm track through Wadi Boran and, a week later, provided a motorable track through Wadi Rabwa. The airstrips Monk's Field, named after Major Monk, and Paddy's Field, named after Lieutenant Colonel Stevens, were built east of Cap Badge and were capable of supporting Beverley medium transport aircraft. Sappers from the Middle East Port Squadron improvised a 1,700ft cable lift from Paddy's Field to the top of Cap Badge. When 24th Ordnance Field Park arrived from Kenya they established logistic support at Thumier and administered supplies ordered from the Ordnance Depot in Aden, a structure that was familiar to quartermasters and resulted in shorter delivery times. Operations were supported by 2 Company RASC with its highly mobile and six-wheeled Stalwarts and armoured Bedfords, by 'A' Air Supply Platoon at RAF Khormaksar, and by trains of mules and camels plodding along the tracks carrying about 1,000lbs a day of non-essential supplies.

Under leaden skies, Lieutenant Colonel Watkins launched a probe down Wadi Misrah on 19 May with two armoured car troops from 4RTR and the FRA and the Centurion tanks. On call was J Battery. In command was Captain D.D.A. Linaker (RTR), supported by James Nash. Unfortunately, the interpretation of an air photograph of fields taken the previous day did not show that each field was terraced on 3ft-high solid sand banks. The plan was to advance to Hadija, but breakdowns and the terrain meant that only Matwil Fawq was reached. Second Lieutenant Smylie recalled:

Everyone emerged very battered and bruised after a couple of miles of this, but found at the valley entrance a position to gladden any Gunner's heart: it overlooks some four miles, and from there we opened up on rebel posts all along the sides of the Valley. After a short and very accurate shoot, we moved down the Misrah, and came under both rifle and MG fire. We soon learned how difficult it is to detect enemy who fire from positions actually in the mountain ridges.

During the fighting, Nash decided to change from his Ferret into a tank and had just clambered in when a bullet entered the turret, narrowly missing him and Corporal Finney, the commander. When Finney flattened a farm house from a range of 300 yards, it was the first time that the 105mm gun had been fired in action and the first time the Centurions had seen action since Korea. Soon after an Auster pilot had warned the force of rain, a sudden thunderstorm reduced visibility to about 30–40 yards and flooded the *wadi*. With several vehicles bogged down, it took until the evening to extract the force. In relation to the rain, Peter Hinchliffe recalled:

My first trip to the Radfan was to Monk's Field, living under camouflage netting for about 8 weeks or so. It was during this time that a monsoon broke filling a *wadi*, rough dimensions 100 feet across and 60 feet deep, within 30 minutes, washing amphibious vehicles downstream. Scary, especially for those out on patrol who were sending up Very signals and were marooned on a hillock. Weapons were lost and vehicles were in a right state. As for those, including me, in Monk's Field camp, the only real shelter we had was our mess tins and these became somewhat dented by the enormous hailstones. It had to be seen to be believed.

Blacker planned to seize Bakri Ridge that spread south-east from Wadi Rabwa and was waiting for 815 NAS Wessex helicopters scheduled to arrive on board HMS *Centaur*, when 1st FRA patrols despatched on 16th May reported two days later that Bakri Ridge was lightly defended. Blacker immediately launched a brigade advance on two axes:

• 3rd Para to clear dissidents on Bakri Ridge and then attack Wadi Dhubsan, an enemy stronghold 2,000ft below the ridge.
• 45 Commando and 2nd FRA to advance through Wadi Misrah with armoured support and open up lines of communication deep into the Radfan.

Much of the western slopes of Bakri Ridge consisted of cultivated terraces surrounded by steep banks. Although Brigadier Blacker had agreed that the ridge would be dominated by Air Control from 21 May, when patrols found a path onto the ridge from Shab Tem, he ordered 3rd Para to probe toward Hajib. Blacker had been intending to commence operations on the 17th, but rain grounded two supporting Scouts and rendered the track through Wadi Rabwa unusable. This meant that the alternative of using Land Rovers to dump supplies to the start line at Shab Tem was shelved, in favour of them being brought forward on foot. This included water, but it is heavy, slops around inside jerrycans and can throw the carrier off balance.

At 7 pm on the 18th, C Company led the 7-mile approach following a steep camel track on to the plateau. Battalion HQ, A Company and 3 Troop, 9th Parachute Squadron followed, each man carrying either a full jerrycan of water or ammunition in a frame, the average load being about 85lbs. Clambering up and down the terraces proved tiring; nevertheless, by dawn the Battalion had covered about six miles and reached Lethoom on the Hajib escarpment. During the day, a Beaver from Thumier parachuted supplies. A Company led the next night. Lieutenant Hew Pike had been about to ambush the south side of the Lethoom and capture a prisoner, when his patrol collided with seven dissidents. A ranging shot from J Battery in Wadi Misrah exploding behind the paras led to the guns being instructed to cease fire. Although surprise had been lost, by dawn on the 20th, 3rd Para had advanced a further six miles and had seized the 2,000ft-high Hajib escarpment. Next day, C Company led, with Anti-Tank Platoon leading. Led by CSM Herbert 'Nobby' Arnold, it advanced down Al Duhira ridge and as it approached Ar Zuqm, three dissidents from a party of twelve slipping out of the village were captured, the first prisoners to be taken since operations began in January. Their interrogation led to the discovery of a path down the 3,330ft escarpment, which 3rd Para followed Parachute Regiment traditions in naming 'Arnold's Spur'.

The RAF were keen to initiate the Air Control next day and proposed that 3rd Para should withdraw; however, discussions between Air Vice Marshal Johnson and Major General Cubbon led to it being moved to an area yet to be brought under control. During the night, small flashing red lights seen by 3rd Para were thought to be dissident signals indicating the locations of patrols. Although the chilly mist clung on to Bakri Ridge, the Scouts continued to fly in supplies. Helped by 9th Para Squadron RE, I Para Battery in Wadi Misrah kept pace with the advance. On 23 May, 3rd Para advanced toward Wadi Dhubsan until C Company was held up by about fifty dissidents armed with automatic weapons located in several stone houses in Al Qudeisha on the highest point of Bakri Ridge. Aided by Hawker Hunters and A Company giving fire support, C Company broke into a village and fought a tough battle; no sooner had one position been overrun than fire opened up from another unexpected direction. The paras eventually captured the village and found a maze of caves, tunnels and escape routes linked to dead ground that had clearly been developed over centuries for self-defence against neighbouring tribes. A Company moved around the left flank and seized the spur overlooking the village, from which the Battalion objective, Wadi Dhubsan, could be seen 3,300ft below. In a week, 3 Para had seized 200 square miles of Bakri Ridge. X Company, 45 Commando was delivered to Bakri Ridge on 25 May.

For Phase Two from 24 to 30 May, Brigadier Blacker ordered:

• 25 May. 45 Commando and 2nd FRA to clear Wadi Misrah and capture Jebel Huriyah.
• 26 May. 3 Para, with X Company under command, to raid Wadi Dhubsan and demonstrate to the dissidents that their stronghold, which had never been entered by a European, was not impregnable. Houses of leading dissidents to be searched and foodstuffs and arms destroyed.
• 25–27 May. 4th RTR to penetrate Wadi Nakhalain and Wadi Niaf in a show of force and deter dissident camel trains from using it as a line of communication route to Yemen.

The advance to Jebel Huriyah involved a six-mile march through Wadi Misrah; however, heavy rain and flash floods saw water levels rise to 8ft, so the operation was postponed for 24 hours, but not before the crews of two armoured cars were rescued by a Navy helicopter shortly before their vehicles were submerged. Y Company lost a Land Rover in the raging torrent.

For the show of force, Lieutenant Colonel Watkins assembled 'WatForce' from B Squadron, 4th RTR, 1st Troop, B Squadron, 16/5th Lancers and B Company and a mortar section from 1st East Anglians. On the 24th, two Centurions fired about 125 rounds at suspected enemy and, after patrols sent out during the night reported no contacts, at 7 am on the 25th the armoured cars led the advance and met no opposition until midday, when about twenty dissidents opened fire with two machine guns at the north end of the wadi. Two Saladins in 11 Troop lost two wheels to mines, and when Trooper Hefferman, a driver, was wounded by a bullet, the medical officer treated him used implements from a fitter's toolbox. During the battle, the two 5.5-inch guns opened fire and the armoured cars fired 250 rounds. The force leaguered behind J Battery of guns and were disturbed by rounds being fired at intervals throughout the night. Mindful that one of the strategic aims of operations was to remind the dissidents that British and Federal forces would enter any area in the Federation at any time, Blacker ordered the operation to be repeated the next day; when no enemy were seen, WatForce withdrew on 28 May. Second Lieutenant Smylie recalled:

> Our time up-country was thoroughly enjoyed by everyone. Morale has never been higher, despite the mass of hard work maintaining the tanks and the daily stand-to at 0405 hours. The tanks had a particularly hard time, as the area was . . . rocky and not good tank country. The most memorable fact was the accuracy of the shooting. [From the Scarlet and Green Journal, 1964]

Blacker then ordered 3rd Para to raid Wadi Dhubsan. Key to the operation was the 5,000ft Jebel Haqla, flat-topped and suitable for Scouts delivering supplies and evacuating casualties. Since the ground below was broken up by steep ridges, the easiest approach was through Wadi Ruheiba and Wadi Dura'a, but it was long, most obvious and therefore likely to be defended. Lieutenant Colonel Farrar-Hockley decided to use the direct route of descending Arnold's Spur in full view of the enemy, not realizing that at the bottom was a 30ft cliff. The plan was as follows:

- C Company to seize Jebel Haqla.
- A Company to break into the village of Bayn al Gidr at the northern entrance of Wadi Dhubsan.
- X Company to descend after being landed by helicopter and to advance as far as of Hawfi, which lay on the far side of a prominent bend in the Wadi.
- The Battalion to be clear of the sector by last light.

Major Banks had urged caution to ensure the advance did not outrun the picquets.

After dark on a wet and cold night on the 25th, C Company secured Jebel Haqla. Then, at 1 pm, A Company scrambled down Arnold's Spur, negotiated the cliff and had seized Bayn al Gadr by dawn. Low cloud and rain grounded the helicopters, and X Company, glad to be on the move, descended the spur and reached at the bottom at about 6 am, 1,000 yards in front of A Company but beyond the range of C Company on Jebel Haqla. In front, the objective of Hawfi was waking up. When C Company reported several dissidents walking toward the village, X Company slowly advanced in eerie silence for the next 600 yards, picquets protecting the flanks. Major Banks had instructed his Troops to spread out in order to degrade enemy fire from high ground. About 400 yards from Al Adhab, a 1 Troop picquet covering 3 Troop on the *wadi* floor spotted about 40 dissidents equipped with several light machine guns tucked into a steep ridge on the right flank and out of control of a picquet. The two leading sections took cover behind a wall and opened fire on the dissidents, sending them scuttling into cover. As the battle rose to a crescendo, a Scout flew down the chimney of the *wadi* and, overshooting 3 Troop, immediately came under heavy fire. The pilot, Major Jackson, banked, but the helicopter staggered as bullets ripped through its skin and as he crash-landed in front of 3 Troop, several Royal Marines dashed forward to find that the helicopter was carrying two passengers, Farrar-Hockley and his Intelligence Officer, who had been wounded. It turned out they had been given the incorrect map reference for A Company.

When it became evident that the dissident position was strong and would require a battalion attack, Farrar-Hockley instructed A Company to picquet high ground north of X Company, while a C Company platoon moved to high ground on the left flank of the Royal Marines. With the 5.5-inch guns and Mortar Platoon already shelling the dissidents, and a Hunter air strike on call, Captain Roger Brind and Quartermaster Sergeant Walton were laying out the red and yellow markers indicating the direction of the dissidents when Brind was wounded in the thigh and stomach; nevertheless, they completed their task, whereupon Brind was dragged into cover by two Royal Marines and treated by a naval Sick Berth Attendant. The Hunters barrelled through the *wadi* at low level at 400 knots in a 30-degree dive, the Rolls Royce engines thundering from *wadi* rocks, and launched 'concrete' rockets and opened fire while still behind the leading companies, showering 1 Troop, still trying to gain high ground, with empty 30mm cases. Marine Kerwick in Corporal Waterson's section was sheltering in an outhouse when he was terribly wounded in the head by a ricocheting case. The leading section, led by Sergeant Clarkson, attracted fire from left, right and centre and lost Marine David Wilson killed and Marine Dunkin wounded so severely in the knee that his leg was later amputated. Meanwhile, under cover of phosphorous grenades, Waterson's section advanced with 3 Troop to several houses high on the southern side of the *wadi* shortly before the track swung into Hawfi. During the early afternoon, 2 Troop moved to the northern side of the *wadi* and threatened the dissidents sufficiently for their resistance to crack. Major Banks was reorganizing X Company, while Sick Berth Attendant Edward

Wade attended the three wounded. A Company advanced to the bend to cover the advance of X Company into the village. Six dead dissidents were found and eleven rifles captured. Farrar-Hockley cancelled the original plan of withdrawing, in order to give REME fitters flown from 653 Squadron AAC Workshops in Little Aden the opportunity to repair the Scout. They had worked all night behind a screen and when Major Jackson pressed the starter, the rotors spun and, to the relief of the troops, the helicopter lifted off in a cloud of dust and returned to Thumier. At the cost of a Royal Marine killed and seven others wounded, 3rd Para now dominated an area of 200 square miles and by capturing an 'impregnable' stronghold, had struck a serious blow to dissident credibility and prestige, particularly when stocks of food were burnt in the village.

X Company relieved C Company on Jebel Haqla, and the next day 3rd Para climbed Arnold's Spur and were flown first to Thumier and then to Aden. On the 28th, the Royal Marines handed over to 2nd FRA and were flown to Thumier by 815 Squadron Wessex helicopters.

The final Brigade objective was the 5,500ft Jebel Huriyah, the highest peak in the Radfan, south of Wadi Tramare, and unclimbed by any European. The approach involved following a reasonable six-mile track and then a four-mile camel track through the steep-sided Wadi Misrah, which then dissolved into several ravines littered with boulders. Brigadier Blacker wanted the *wadi* clear of dissidents so that he could open a line of communication route and assault the *jebel*, which was expected to be defended as a matter of prestige, especially after the dissidents' defeat at Wadi Dhubsan. He assigned the task to Lieutenant Colonel Jack Dye, who commanded 1st East Anglians, and gave him 2nd FRA and D Squadron, 4 RTR. Dye had been commissioned into the Royal Norfolk Regiment in 1940 and had been awarded the Military Cross during the advance through Germany. In 1962, he took command of 1st East Anglians when it reformed from the amalgamation of the Royal Norfolk and Suffolk Regiments.

At 10 pm on 29 May, Dye issued his orders for a four-phase operation. He did not issue timings for Phases 2 to 4 because it would take time to picquet the heights:

Phase One
• C Company, 1st East Anglians to picquet as far as Moba'a by first light on 31 May.
• A Company and a Saladin Troop to clear by the wadi by midday on 2 June.

Phase Two
• 2nd FRA to picquet north side of the wadi.
• B Company to clear as far as the junction of Wadi Bulbar and Wadi Tramare.

Phase Three
• 2nd FRA to secure southern limits of the ridge.
• C Company to seize Ice Cold as a start line for the assault on Jebel Huriyah.

Phase Four
• A Company and elements of 2nd FRA to seize Jebel Huriyah.

Phase One was completed without incident. A patrol briefly entered Mogga. On the 4th, B Company picqueted the advance of two FRA companies to Mogga, while C Company and the other two FRA companies covered the advance through the *wadi* to Al Surata, which was reached in the late afternoon. During the early stages of Phase 2, a mine damaged a Land Rover near Mas Magar, and a seriously wounded military bystander was flown direct to BMH Aden. Next morning, B Company secured the junction of Wadi Misrah and Wadi Tremare; D Squadron then patrolled Wadis Tremare and Bulbar up to a distance of 1,000 yards, without incident.

Phase 3 opened on the 7th. At about 10 pm, 2nd FRA were advancing up the slopes of Jebel Huriyah when dissidents in Shaab Sharah opened fire across a 600ft-deep valley at a range of 600 yards. Captain Tim Thompson, who was the Forward Observation Officer with two signallers, recalled:

We were with the leading coy of 2 FRA and soon after we had started to climb the lower slopes of Jebel Huriyah at the head of the *wadi*, we came under fire from several enemy positions hidden amongst the rocks and difficult to identify. I knew we had two section of J Battery RHA guns sited back on the *wadi* floor and also a section of two 5.5-ins guns further back but all within range of potential targets, so having failed to make much of an impression with one section, I left that firing on a presumed target and set using other gunner assets. My signallers soon proved adept at mastering an improvised procedure as we adjusted the fire of all three sections, spreading it around the likely enemy positions. Eventually the enemy fire dwindled. Many cries of 'Murrawahhed timan!' were heard from our supporting infantry in praise of the guns.

In spite of enfiladed fire from above and on its flanks, the FRA company descended into the valley, fought their way up and by the end of the day had overrun three positions. Supported by Hawker Hunters and artillery, the FRA entered the village at first light on 8 June. A feature of the fighting was that the insurgents and dissidents held on to their positions until the last moment. From FRA Ridge, as the ground became known, Ice Cold was visible and apparently undefended. With C Company some distance from the FRA, Blacker instructed 5 Company to seize the start line, which they achieved by 2.30 pm. Lieutenant Colonel Dye expected the dissidents to defend Jebel Huriyah and Shaab Sharah tenaciously and, planning a Battalion attack, over the next two nights he brought his C and A Companies forward and spent two days bringing up his supplies. During this time an 815 NAS Wessex crashed killing one person and injuring ten others; a Scout arrived on the scene within 15 minutes, even though the pilot had been in the Mess and the medical officer in the Casualty Clearing Station at Thumier.

At 2 pm on 10 June, Dye instructed C Company to secure the ridge from the west while A Company was to seize the summit. Twelve hours later, on a moonless night broken by Shackletons dropping diversionary flares eight miles away, the East Anglians crossed Ice Cold and picked their way across the rocky terrain. Two hours later and just ten minutes behind schedule, it went firm to allow Tactical HQ and A Company to pass through and seize the summit, the lights of Aden twinkling forty miles to the south. At 6 am, a Scout delivered a flagpole from which were flown the Regimental flags of the East Anglians and the FRA. A lone sniper was silenced by Mortar Platoon. The East Anglians remained on Jebel Huriyah for the next week of hot days, rainstorms at 6 pm and chilly nights, until relieved by 1st FRA. The battle at Shaab Sharah and seizure of Jebel Huriyah were both high points in the Radfan campaign. While the dissidents may have fought to preserve their independence, British and Arab soldiers had proven their impregnable fortress could be breached, however much the insurgency threat remained.

At the height of the fighting in the Radfan, the Yemenis launched a Second Front in May by threatening the State of Audhali, with the aim of spreading the Federal defensive posture (a 'Front' in Soviet military terminology was a theatre of military operations). Audhali was selected because it had retained its autonomy within the Federation and was seen by the Yemenis to be susceptible to their republican vision. 'Sam' and dissident elements of the Shamsis to the north-east were seen to be candidates for spreading revolution. Arms and ammunition flowed across the border and several forts were attacked, but FRA counter-attacks saw the tension checked, and several

Yemenis were captured. The Second Front then crumbled when FRA operations forced the insurgent supply routes from Beidha to use Wadi Merkha and other tracks, where they were ambushed. The only British troops in the area were three Royal Signals from 222 Signal Squadron (Air Formation) supporting the FRA Arab Forward Air Controller based at Mudia FNG fort directing Hunter strikes in the region of Jebel Khuder, north of Radfan. This was the 'British invasion force' claimed to exist by the Yemenis. Strikes continued into September. In June, the Chiefs of Staff reported:

> More Egyptian-trained tribesmen could be infiltrated as potential trouble makers; more weapons and money could be provided; a policy of assassination could be encouraged. There have been several reports that the number of intelligence officers in the Yemen has increased and that the Egyptians are providing increased material aid not only for dissidents but also for terrorism by extremists in the Federation, including Aden State. As activity in the Radfan has shown recently, dissident forces are likely to be increasingly sophisticated in their equipment, training and discipline.

On 14 June, Brigadier Blacker handed command of HQ 39th Brigade to Brigadier Chandos Blair MC. Commissioned into the Seaforth Highlanders in 1939, he was captured when the 51st Highland Division surrendered at St Valery in June 1940. Sent to a prison camp in Germany, he was the first officer to escape and reach England via Switzerland, Spain and Gibraltar. He then fought in Normandy and Germany and commanded the 4th King's African Rifles in 1959, before being posted to HQ 39th Infantry Brigade. Blair consolidated the gains made since January by dividing Radfan into three battalion tactical areas of operations to prevent insurgency and to conduct a pacification programme. The areas were:

• Wadi Taym – 1st KOSB.
• Cap Badge and Danaba Basin – 1st Royal Scots.
• Jebel Huriyah and Wadi Misrah – 1st FRA.

When intelligence emerged of groups of uniformed insurgents infiltrating into Radfan, Blair instructed that the tactical areas be smothered with company and platoon bases, from which patrols, OPs and picquets could dominate the ground with ambushes and mine clearance. From 14 to 18 June, 1st Royal Scots and D Company, 3rd Para under command, shortly before it returned to Bahrain, conducted a recce in force to Shaab Lashab and encountered sniping. On the 27th, 3 Company, 1st FRA found Jebel Widina to be empty; however, 1st KOSB patrols then found evidence of infiltration in the vicinity of Jebel Widina and Jebel Sababah.

Brigadier Blair now launched Operation Test Match. A Company, 1st East Anglians and an 81mm mortar section commanded by Captain Abbott were to seize both Jebel Widina and Jebel Sababah, supported by 2nd FRA securing their start line of Arnold's Spur. The plan was for two 653 Squadron Scouts to fly an advance guard of 36 men to secure a landing site on Jebel Widina by midnight on 23/24 August and for the remainder of the company to be delivered at first light next day. A platoon would then seize Jebel Sababah. Ten years earlier, during the Cyprus Emergency, Sycamore light helicopters had delivered small patrols to seize high ground in the Troodos Mountains. This proposal is thought to have been the first British helicopter night assault. But when one of the Scouts suffered engine failure on Arnold's Spur and the contingency plan of a 6-hour march looked likely, Staff Sergeant Scott, the pilot of the second helicopter, offered to ferry the advance guard to Jebel Widina. He completed the transfer, without lights, just after midnight in a turnaround time of eight minutes (thirty seconds at Arnold's Spur, five seconds on Jebel Widina and the rest flying time). A platoon found Sababah to be unoccupied. A Company patrolled the area until the 28th, when it was withdrawn.

Battalions generally served three months in Radfan, with companies rotating through patrolling and guarding bases. Generally, company bases supported three platoon picquets, for instance in the Wadi Rabwa/Wadi Taym Sector platoons overlooked Danaba Basin from Cap Badge, Piccadilly and Hotel 10 (unnamed peaks were given nicknames), the latter only reached by helicopter. Platoon bases were about three-quarters the size of a soccer pitch. The perimeter was defined by a sandbag wall and several sandbagged OPs equipped with machine guns and sheltered from the sun by hessian. Tents (160lb) were usually protected by a 2ft-high mortar blast wall. Inside, camp beds were laid in slit trenches to give additional protection. The Well Drilling Troop of 63 (MELF) Park Squadron was helped by information from Army Emergency Reserve geologists in UK. Water was piped to Dhala for the first time. Since the deep pits of latrines were a health hazard, one method of suffocating flies and insects was to throw a smoke grenade into the pit. Urinal pipes shoved in the ground were known as 'Desert Roses'. The latrine on Cap Badge was outside the perimeter, and once the evening stand-to had been ordered, it was not used because any movement was regarded as hostile.

Daily routines started with a dawn stand-to. Afternoons were generally spent preparing for night activities. Ambushes might mean securing shirt and jumper sleeves with masking tape to ward off insects and 'creepy-crawlies'.

Fighting patrols might include practice section attacks using live ammunition. Recce patrols looked for ambush sites and evidence of mines and booby traps buried in the vicinity of tracks. Psychological Operations visits to villages often included a medic. Artillery and mortar Defensive Fire missions were regularly registered and checked at night. Several airstrips capable of handling fixed-wing transport aircraft, for example Twin Pioneers, were built, Blair's Field being named after Brigadier Blair. The aircraft using Monk's Field had a short strip and, depending on the wind direction, the pilots just about cleared Coca Cola or Pepsi Cola.

Every other day a convoy of about 100 vehicles left the FRA Training Battalion camp at Lake Lines at 6 am bound for Thumier/Habilayn, which meant passengers and the infantry and armoured car escorts either arrived at night or had an early start. The first five miles of tarmac petered out into sand, which might mean engaging four-wheel drive. In the vicinity of Lahej conditions improved along a hard track flanked by irrigation ditches feeding green fields and groves. At the company base at Nobat Dakin the track forked with the Sacred Road to Dhala, becoming hazardous from rocks and boulders as it entered the mountains and making for an uncomfortable ride in the backs of dusty vehicles. About six hours after leaving Aden, convoys stopped at the white-painted Government Guard fort at Thumier, where traders sold fruit, biscuits and tea at inflated prices amid mutterings of '*Nasser tamaan!*' (Nasser good) and '*bakshesh*' (a Persian word meaning a tip or bribe to expedite service and common military slang for 'no cost').

The convoy sometimes split, with some vehicles driving through *wadis* to supply the forward operation bases, such as Monk's Field. Those bound for Dhala took the old Turkish road that twisted beneath high, jagged mountainsides, on which picquets dominated the heights. By now, the drivers had been at the wheel for about eight hours, when they were faced with the Khuraybah Pass, a hazardous series of hairpins on a track that was so narrow that lorries often had to reverse back and forth to negotiate the bends. Convoy commanders often released vehicles at two-minute intervals, in order to avoid casualties if one overturned. Escorts and passengers usually walked up the footpath. When mines started causing losses of vehicles and casualties, Ferret Scout Cars provided by the Armoured Car Squadron for convoy commanders took the lead. Lieutenant David Pepperell was serving with 2 Squadron RCT when Stalwarts were then adopted as the command vehicle:

They [the Ferrets] were losing so many vehicles (and particularly commanders because of their exposed position in the vehicle when hitting mines) that they repositioned to the centre of the convoy, ironically because the mines were so unreliable it was rarely the front vehicle that got taken out. The main benefit of the Stalwart was the heavy, shaped hull which deflected mine blast from the crew.

In effect, the Stalwart was an early, if accidental, variant of the Mine-Resistant Ambush Protected vehicles that preceded the Rhodesian Rhinos and Cougars seen in Iraq and Afghanistan.

At the top of the pass near Dhala, the track passed through a plateau of cultivated green terraces at an altitude of 5,000ft. The low humidity was a welcome change from the clinging heat and dust of Aden and the convoy. The British tented company base was on a small ridge about a mile north of the town beside the road, 300 yards away on another ridge was the APL camp and a mile away was the airstrip.

In September, after fourteen months, J Battery handed over to 19th Light Regiment with its full complement of eighteen Pack Howitzers, in the knowledge that it had enhanced the reputation of the Royal Artillery. The gunners had fired over 20,000 rounds, with many of the officers and NCOs working 'one up', for instance warrant officers and sergeants acting as Gun Position Officers instead of officers, although in Beihan this had been a lance bombardier's job; 4th RTR also handed over to the 10th Royal Hussars. In its account of operations, credit is paid to its REME Artificers and Vehicle Mechanics for keeping the lorries, Land Rovers and armoured vehicles maintained and repairing battle damage, frequently hundreds of miles from Light Aid Detachments. When a Saladin lost a complete wheel station to a Teller mine during Operation Nutcracker, the REME fitted it with a Saracen wheel station within three days, 'not bad some 450 miles from the nearest recovery vehicle'. The Saladin, Saracen and Stalwart all came from the same basic six-wheel design manufactured by Alvis.

The Hussars, nicknamed 'The Shiny Tenth', had spent six years on Centurion tanks in West Germany before converting to the Armoured Car Regiment in support of 5th Infantry Brigade at Tidworth in 1964. Regimental HQ and two squadrons joined 24th Infantry Brigade in August, while C Squadron deployed to Sharjah. Initially, their armoured cars supported convoys supplying the company bases at Ballpoint, Holdfast and Monk's Field. On 1 July, soon after 1 Troop took over from 4 Troop in Hayaz, a hill in the desert five miles from the border overlooking a route used by insurgents, a flash flood swept through their positions. Crews usually pitched their tents beside their Saladins and slept in an order that enabled them get out into the armoured car quickly: the driver at the back, then the gunner and at the opening, the commander. Trooper Chris Dunning recalled:

A flight of RAF medium tactical transport Argosies fly over Crater. Top right is the island of Sirrah. On the surrounding cliffs is evidence of the Turkish forts. (*Robert Egby*)

Steamer Point in 1966. This heart of Aden Settlement evolved into a thriving port. Top right is Command Hill with HQ Middle East Command. In the centre is the white Catholic Church. (*Brian Harrington Spier*)

1964. A Beverley and a Wessex helicopter embark troops on the parade ground in front of HQ Middle East Command, the Royal Navy signal station and accommodation blocks for the WRAC and WRAF. (*Jenny Holmes*)

The town of Lahej in 1963. The Sultan governed Aden before transferring it as part of compensation in 1939. The town was the scene of a British defeat in 1915.

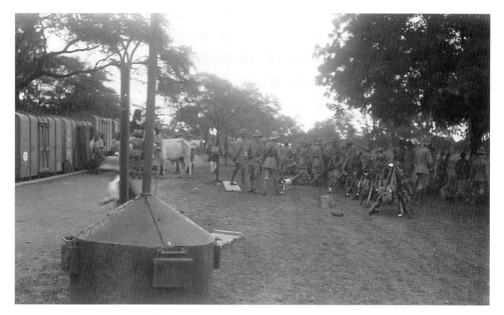

1915. The 1/1ˢᵗ Brecknockshires (TF) return to India after their year in Aden. (*Regimental Museum of The Royal Welsh*)

1919. Turkish prisoners in railway trucks arrive at Sheikh Othman from Lahej to be repatriated by ship to their homelands.

Fairey F-3. Entering service with RAF and Fleet Air Arm service in 1927, it was used by No. 8 Squadron in Air Control before the Second World War.

Yemen, 1963. Royalist forces training. In the background wearing a beret and with a handlebar moustache is a member of the British Mercenary Operation.

Aden, Radfan 1963. Lt. Col. David Court, CO 4 FRA, chatting to a local sheikh and his escort, most armed with .303 Short Lee Enfield and Mauser rifles. With Court is his FRA close protection. (*Bill Briggs*)

The Yemen border, 28 May 1964. Soldiers from the RHA and 4 RTR recover a Saladin damaged by a German Teller mine. Rain in the mountains had produced a 'seil' that had flooded the dry riverbed. (*Bill Briggs*)

A 26 Squadron RAF Belvedere helicopter lifts a J Bty 105mm Pack Howitzer during a training exercise. Since flying conditions in Radfan were hot and high, moving underslung loads was hazardous. (*Peter Cronk*)

Operation Nutcracker, January 1964. 16/5th Lancers Centurion tanks supporting the FRA in Radfan. (*Queen's Royal Lancers & Nottinghamshire Yeomanry Museum*)

Operation Nutcracker. FRA soldiers assist 12 Troop RE construct the road from the Wadi Rabwa. Gunner Godfrey, of J Bty, uses a petrol cooker to make a brew. Lt. Mike Bremridge, in beret, moves forward to lend a hand. The track was destroyed by dissidents after the operation. (*Bill Briggs*)

Radfan, 20 March 1964. J Bty RHA guns are manhandled up the zigzag track from Wadi Rabwa into Wadi Taym. (*Tim Thompson*)

Radfan, 6 May 1964. Two J Bty howitzers on Coca Cola positioned by helicopter to overcome the problems of shells hitting crests held by friendly forces, in this instance Cap Badge (in the middle distance). The Danaba Basin is below the guns and in the distance is Sabrina. (*Richard Mountford*)

Bakri Ridge, May 1964. Behind the J Bty radio operator are the farmed terraces that typically stretched from Radfan *wadis* to the summits of peaks. The terraces made movement very arduous and tiring. (*Tim Thompson*)

Bakri Ridge, May 1964. A typical Radfan 'fortified' village. A network of underground stores and tunnels connecting houses made fighting difficult. This village was sited with a 1,000ft sheer cliff on one side. (*Richard Mountford*)

Jebel Huriyah, 9 June 1964. 2 FRA hoist their flag on the 6,500ft peak after a tough two-day battle with dissidents. (*Patrick Daniell*)

Radfan. A 2 Sqn RCT convoy stops in a *wadi* en route to Habilyan after a Bedford lorry at the rear had hit a mine. The vehicles are escorted by Ferret Scout Cars and led by a Stalwart. This convoy was commanded by Lt. David Pepperell. (*Lt. Col. David Pepperell*)

A Stalwart leads a convoy. Its high profile proved a useful protection against mines.

Radfan. A camel train passes a Saladin armoured car stopped in a stream. (*Movement Control Organisation*)

An 8 Squadron Hawker Hunter F9 Fighter Ground Attack at RAF Sharjah in 1963. Its weapon fit includes practice concrete-headed rockets that proved particularly useful against stone houses in Radfan. (*Courtesy of Ray Deacon*)

1966. The company base outside Dhala on a plateau that commands the ground to the border.

Aden, 1966. A 1st PWO patrol in Tawahi. Notice the narrowness of the streets that made grenades so dangerous. (*Brian Harrington Spier*)

A Cameronian patrol protects British schoolchildren crossing a road to meet their parents. (*Movement Control Organisation*)

Aden. Ma'alla Straight, which housed many Service dependants. (*Movement Control Organisation*)

Aden. The district of Sheikh Othman with the dominating Damascus Mosque in the foreground. (*Movement Control Organisation*)

Sheikh Othman. The junction of Hunters Road leading from Radfan Camp that became known as 'Grenade Corner'. (*Brian Harrington Spier*)

The Border Post between Sheikh Othman and the State of Lahej was controlled by the Aden Police. The military Checkpoint Golf was in close proximity. (*Brian Harrington Spier*)

Main Pass at the top of Queen Arwa Drive which runs through Crater. (*Movement Control Organisation*)

Sheikh Othman. 13 Pl, D Coy, 3rd Royal Anglians prepare for another day of patrolling using Armour Plated Bedfords and Land Rovers. (*Brian Harrington Spier*)

1967. 3rd Royal Anglians 'Bravo Mobile' and the Aden Armed Police on stand-by for the daily disturbances in Sheikh Othman in the compound of Mansoura Police Station. (*Brian Harrington Spier*)

Sheikh Othman, 1966. Captain Martin Lewis, 3rd Royal Anglians, with a haul of terrorist weapons and the not too worried suspect. (*Brian Harrington Spier*)

Crater, 1967. A Royal Northumberland Fusilier and a civilian wounded by a 'Cairo Grenadier' are treated by other members of the patrol.

Left, an Intelligence Corps NCO attached to B-Group has drawn his pistol after an attack on a military Land Rover. (*Military Intelligence Museum*)

20 June 1967. 2 Lt. Nick Beard shortly before the ambush from Champion Lines on the 60 Sqn RCT range party. Behind him are SSgt. E. Butler and Sgt. R. Garth, who were both killed. Beard was lucky to escape injury when a bullet lodged in his First Field Dressing attached to his belt. (*Colonel Nick Beard*)

The Aircraft Carrier HMS *Eagle* off Aden during the Withdrawal. (*Movement Control Organisation*)

Members of 8 Pl, Y Coy, 1 RNF in Aden. On the left is 2 Lt. John Davis, who was killed in Crater on 20 June 1967. On the embankment are Fusiliers Archie Moor and Harry Wiltshire. In centre, wearing his beret, is L Cpl. Jim Carroll. On his left with his hands in his pockets is L Cpl. Keith Kelly. Both survived the Armed Police ambush. On the right is Fusilier P. Dennis. (*Courtesy of Jim Carroll*)

The 12th of September is a day I will never forget!! Coming back from Dhala, we went on ahead to pick up the Infantry who were up on the ridges (to cover the convoy through the *wadi*). We had just passed Milestone 36 when we hit two anti-tank mines and 25lb of plastic explosives. It picked the 14 tons of armoured car and threw us about 25 feet into the air, leaving a crater 30 foot wide and 10 foot deep. We were very lucky the armour did not split open as we were fully loaded with all our shells and bullets.

The crew were flown by a Scout to BP Camp for treatment. During the next week, 4/7th Dragoon Guards relieved the 10th Royal Hussars, some of whom returned to England in one of the first VC-10 flights. Dunning returned on a Britannia via Bahrain and Istanbul.

Throughout the Yemen civil war, London struggled with its presence in Aden. The Private Secretary to Prime Minister Alec Douglas-Home, Oliver Wright, wrote to the Prime Minister on 18 July 1964:

Nasser has been able to capture the most dynamic and modern forces in the area while we have been left, by our own choice, backing the forces that are not merely reactionary, but shifty, unreliable and treacherous.

Royalist forces supported by the British Mercenary Organisation were having considerable success in tying down Yemeni and Egyptian troops; however, the steady supply of weapons was always problematic, as it had been to resistance movements during the Second World War. When the British Government shelved supplying arms, High Commissioner Trevaskis wrote a strongly-worded telegram to the Colonial Office suggesting that the greatest threat to British interests in South Arabia was a stable Yemeni government influenced by Nasserism and that therefore everything should be done to destabilize Yemen. Then Israel stepped in. During the late 1950s, the Israeli Defence Force had been modernized, which meant stockpiles existed of obsolete but serviceable weapons. In Operation Mango, an Israeli Air Force Stratocruiser capable of heavy drop left Eilat Air Base in southern Israel in February and, at low level to avoid Egyptian radar, picked up the Red Sea as a way marker until it reached the port of Hodeidha, then banked inland. Johnny Cooper was on the ground to observe it:

The huge aircraft came in for the actual drop and as it passed 60 parachutes spewed out of the back. It really was excellent dropping, real professional stuff. Abdullah bin Hassan, a Royalist commander, was delighted. He had the mortars and bombs he needed, together with a plentiful supply of small arms including German Schmeisser sub-machine guns. The source of these weapons was brilliantly concealed. Every serial number had been scored out, the parachutes were of Italian origin and even the wood shavings used in the packing had been imported from Cyprus. Even the most expert intelligence analyst would have had a job to unravel that Israeli support was not just restricted to the delivery of arms supplies.

In return, Colonel Smiley briefed Israeli intelligence on Egyptian military capabilities and passed items of Technical Intelligence interest, including casings that had been used by Yemeni artillery to fire gas-filled shells, a war crime that drew little comment at the UN. He was also permitted to interrogate an Egyptian MiG-21 fighter pilot who had defected with his aircraft.

CHAPTER TEN

The Rise in Terrorism

Although the grenade attack in December 1963 at Aden Airport did not induce an immediate breakdown in internal security in Aden State, on Christmas Day the NLF opened a brutal terrorist campaign to destroy the intelligence infrastructure by murdering Special Branch Inspector Fadhi Khalil, shot in his car in Qat market in Crater, because, as Radio Sana'a claimed, he had ignored warnings not to cooperate with the British.

Terrorism can be defined as a calculated act of violence designed to generate fear and intimidate governments in the pursuit of an ideological, political or religious goal. It is generally regarded as a crime. The response is Internal Security in keeping the peace, and for armed forces, this generally means 'military aid to the civil power' by supporting the police to preserve law and order, until such time as public safety can be restored. While 1964 in Aden was generally a quiet year compared to 1965 and 1966, the NLF still recruited young men and militant women to distribute subversive documents, carry messages and move weapons, with the overall aim of installing a revolutionary government and forcing the removal of the British military presence. The nationalists constantly reinforced the notion that anyone who expressed support for the Federal authorities would be regarded as a traitor. Their strategies were typical and in general terms aimed to:

• Discredit and harass the British and Federal Security Forces.
• Intimidate Federal bodies with subversion.
• Destroy Federal intelligence assets, in particular Special Branch.
• Intimidate the local population into supporting the revolution.
• Develop national and international support using propaganda to influence politicians, activists and media editors.

While the British were experienced in developing military and political command and control, far less familiarity with coordinating the civil, military, police and intelligence components was shown by the Federal response. The British Government had overall responsibility for Aden through the Colonial Office and the High Commissioner. The Chief Minister of the Aden State Government had government responsibilities, except for internal security, which lay with the High Commissioner; this was because Aden was still a colony and its security was closely linked to Aden Base. The Federal Minister of Internal Security was responsible for the coordination of security policies within Aden with those in the remainder of the Federation. Within his directorate was the Aden Police, which had been formed in 1857 as part of the Bombay Provincial Police Department and had stations on Perim and Kamaran Islands. Special Branch had a cohort of Arab, Indian sub-continent and Colonial police officers able to address subversion and collect political intelligence. It was not involved in criminal investigation. The small Federal Armed Police, recruited from the States and trained in riot control, was based in barracks near the prison in Crater.

The mauling of Special Branch over the next eighteen months saw its cohort almost eliminated. Sixteen Special Branch members were murdered or wounded, and others were intimidated to the extent that the police intelligence contribution to the Aden Intelligence Centre (AIC) became progressively less reliable. Key features of such murders were to attack in public, leave a note announcing that the execution had been carried out by the NLF and warn that cooperation with the British risked death. It did not take much detection to deduce the presence of NLF sentiments within the Aden Police. The AIC reported to the Minister of Internal Security and the High Commissioner from its offices near the Armed Police Barracks in Crater. Its role was to fuse the collection, analysis and dissemination of information into intelligence. In modern terms, it was a fusion cell. Although Colonial Police and police officers seconded from British constabularies helped fill the gap, they did not have the same 'feel' as the local Special Branch.

As soon as he declared the Emergency, the High Commissioner established the Security Policy Executive. Its permanent members included the Minister of Internal Security, the Commander-in-Chief, the Security Commander and Chief of Police. Reporting to it were:

• The Security Executive Committee. This civil and military planning body oversaw innumerable matters, including key point security, movement control and Emergency legislation. Members included the Security Commander, Chief of Police, Chief of Intelligence and Ministry of Internal Security officials.

• The Operational Executive. Chaired by the Security Commander, it exercised military control of operations in support of the civil authorities to counter terrorism and insurgency and protect life and property.

• G (Operations), HQ Middle East Command. Controlled Aden and 24th Brigades exercising internal security control through District Security Committees in their areas of responsibility. No matter what they did, appeasement governed the response.

• Security Secretariat. Coordinated the bodies by issuing meeting minutes and following up actions.

From the inception of operations, in the knowledge that lapses would be exploited by Egyptian and Yemeni propaganda, the British adopted their usual policy of minimum force, even though it was a frustration for soldiers facing an enemy uneducated in the Laws of Armed Conflict. Federal forces were expected to adopt the same principles.

Intelligence organisations have a troubled history of being dysfunctional. Aden was no different. At the top of the tree was the Joint Intelligence Committee in London advising Her Majesty's Government, usually in the shape of the Foreign Office and Colonial Office. The Joint Intelligence Staff at HQ Middle East Command focused on regional intelligence and security. In Aden, there were at least ten civilian, police and military intelligence and security organisations, yet there was no Director of Intelligence until Brigadier Tony Cowper arrived in early 1965, tasked to unravel the web. Significant factors were weak FRA intelligence and security sections and the absence of Special Branches in the states, although this was alleviated by the political officers as usually reliable sources of information and Military Intelligence Liaison Officers providing links between the police and Army. While the FRA was generally respected, it was also susceptible to tensions between younger soldiers who saw themselves as representatives of the emerging middle class of an independent nation and senior ranks favouring regulated progress and expecting respect. Of some concern was that the Adenis were generally unrepresented. On 18 September 1964, Major Mike Pearman (The Staffords), the FRA Garrison Major at Mukeiras, went for a walk along the Audhali plateau escorted by Private Mohammed Saleh Mahwari, a Fadhali of about nine months' service. The garrison was a regular rendezvous for visiting the border. Next morning, Pearman was found shot dead with a .303 rifle bullet of the type used by the FRA. Of Mahwari there was no sign, except that he was later sighted in Beidha in Yemen. While the murder horrified the FRA, it had also broken local custom that one does not murder someone with whose safety one has been entrusted. However, the incident must be set in the context of rising terrorism, endless stream of vitriolic propaganda and witnesses claiming, 'I saw the British soldier throw the grenade . . . But even if I did not, I know someone who did'.

After the AIC was hit by a Blindicide projectile in August 1964 and Special Branch Superintendent Arthur Barrie was murdered as he was driving to work in his yellow Mini on the 29th, Cowper moved the organization to a building owned by Shell Oil alongside HQ Middle East Command. The Belgian Rocket Launcher 83 'Blindicides' fired a 1.6kg projectile with a 0.5kg warhead to a range of 400 meters. It and the Soviet anti-tank Rocket Propelled Grenade 2 (RPG) were also used to attack married quarters as part of the NLF strategy to degrade morale by intimidating Service families and stretch military deployment to guarding families.

In October, HQ 39th Infantry Brigade handed control of Radfan operations to HQ 24th Infantry Brigade, which had moved from Kenya to Little Aden. Within three years, it would be fighting the Irish Republican Army for the 37 years of the Northern Ireland Troubles. Included in the 24th Brigade Tactical Area of Operations were the BP oil refinery, the Federal Government complex at Al Ittihad and the border. With intelligence suggesting insurgents were crossing the border, its role was to work with the Federal authorities, prevent the infiltration of arms and insurgents and disrupt the spread of subversion and terrorism into Aden. While the border remained tense and clashes were frequent, the Security Forces were playing at home, and insurgents risked ambushes, artillery shelling and mortar 'stonks'. In October 1964, 2nd Coldstream Guards arrived in Aden and was the first to move into Salerno Lines in Little Aden, from where it spent most of its tour on the border. On 15 January 1965, the London Gazette published this citation for the George Medal to Guardsman Andrew Norton:

On the afternoon of the 24th October 1964, Guardsman Norton was the driver of a Land Rover in which Captain Fazil was the only passenger. After passing the Arab Village of Gadir Khaysa, the vehicle blew up on a mine. Captain Fazil had his left leg blown off above the knee and suffered other injuries. Guardsman Norton suffered from burns, bruises and shock and temporarily lost the sight of one eye from the blast. At first his legs were pinned inside the vehicle, but he managed to get out, and immediately set about helping Captain Fazil. He first applied a tourniquet with a towel, and then looked for help. Although several Arabs were about, none would help, and to make a better tourniquet he had to remove the belt from one of them. He then left Captain Fazil, having put him in what shade there was, under the vehicle, and found an Arab with a car. He would not lend it to him, but Guardsman Norton jumped into it and drove it off. As soon as he found another military vehicle — a Land Rover — he brought it back to the scene of the explosion. Knowing well that there could be more mines about, he and the driver brought this vehicle as close as they could to where Captain Fazil lay. They secured him in the vehicle with sandbags to keep him still, and with his head down and his legs up to reduce the loss of blood. During a desperate drive of about 20 miles, Guardsman Norton tended Captain Fazil, and kept the tourniquet in place. Not until he handed Captain Fazil over to the hospital staff would he accept any help for himself. Without any doubt Guardsman Norton saved. Captain Fazil's life. He did so partly by his firm dealings with a surly crowd, and by his disregard for his own safety when he drove back into the mined area. But as well as this he showed the greatest possible presence of mind in every action he took to reduce the amount of blood that Captain Fazil was losing.

The July 1964 Defence White Paper stated that London intended to retain Aden Base and declared that South Arabia should have independence 'not later than 1968'. Colonial Secretary Duncan Sandys agreed a defence treaty at a Constitutional Conference with the Federal Government. When the Labour Government won the General Election on 16 October with a slender majority, it was expected that administration of the new Prime Minister Harold Wilson would last only a few months; however, it had energetic leadership committed to supporting emerging states.

The announcement on 6 November that Mr Anthony Greenwood, the new Colonial Secretary, would visit Aden exposed a serious disagreement within the Aden Legislative Council about the development of a unified democratic state: the hereditary Protectorate rulers proposed that they form an upper house, an idea rejected by Adeni politicians. The NLF exploited this disagreement as a suitable opportunity to open the terrorism, into which Aden would sink and from which it has not surfaced. Four days later, a grenade was thrown at a group of soldiers outside a restaurant in Steamer Point; then, on the 28th, Signalman George Slater was killed by a grenade exploding inside the Oasis, a bar in Ma'alla frequented by those living in the married quarters. Over the next six weeks, the NLF claimed responsibility for eleven incidents in which thirty-four military, police and civilian were casualties. Grenades became a favoured weapon – easy to hide, easy to throw, devastating in narrow streets, indiscriminate in their damage to the target and bystanders – in fact, a predecessor to the suicide bomber. The throwers were nicknamed the 'Cairo Grenadiers'. Although protective 'flak' jackets appeared with US Forces in South Vietnam, they would not be on general issue to the British until about 1970 in Northern Ireland. The only protection for the soldier was his thin shirt. Most grenades were either British 38 Mills bombs left behind in Egypt or Soviet RG-4 hand grenades packed with 105 grams of TNT and fitted with an impact fuse and sold to Egypt with markings in Arabic. The RG-4 had a typical throwing range of 35 metres and a blast radius of about 13 metres; it could also be fitted with a fragmentation sleeve that widened the effective blast radius to 25 metres. Initially, the concept of handling a live bomb with a short fuse frightened the average 'Grenadier', and it was not unknown for them to throw grenades indiscriminately and run. It was also not unknown for the pin to be lobbed and the grenade dropped.

Squadron Leader Jack Riley, of Joint Movements Planning staff at HQ Middle East Command, arrived in Aden in 1963 on the troopship *Nevasa* and moved into a married quarter at Ma'alla. He recalled the situation at the time:

> Meanwhile the locals proved rather less than welcoming with such outrages as dragging a Warrant Officer from a bus and setting fire to him in front of his wife and family and lobbing a hand grenade over the verandah of the PMO's house. [From the UKMAMS Old Bods Association]

Gillian Sidey, aged sixteen, was the daughter of Air Commodore Ernest Sidey, the Principal Medical Officer, Middle East Command. On 24 December 1964, two days after she had joined her parents from boarding school in England for the Christmas holiday, Gillian was at a private teenagers' dance in the married quarter of Lieutenant Colonel W.D.C. Holmes at RAF Khormaksar, when a terrorist threw a grenade through a window killing Gillian and wounding Holmes, Guy Harington, the teenage son of Major General Harington, another teenage boy and a servant.

CHAPTER ELEVEN

Deterioration in Internal Security, 1965

An early result of the change of government was the replacement, on 20 January 1965, of Sir Kennedy Trevaskis by Sir Richard Turnbull as High Commissioner. Nicknamed the 'Hammer of the Mau Mau' for his stance during the Kenyan Emergency, Turnbull had negotiated the constitutional transition when Tanganyika gained independence as Tanzania. It was hoped that his understanding of nationalist movements could be put to good use in South Arabia.

As the NLF had become more confident, violence increased. A grenade landed on a table during an open air dinner night in the Tarshyne Officers Mess and wounded six officers; another grenade thrown at an FRA Officers Mess film night killed one officer and wounded two others; and fourteen were wounded when one exploded in the Army Kinema Service cinema in Waterloo Lines. There were also unintended incidents. A terrorist placing electrically-detonated explosive under the floor of the Tarshyne Officers Mess mixed up the connecting wires and demolished the building. A friend of Lance Corporal Jenny Wileman (married surname, Holmes), posted to 28th Independent Company WRAC as a clerk in the Technical Branch, HQ Middle East Command, was wounded when a grenade tossed into a bar wounded her and several others. Attacks on and intimidation of Special Branch by the NLF continued to destabilize intelligence; and the Aden TUC called strikes at every opportunity, some of which led to riots.

Lord Louis Mountbatten, the Chief of the Defence Staff, visited Aden in February. On his staff as a 'briefing officer' was Lieutenant Colonel Colin Mitchell. Commissioned into the Argyll and Sutherland Highlanders, Mitchell was wounded at the Battle of Monte Cassino in 1944 and during a friendly fire incident in the Palestine Emergency. He served in Korea and Cyprus and had been seconded to the Kings African Rifles in East Africa. After passing out top at Staff College, he was posted to the Chief of the Defence Staff. With a reputation for being forthright, Mitchell believed that Britain was losing the will to govern its colonies and that a strong stand should be taken against terrorism. He also believed that South Arabia was not anti-British and deserved stronger political leadership; however, while the Government made 'soothing noises' about decolonization at the UN, a plebiscite on independence had yet to be held. He was critical of the level of casualties among those guarding Service families and was affronted that the NFL had made Crater their headquarters. Mitchell returned in April on the staff of Air Chief Marshal Sir Alfred Earle, who was accompanying the new Secretary of State for Defence, Denis Healey, on his only visit to Aden.

In February 1965, HQ 24th Infantry Brigade transferred its border tactical areas of operations to HQ FRA, which was now commanded by Brigadier Gordon Viner (Royal Hampshires). He had commanded 1st FRA between 1960 and 1962 and would later raise a fifth battalion. Viner divided his area of responsibility into two battalion sectors:

• Area HQ (West) – Dhala area and Radfan
By the end of 1964, the dissidents in Radfan had accepted that their disagreement with the Amir of Dhala had been counter-productive, and in the time-honoured tribal tradition they offered hostages as insurance for peace and tranquillity. Most were guarded by the Federal National Guard in Dhala. The Mahli and Dairi communities living in the Danaba Basin remained troublesome, attacking bases, sniping and laying ambushes and mines on roads and well-used tracks; nevertheless, by the middle of 1965, the area had been pacified to such an extent that Area HQ was transferred from Thumier to Dhala in order to ease negotiations. The British and FRA battalion groups were based at Thumier, since renamed Habilayn.

• Area HQ (East) – Beihan
The state faced air incursions, culminating in armed Egyptian helicopters attacking the Federal National Guard post at Bulaiq. The problem remained that by the time Hunters had been scrambled from RAF Khormaksar, the enemy aircraft had returned to the sanctuary of Yemen. To resolve the issue in 'tit for tat' retaliation, Hunters destroyed the fort at Al Qala on 24 March 1965. Although prior warning had been given, the international uproar about this attack was considerable – although nothing was said about the original raid from Yemen.

The number of battalions sent to South Arabia was raised to five. As a general rule, the two that supported 24th Brigade were based at Anzio and Salerno Lines at Little Aden. They were in addition to 45 Commando at BP Camp, which essentially became the Force reserve. Aden Garrison was converted into an operational Brigade of three battalions, each with a Tactical Area of Operations on a mix of one-year and six-month roulement tours. Brigadier Hargroves was the Security Commander at Brigade HQ in Singapore Lines. The tented Radfan Camp was built by Royal Engineers to accommodate the extra battalion. Generally, the deployment was as follows:

• Singapore Lines Battalion. Area West – Steamer Point and Tawahi. Inside this was Government House and HQ Middle East Command.
• Waterloo Lines Battalion. Area Centre – Crater and Ma'alla.
• Radfan Camp. Area North – Sheikh Othman and Al Mansoura. This contained the Al Mansoura Detention Centre.

Several battalions provided reinforcement companies, such as B Company, 1st York and Lancasters from February 1966 for four months, as did the battalion based in Bahrain. The Aden battalions also supplied companies to the Dhala and Mukaries bases, usually for a month, which offered a welcome change to patrolling in Aden. Troops were issued with a several cards:

Pink Card	Internal Security Arab Phrases
Yellow Card (until February 1965)	Instructions to Servicemen Employed on Guard Duties, Internal Security and Duties in Aid of the Civil Power. For instance: 3. How To Fire; a) Fire only aimed shots b) Aim at the target, e.g, middle of the body c) Fire only the minimum number of shots necessary to achieve your purpose
Blue Card	Middle East Command for Opening Fire in Aden – this included warnings to be shouted in English and Arabic.
Pink Card	Wanted Persons (a photograph and brief description).
White Card	Vigilance Card (for new Service personnel and their families).

Battalions generally settled into a routine of rotating their companies about every six days. Of the three rifle platoons and one support platoon of the Operational Company, three provided anti-arson OPs, foot and mobile civil protection patrols and conducted roadblocks. The fourth platoon was on 'stand-by and immediate notice', particularly when it returned to its camp. OPs placed above street level had been developed during the Cyprus Emergency and again proved effective in dominating sectors. Patrolling meant showing an armed presence and had little identifiable tactical value except to dominate streets. Foot patrols included 'finger patrols', in which two sections patrolled two parallel streets, with the third section in reserve. Major Michael Tillotson, of 1st PWO, developed the concept of having obvious cut-offs as a deterrent. The Crater Battalion patrolled RAF Khormaksar area, although some Army officers queried why the RAF did not guard their own airfield. Officers manned the Battalion Operations Room.

Mobile patrols were conducted in open-top Land Rovers shielded from grenades by a wire frame. Other vehicles included the Humber 1-Ton Armoured Personnel Carrier (APC), capable of carrying a section, nicknamed the 'Pig' because of its long bonnet and square windscreen and usually driven by the RCT. It could also be difficult to drive. Second Lieutenant Nick Beard, who was in 60 Squadron and had recently graduated from Sandhurst, recalled:

APB were locally mine-plated Bedford 3-tonners. The passenger seats were removed. Underneath the driver, a mild steel sheet was welded and a piece vertically up from the floor to the left of the driver, the principle being so that if the nearside front wheel detonated the mine the blast would be free to go upwards without hitting the driver, and that if the offside front detonated the mine, the driver would be protected by the mild steel plate underneath him and again any further blast would have an exit route on the passenger side. The whole of the rear cargo compartment had sandbags placed over the floor, with two double lines of sandbags over the rear axle; only a maximum of 10 people were allowed to travel in the back of the vehicle and then forward of the rear axle.

'Bathtubs' were a more sophisticated Military Vehicles Experimental Establishment design. The whole of the front cab was taken off and a welded mild steel open-topped 'bath' constructed in its place, with just the steering column and pedals coming through. The driver and passenger sat on aircraft-type seats with aircraft straps to hold them in place in the event of a mine going off and throwing the vehicle around.

'Bathtubs' were still evident in Aden in 1997. Six-wheel Alvis Saracen APCs, capable of carrying twelve soldiers, were frequently allocated to companies from the Middle East Armoured Car Regiment with their drivers. These came from same family as Saladin armoured cars and Stalwart high-mobility load-carriers.

The main tactical radios in use were the Larkspur VHF range. First issued in the mid-1950s, their principal feature was the capability to pre-set frequencies, as opposed to 'Tune and Net Call' on previous radios, a gift to signals intercept. Platoons and sections were issued with A-41 manpack radios carried on a frame, while battalion and company HQs and armoured cars used C-42 radios. Communications between armoured vehicles was by B-47s, and C-11/R210 HF radios were used for long-range communications, a key feature being the positioning of the Skywave antenna. The nature of Aden, with its streets and alleyways, meant that communications were often poor; therefore, if a patrol did not acknowledge a message, it would be relayed to the Battalion Operations Room to resolve.

Riot control centred on a platoon adopting a disciplined box formation designed to be psychologically powerful in comparison to a mob of scruffy and undisciplined rioters. Squad were usually formed from two sections wearing steel helmets and armed with batons, shields and tear-gas grenades; respirators were also quickly available. Two soldiers carried a banner on 10-foot poles which, when unfurled, read in Arabic, 'This is an unlawful assembly and you must disperse immediately'. If the warning failed to impress, the two soldiers crossed to display on the rear of the banner: 'If you do not disperse now, we will fire tear gas'. The third section in the rear up brought frames of barbed wire and stretchers.

The standard uniform for the Army on patrol was a Khaki Drill (KD) shirt and denim or KD trousers tucked into ankle gaiters or puttees, and black, hobnailed leather ankle boots. The introduction of rubber Directly Moulded Sole (DMS) boots in 1965 proved invaluable, because soldiers could then hear strikers being released as grenades were thrown. Around the waist was worn a webbing belt on which was suspended an ammunition pouch for a spare magazine and a water bottle. Inside the bases, 'bare buff' of blue physical training or khaki shorts was common.

The third company managed administration and training and education courses, and organized rest and recuperation. Battalions in Aden also reinforced operations in Radfan by manning the company bases at Dhala and Mukeiras, and provided a platoon to garrison Perim Island.

By 1962, long haul air trooping by RAF Comet 4s, VC10s, Britannias and contracted aircraft was replacing the troopship. Civilian clothes were worn.

A common theme, particularly for those departing in mid-winter from Britain, was the suffocating heat of Aden. James Gallagher, an RAF mover, arrived in 1967 in a British Eagle Britannia via Istanbul, Bahrain and Aden. When the aircraft door opened:

> A rush of suffocating heat gushed into the fuselage which was like a furnace in seconds. My own body seemed to sprout liquid and trickles of sweat ran down my back. I was wearing a Harris tweed jacket, just the sort of apparel for the environment. Within minutes I was a wreck, and with the dreaded jacket clinging to my soggy frame, I limped off the aircraft . . . 'So, you've come for a spot of sun, have you', was the opening at the briefing next morning. [UKMAMS Old Bods Association]

The usual working day in Aden lasted from 7 am to 1 pm, but as the security situation deteriorated, work was extended for as long as necessary. Menus were supported by locally purchased fresh fruit and vegetables. Fatigue parties supported cookhouses by washing up and disposed of rubbish. Initially, entertainment in Aden was unrestricted, but the Colony became progressively declared out of bounds. Sport remained an important part of military life, with inter-unit competitions in cricket, soccer and rugby. Inevitably, water sports and fishing were popular. Beaches used by the military were divided into three lidos, one for officers, one for senior non-commissioned ranks and one for junior ranks, and their families. Royal Engineers built and maintained shark nets. The Army Kinema Corporation cinema frequently showed recently released films. There was no general restriction on alcohol, as there was in other theatres (theoretically, the equivalent of two cans per day). Kenya was a popular destination for those taking advantage of the Aden Leave Scheme Service at the Aruba Safari Lodge at Tsavo Eastern National Park and the Silversands and Lawfords Hotel at Malindi, on the coast north-east of Mombasa. Jenny Wileman was one of several Servicewomen invited to a cattle farm and private beach owned by the Pope family for a second spell of recuperative leave. The Service postal arrangements were efficient, with soldiers and dependants able to use lightweight envelopes known as 'blueys'.

The Dhow was the Middle East Forces newspaper providing local news of interest to Middle East Command and rebutting terrorist propaganda. Discussing terrorism in October 1965, its issue of 11 November 1965 noted:

NLF CLAIMS	THE TRUTH
140 Security Forces killed 74 wounded	1 Security Forces killed and 5 injured in Aden 18 wounded in the Federation, of whom 12 were Federal Forces
	17 civilians injured, including a 20-month-old girl in Ma'alla and two Arab nursing assistants in Lahej when their ambulance struck a mine.
	4 terrorists/insurgents killed Of 29 captured, 24 were in Aden State. 38 surrendered, 32 in Dhala.
Transport plane with 50 paratroopers on board shot down. Secretariats of Beihan and Yafa destroyed.	On 22 November 1966, an Aden Airways Douglas DC-3 crashed after a bomb on board exploded, killing all 30 passengers. The bomb had been planted by the NLF son of the Prime Minister of Wahadi.
	Security Authorities have recovered 10 pistols, 18 mines, 10 grenades, one bazooka and a quantity of explosives

The British Forces Broadcasting Service (BFBS) also provided accurate news. In 1966, the station in Aden became the only one to be attacked, with grenades and a rocket, in all the insurgencies facing British rule since 1945.

The security threats in Aden were assessed to be sufficiently serious that it should be an unaccompanied posting; however, the 1960s was an era in which military separation was common and the presence of families for those on long tours was considered beneficial. Eventually, about 9,000 dependants of Servicemen and civilians associated with Security Forces were placed in base married quarters and in hirings, such as in Ma'alla. They were supported by schools, medical centres, NAAFI shops and clubs. Families faced the risks with the same resilience as their predecessors in the Cyprus Emergency and were exposed to terrorism of a kind which would be continued by the IRA in England, West Germany, Belgium and Holland.

A major intelligence asset in internal security and counter-insurgency operations is Human Intelligence collected by patrols from snippets of information, conversations with informants and sources and interrogation. Since 1945, the ancient art of interrogation had been under frequent accusations that its methods equated to torture. Effective interrogation following the principle of no violence is enshrined in the Laws of Armed Conflict. Violence is, in fact, generally counter-productive. During the Second World War, British high-level Combined Services Detailed Interrogation Centres had used cunning by recording the conversations of prisoners. Interrogation had been a key operational asset during the Malayan and Cyprus Emergencies, and in Borneo was being used to identify future targets, undermine Indonesian operations, unearth organisational structures and provide opportunities for Human Intelligence exploitation. Under the emergency powers in Aden, the ability to detain and deport proved powerful levers in the pursuit of information.

In September 1964, the commanding officer of the Joint Service Interrogation Wing and his Army warrant officer instructor, both Intelligence Corps, arrived in Aden with instructions to reinvigorate interrogation. They found that the military interrogation centre at the Fort Morbut coastal battery was unsuitable because some parts were overlooked by the Corporals Club at Steamer Point; therefore, isolating prisoners was impossible, and the quality of the Aden Police guard force was poor. While arrangements were made to improve Fort Morbut, interrogation was transferred to a house at Ahwar in the state of Lower Aulqui, about 130 miles east of Aden. Within about three weeks of the arrest of several NLF suspects in Aden, interrogators untangled a web of lies and half truths and built a breakdown of the NLF political wing, along with the name of the senior Yemeni agent in Aden. One suspect was unable to control his body language and regularly scratched his elbow when he struggled to promote a lie. At Fort Morbut, Royal Engineers created six cells, a suspect-holding centre and a collation cell and control room on the upper floor, all of which Ian Cobain, in his book *Cruel Britannia*, describes as 'chambers'.

In February, the Chief Minister of Aden State, Seyid Zeid Baharoon, resigned from the Legislative Council after a disagreement about the Eastern Aden Protectorate, which had not joined the Federation; he was replaced, as protocol demanded, by the person with the most support. This turned out to be Abdul Qaim Mackawee, the leader of the Opposition, a man totally opposed to the Emergency who took every opportunity to discredit the British and Federal Governments by promoting Nasserism and refusing to support measures to control terrorism. His ministers included Khalifa Abdulla Hassan, who had just been released from months' detention on suspicion of involvement in the murder of Gillian Sidey. Mackawee accused British soldiers of throwing the grenade that killed her. As the internal security situation deteriorated, High Commissioner Turnbull introduced a second and rigorous set of Emergency Regulations in Aden State that included detention without trial for six months or longer, to counter the difficulty of persuading witnesses to testify in court, and the proscription of organizations suspected of involvement in terrorism. The NLF was at the top of the list. Mackawee objected with vigour, as he did when banning the proposed visit of the Constitutional Commission in July to examine independence, claiming that its members were 'undesirable immigrants'. He also refused to negotiate at a conference in London in August.

By April 1965, colonial confrontations were sucking in troops, particularly in Borneo, where Major General Walker was sending men across the border into Indonesia in the secret Operation Claret. In the autumn of 1962, the Conservative Government had formed the Territorial Army Emergency Reserve with an establishment of about 7,000 reservists available to be called up to reinforce the Regular Army in return for an obligation to serve up to six months with a bonus. Many were former Servicemen, known as the 'Ever Readies'. Hitherto, none had been called up. In April 1965, Defence Minister Fred Mulley informed the House of Commons that under the Army Reserve Act, 1962, 175 Ever Readies were put on four weeks' notice for service in the Middle East, Far East and with the United Nations Force in Cyprus, and that those selected were guaranteed their civilian employment under the National Service Act. He qualified his statement by saying that the Army had been engaged in emergency operations overseas for over two years, which meant that soldiers were spending long periods on active service away from families and unable to attend courses. Collectively, this was leading to a detrimental effect on recruitment and re-engagement. Most affected were the Strategic Reserve brigade HQ in Borneo: nine infantry battalions, two armoured car squadrons, an artillery regiment and two engineer squadrons, totalling about 600 individuals. An example is that the Queen's Royal Irish Hussars, sent to the Middle East as the Armoured Car Regiment in 1961, was then posted to Malaya in October 1962 before being deployed in December for the Brunei Revolt, and was now involved in Confrontation with Indonesia. Mulley said that the Ever Readies would be Infantry, from the Home Counties Brigade, Royal Artillery, Royal Engineers, Royal Electrical and Mechanical Engineers, with the Intelligence Corps providing interrogators. In spite of the Joint Service Interrogation Wing's teaching of no violence, a Maltese Reservist officer was particularly crass when he showed off by hitting with his swagger stick a prisoner captured by B (SAS) Squadron up country. The Home Counties Brigade consisted of the Queen's Royal Surrey Regiment, Queen's Own Royal West Kents, Royal Sussex Regiment, the Middlesex Regiment, and their associated TA battalions. Several members of 144th Parachute Field Ambulance (V) also served in Aden. During the year, the Service variant of the SRN-5 Hovercraft was given its desert trials in Aden and jungle trials in Sarawak.

Operations in Radfan continued, with aim of containing the dissidents and minimizing insurgency seeping into Aden. The fighting was conventional, with attacks on bases, patrols and OPs, ambushes and psychological warfare operations. During the night of 18/19 March, two Pack Howitzers of 28 Battery RA commanded by Lieutenant Martin Proudlock in Wadi Adad were attacked on a bright moonlight night from a range of 300 yards. Proudlock moved the guns into open ground in order to engage the enemy over open sights, which meant that ammunition had to be carried to the guns under fire. There was a final short burst of firing at 2am and then silence. Lieutenant Proudlock was awarded the Military Cross. The following night, a 3-inch mortar pit occupied by men from 2nd Coldstream Guards received a direct hit that killed three guardsmen and ignited a fire that threatened to detonate the ammunition. Following the increased threat in Radfan, 1st Royal Sussex in Malta was warned for a six-month emergency tour in South Arabia to begin in May and requested about thirty Ever Ready reinforcements. Most of these selected had trained with the Battalion in Hong Kong and in Munster, West Germany.

Corporal Malcolm Milhan had served in the Royal Navy as a Yeoman between 1951 and 1959 and, finding it difficult to settle down with the responsibility of two children, took the advice of his brother-in-law and enlisted in the Territorial Army. Signing on as an Ever Ready, he assured his wife that the odds were stacked against his having to serve – until a smiling postman handed him a large brown On Her Majesty's Service envelope containing his mobilization papers. Early in May, he reported to the Regimental Depot at Howe Barracks in Canterbury, drew his kit and flew to Aden as a Section Commander in 3 Platoon, A Company, which was commanded by another Ever Ready Lieutenant, Joseph Smith, normally known as Jock. The Platoon Sergeant was Sergeant Charlie Tierney, a Regular. The first person that Milhan met on arriving at RAF Khormaksar was a cousin, a Regular in the Battalion. After a week of training and acclimatization, Milhan led several Internal Security patrols in Aden until, a week later, A Company joined 45 Commando at Habilayan, near Thumier. The drive was in Bedford lorries, with the driver's seat and the doors and windscreen protected by armour plating. Sandbags on the floor of the cargo compartment protected the ten soldiers per truck, who were warned not to sit over the rear wheels. As the convoy climbed into the mountains, armoured cars and helicopters escorted it though a chain of mountain-top picquets.

As the Company deployed to Monk's Field, the outgoing unit warned them they would be welcomed. Within the hour, 3 Platoon came under machine-gun, rifle and RPG fire from a wadi entrance, shredding tents, showers and the cookhouse. Fortunately, several RPG projectiles fell short. Section commanders worked hard to resolve the initial ragged fire control until Private Nobby Clark crawled 200 yards to his Wombat Anti-Tank Gun and fired into the centre of the enemy position, followed by 19th Field Regiment shelling the wadi. A follow-up patrol found abandoned weapons. Stand-to at sunset was something that most looked forward to because it included a dramatic and widely practised event in which the artillery fired on to targets and every soldier fired his weapon – 9mm Browning pistol, SLR, Bren Gun, 81mm mortar and Wombat – as fast as possible for two minutes. On alternative nights, Shackletons and Hunters bombed tracks known to be used by the insurgents. Whenever aircraft carriers anchored off Aden, Royal Navy aircraft then lurked overhead to demonstrate that combat air patrols could arrive within ten minutes. At night, the company tactical area was subjected to curfew and anything that moved outside the perimeter was shot at on sight, including packs of baboons. The shelling often drove insurgents into ambushes and restricted their freedom of movement.

On one occasion, Lieutenant Smith laid an ambush on a regularly used track about 600 yards from the camp. A bright moon rose shortly after 8 pm, and then, about two hours later, dogs barked in a village and a donkey brayed. Corporal Linham was worried because the noise was to his front, which covered the rear of the ambush. Some rocks then tumbled down a slope, a tin can filled with stones rattled and someone whispered in Arabic. Lieutenant Smith then committed a cardinal sin by moving the killer group so that it overlapped the cover section. Linham saw armed men about 200 yards away approaching in single file, seemingly unaware of the readjustment of the killer group. He recalled:

> We waited until it seemed they would walk into us, then at about 50 yards distance they turned to their right and walked across our front. I counted nine, five, a gap then four, and then our patrol opened up. They were well-trained and those still able to dashed into the rocks at our feet. We were receiving rifle fire from somewhere to our front, but were concentrating too much on the rocks below to take much

notice. Suddenly, the survivors from the first bursts of fire made a dash for it in various directions, and all hell broke loose with people taking the nearest target to them. Strangely, both of our light machine guns picked on the same guy running to the right trying to get down the wadi, and the tracer bullets were crossing just an inch or so in front of him, but seemed to keep at that distance as he ran. Would they never get him? Suddenly he appeared to blow up, there was an almighty flash and bang in front of him and down he went. At this moment I got the message that my Number 2 on the machine gun, Private Terry Sullivan, another TA soldier, had been hit and thrown about ten feet away. I crawled to him and he was rolled up in a ball holding his arm to his chest. I asked where he was hit and he replied the arm. Having checked as best as I could there was no major bleeding, I got down to Lieutenant Smith to report and to get morphine for Terry. As soon as this was administered, I was ordered to take the patrol back to our Final Rendezvous Point and wait for Lieutenant Smith and the radio operator. As we waited, Lieutenant Smith directed the Defensive Fire Mission down on to the location and got out fast to join up with us, and we returned to base to await the dawn. Sullivan had his wounds dressed and awaited casevac the next morning; his main moan was that he had lost his new tattoo, which he had only had a couple of months. [www.britains-smallwars/Aden]

A first-light patrol found two bodies at the ambush site, and six more were later discovered hidden under rocks or in crevices after blood trails were followed. One had been a Bren gunner. Lieutenant Smith was awarded the Military Cross. A Company later moved to the base at Mukeiras, where the soldiers witnessed a mine damaging an airfield roller, were shelled from Yemen and had a patrol ambushed. In late October, the Battalion returned to Canterbury and the Ever Readies to their civilian employment.

Between 1964 and 1966, Regular and Territorial Army Royal Engineer squadrons spent nearly three years improving the quality of the Dhala Road by laying tarmac, so that, with the exception of a four-mile stretch in Wadi Matlah, it became a two-way, all-weather surface from Aden to Habilayn. Tarmac hindered the ability of dissidents to bury mines. Playing a key role were 19 Topographical and 13 Field Survey Squadrons, initially based in Little Aden and later Normandy Lines. Maps were drawn and printed 'in the field' by 13 Squadron from mobile reproduction offices in semi-trailers towed by Leyland prime movers, nicknamed 'the Print Train'. Sapper Peter Woods:

One of the map series was to update was the 1:100,000 mapping of the Middle East. Much work was also carried out by the field surveyors in the Radfan area, including the Dhala road. Meanwhile, back at base, the reproduction team spent quite a lot of time producing the Radfan Report – a military appreciation of the developing dangerous situation in the Radfan and the Yemen border.

The work was originally estimated to take nine months. Tracks through several *wadis* in Radfan were upgraded to take vehicles and although the work was protected by picquets and patrols, nevertheless there were casualties. Between 1 and 14 April, about 300 soldiers from 131st Parachute Field Engineer Regiment (TA) helped 24th Field Squadron RE during its annual camp, based at Al Milah. On the 9th, a Bedford lorry hit a mine and a soldier in the cab was injured. Major Clive Samuel RAMC, a Medical Officer, ignored the threat of other mines and, walking to the lorry, treated the soldier, saving his arm from amputation. Two days later, the camp came under sustained fire at midnight for about half an hour, during which Warrant Officer Two John Lonnegan, the 300 Squadron (V) Squadron Sergeant Major, and an RAPC sergeant were killed, and several others wounded. Major Samuels ignored the firing and treated the wounded, including saving the life of a very seriously hurt sapper. In a bizarre decision of the kind that shrouded awards in Aden, Samuels was awarded the MBE for gallantry. In other circumstances, he would have probably have received the MC.

In May, Major General John Willoughby took over as GOC Middle East Land Forces from Major General Cubbon. Commissioned into the Middlesex Regiment, he had been evacuated from the beaches of Dunkirk and had served with the Lethbridge (220) Military Mission developing tactics to defeat the Japanese in the Pacific and Burma. He had fought in Korea and commanded his Regiment during the Cyprus Emergency. A month later, he assumed responsibility as the Security Commander reporting directly to the High Commissioner, thus releasing Brigadier Hargroves to concentrate on internal security operations in Aden.

On 29 August, Superintendent Barrie was shot dead and then the highly-respected Sir Arthur Charles, Speaker of the Legislative Council, was murdered, both in Crater. On 17 September, a terrorist threw a grenade at 73 British children and their parents waiting to board an aircraft after the summer holidays, injuring two seriously and three less so. After a cordon and search operation in September resulted in arrests of a NLF cell headquarters, interrogations again crippled the main headquarters in Aden; and although the organisation regrouped, it suffered another disaster in December when two armed terrorists from a group escaping after an incident were captured at a roadblock and revealed a cache of buried weapons and other war stores. The increased tempo of terrorism, and Mackawee's demands that the NLF be recognized as a political party, led to High Commissioner Turnbull dismissing him as Chief Minister on 26 September and suspending the Constitution. Enforcing direct rule, he ordered a 6 pm to 5 am curfew.

The 1st Prince of Wales Own Regiment of Yorkshire (1st PWO) had returned to Aden in August and was taking over the Ma'alla/Crater sector from 1st Royal Anglians, when it was quickly pitched into an operation in which Tactical HQ and two companies searched Al Waht for a known terrorist. It was later learnt that he had fled to Yemen. A general strike between 2 and 4 October was so destructive that the Battalion was reinforced by two 1st Para companies and two FRA platoons. A 3rd Wing Army Air Corps Scout helicopter spotting from above the streets and alleys helped the Battalion to take prompt action. On the 2nd, 248 rioters were detained in three cages and 97 were later deported to Yemen, 29 were charged and 122 released. Many of the rioters were children.

One problem faced by law-abiding governments tackling terrorism by prosecuting suspects is that the judicial process can be compromised by witness interference. Aden was no different. This led to suspects being detained at the Al Mansoura Detention Centre, where the Military Provost Staff Corps provided about eight warders while the Sheikh Othman Battalion provided the guard company based in a fortified camp outside the twelve-foot high, five-foot thick stone walls surmounted by towers equipped with GPMGs and searchlights. Private Cliff Sweeting was serving with A Company, 1st PWO:

> After breakfast, there would be a rush for the truck running a shuttle service to the Dolphin Club at Elephant Bay, set within the secure cantonment of HQ Middle East Command. Here we could relax with a swim in the crystal-clear waters of the Gulf of Aden, sip luxuriously at a tall, ice-cool Tom Collins, stretch out on the pristine white sand, and . . . sleep! Nobody could warn us sun-starved young Brits about the combined effects of fatigue, sun and alcohol. The start of the next night increment guard would be a harsh lesson, as coarse denim trousers and khaki flannel shirts abraded fresh sunburn on legs, backs and shoulders. Cries of agony would ring around the prison as the sufferers slowly climbed their fifty feet of metal ladder, laden with SLR, three full magazines, Very pistol and flares, and a fresh radio battery for the A40 short-range set. Nobody dared report sick –

'Rendering himself unfit for duty' was a chargeable offence, and sunburn fell well within that category. [www.britains-smallwars/Aden]

One night, Sweeting was in a guard tower admiring the sunset while the *muezzin* called the faithful to prayer from the mosque across the road, when the Pig returned. He watched as the soldiers debussed, unloaded their weapons and made their way to a modest canteen on the left side of the main entrance:

> We didn't see the battered blue sedan which cruised in from the direction of Little Aden. Mere minutes after the finger patrol had returned, a tongue of flame jetted from the right rear window of the vehicle, as a yellow-green streak of fuel trailed the rocket on its way to the gate of the prison. The bane of our existence in Aden – apart from the often fairly inept grenade-throwers – was the Blindicide rocket launcher . . . From the outer gate came a huge 'Ker-langg!!' as the High Explosive Anti-Tank rocket slammed into it. Three inches of hardened steel finished up with a hole in it nearly four inches wide, narrowing down to a 'keyhole' of about 3/4 of an inch. Luckily, the blast dissipated after the projectile penetrated the gate . . . Nobody was standing behind the gate at the time – although the watchers in the guardroom did not hear too well for the next day or so. [www.britains-smallwars/Aden]

After nine months in Crater, 1st PWO was sent to Habilayn Camp where B Company deployed to the picquets around the airfield. For several weeks before the Battalion arrived, HQ 24th Brigade had considered abandoning the company base at Mukeiras; thus, when Captain A.J.M. Nevile arrived with part of A Company and elements of the Motor Transport, Assault Pioneer and Recce Platoons, under command of 1st Irish Guards, they found it in a state of disrepair. Nevile also received a letter from dissidents:

> We welcome Capt Nevile and his Company to the plateau and wish him a good tour. Unfortunately, we shall have to disturb a few of his nights with mortar fire, as we need target practice.

Replying to the 'generous welcome', he assured the writer that he would be delighted to demonstrate the accuracy of his mortars. When a lorry negotiating the Thirra Pass slid several feet into a ditch, Nevile, Sergeant Wallace and Craftsman Plaice straightened a badly bent track rod with the 'judicious use of a heavy rock'.

C Company joined 2nd FRA at Dhala and D Company was a mobile reserve. On call was E Battery, 1st RHA. Within a day of arriving, Corporal Geoffrey Auker was commanding a three-man OP on top of a house about 600 yards south of Habilayn when, during the night, dissidents fired several Blindicides from the south. Unable to fix a compass bearing of the enemy position, Auker ran to a sangar occupied by an FNG section and obtained a bearing, which he passed to support weapons at Habilayn and a picquet equipped with a machine gun. Returning to his OP, he continued to supply Company HQ with accurate reports. Private Kenneth Proctor lost a hand and George Cornell, also of C Company, lost an eye on 9 July when a pencil mine secreted in their sandbagged sangar exploded. Fortunately, a Sioux of the Battalion Air Platoon was in the area, and they were treated at the RAF Hospital at Steamer Point. Ten days later, Operation Cover Point was launched against Ar Rikab in Wadi Taym, which was thought to be sheltering insurgents. Supported by the 2nd Para Patrol Company, two troops from 4/7th DGs and an FRA patrol, D Company and parts of Support Company were taken by Stalwarts to Monk's Park, then flown by helicopters to a landing site near the village from where they killed several gunmen and captured others in an attack on the village. On the 27th, after dissident activity had been seen near a track one mile east of Habiliyan for the fifth night in a row, 7 Platoon, B Company commanded by Lieutenant Peter Orwin laid an ambush on it. At about 11 pm, the section covering the rear of the position saw about fifteen dissidents deploying to attack and opened fire. The enemy reacted with four Blindicides fired at short range, killing Lance Corporal Bryan Foley, a former National Serviceman, wounding two soldiers and stunning the Platoon Sergeant. Orwin, with the killer group, instructed a GPMG to engage the dissidents moving towards his right flank and, after dragging two wounded into cover, then attacked the Blindicide team with grenades. He then directed mortar fire on to the enemy and forced them to withdraw, leaving behind one killed, one fatally wounded, six wounded and a wrecked rocket launcher. Orwin was awarded the Military Cross. Foley was married with a daughter. Private Berryman was flown to a military hospital in UK with very serious wounds. On the 29th, when about fifty insurgents infiltrated between HQ C Company and an FNG position and fired rockets at the Amir's palace, 11 Platoon cut the enemy withdrawal route and directed harassing mortar fire.

In October, Sir John Prendergast was seconded, at the request of Sir Richard Turnbull, from his appointment as Head of Intelligence in Hong Kong to review intelligence in Aden. They had known each other in Palestine and Kenya. As Head of Intelligence in the closing stages of the Cyprus Emergency, he had reinvigorated a Special Branch crippled by terrorism and had reorganized a dysfunctional intelligence organisation. Within a month of undertaking his review, Prendergast circulated the highly classified Review of Aden Intelligence on a strict need-to-know basis. He was typically forthright, his findings and his recommendations replicated those in Cyprus:

- The intelligence community lacked urgency, purpose and direction.
- There was no centralized control within the intelligence community.
- The application of the Need to Know meant that information was not being shared within the civilian and military intelligence community, who should know.
- Brigadier Cowper had been marginalized by other intelligence and security officials.

The failings were not new and would be repeated. Many reflected the view in the War Office that while intelligence was a wartime specialist skill, as with gunnery and medicine, it is not required in peace. Ad hoc intelligence organisation had been cobbled together in 1914 and 1940, and the Intelligence Corps had nearly been disbanded in 1945. The Cold War and the unpredicted nationalist campaigns had seen a reluctant change of opinion. The Joint Intelligence Committee had also published several reports on the state of intelligence in the Middle East, and there was general agreement on the need for an effective intelligence system in South Arabia. Prendergast recommended:

- A Chief of Intelligence be appointed as the focal point for the centralized intelligence strategy.
- The Aden Intelligence Centre be disbanded.
- Closer links be developed between Special Branch and the SIS with the overall aim of infiltrating the headquarters of both the Egyptian Intelligence Service and NLF in Taiz.
- The Federal Government to form Special Branch and military intelligence organizations, including in Eastern Aden Protectorate.
- The Fort Morbut Interrogation Centre to report direct to the Chief of Intelligence.

Inevitably, some recommendations were rejected in Aden, notably by Mr Donal McCarthy, the political advisor to Major General Willoughby, who disagreed with the concept of a Chief of Intelligence. Interestingly, McCarthy's experience in the handling of operational intelligence was limited; indeed, he had criticized the performance of the two Intelligence

Corps interrogators, whereas Prendergast suggested that they had produced valuable intelligence.

In October, 1st Coldstream Guards replaced 2nd Scots Guards and took over the outer defence of RAF Khormaksar, which had become increasingly vulnerable to mortar attacks from Sheikh Othman, where it was not difficult to set up a simple mortar, fire twenty bombs and hide it before Security Forces patrols arrived. Although roadblocks helped to deter attacks, the miles of open desert meant that follow-up searches were not easy. The second-in-command, Major Stewart-Richardson, had the idea of placing the RAF base out of range of mortars by building the 11-mile barbed-wire 'Scrubber Line' (the major's nickname was 'Scrubber'), a fence from coast to coast north of the Pennine Chain. In November, increased dissident activity saw C Company, 1st PWO reinforce the Welsh Guards. On 7 December, elements from 1st Coldstream Guards and 1st Welsh Guards dispensed medical care in a pyschological operation in the village of Dohl El Wahab in Wadi Rabwa to remind caravan traders of the British military presence. Thirteen schoolchildren who lined up for an inspection were rewarded with Smarties chocolate buttons. Next day, a Land Rover was very seriously damaged by a mine when its occupants, two sergeants, were visiting picquets.

By the end of 1965, 286 terrorist incidents had been logged with British military casualty statistics in Aden, resulting in six killed and 83 wounded, against 18 terrorists killed and 86 wounded. Local Security Forces experienced nine killed and wounded, and two British civilians were killed and 28 injured. There was no lack of targets for the terrorists, as foot and mobile patrols slowly negotiated the streets of Aden and Service personnel and dependants continued to use the shops, bars and cafes.

In December, Admiral Sir Michael Le Fanu KCB DSC arrived as Commander-in-Chief, Middle East Command. He had fought as a gunnery officer in the Home Fleet during the 1940 Norwegian Campaign and had served in the Mediterranean and Far East. After the war, he had commanded a frigate, a training establishment and an aircraft carrier.

Meanwhile, in Yemen on 18 April, Royalist forces had launched an operation in Wadi Humeidat and forced the republican garrison in Marib to surrender four months later. For the first time since the 1962 revolution, it was possible to travel from the Federation to Saudi Arabia across territory held by Royalists. So far, the Egyptian Army had suffered 17,000 killed in Yemen; indeed, the civil war was fast becoming Nasser's 'Vietnam' and there was unrest in Egypt about it. In August, King Faisal of Saudi Arabia brokered the Jeddah Agreement, under which Nasser undertook to disengage by withdrawing 10,000 troops monthly, thus contributing to the Federation's continued existence as a sovereign entity.

CHAPTER TWELVE

The 1966 Defence
White Paper

On 7 February 1966, Brigadier Hargroves handed command of Aden Brigade to Brigadier Richard Jefferies (Royal Irish Fusiliers). Three weeks later, Secretary of State for Defence Denis Healey presented his Defence White Paper, in which he detailed that while the previous Government had allowed an annual expenditure increase of 3 per cent, in 1964/65 spending had risen by 8.7 per cent and was projected to rise to 8.9 per cent for 1965/66. He therefore concluded that the Armed Forces were overstretched and underequipped, and that military capability did not necessarily match political necessities. While instability in Africa and the spread of communism in the Far East were of concern, the principal threat to the UK was nuclear and from the Soviet Union; therefore, he intended to revert to the historic strategy of defending the nation by fighting in Europe. Healey then merged the three Service ministries into the unified Ministry of Defence to be commanded by a Chief of the Defence Staff. In another round of mergers, famous regiments disappeared into history, and a review of the Territorial Army between 1965 and 1967 saw it reduced from 120,000 to 50,000 all ranks and renamed the Territorial Army Volunteer Reserve. Healey accepted the necessity for research and development and indicated that international collaborative projects would be promoted. The Services' rejection of a Forces Supply Corps led to the RASC disbanding, with its vehicle, maritime, air and animal transportation services transferred to the new Royal Corps of Transport (RCT), while logistic supply, clerical duties and barracks and married quarter accounting were transferred to the RAOC.

In terms of the two major operations, Confrontation (Borneo) was nearing victory and Aden was beset by terrorism and insurgency from Yemen; nevertheless, Healey surprised President Nasser by declaring:

South Arabia is due to become independent by 1968, and we do not think it appropriate that we should maintain defence forces after that happens. We therefore intend to withdraw our forces from Aden Base at that time.

Several days before the announcement, Lord Beswick had briefed the Federal Government at Al Ittihad and had to face their sense of betrayal after the assurances given by previous British Governments of a continued military presence in Aden. The Federation and South Arabia were doomed. Nasser immediately abrogated the Jeddah Agreement in the knowledge that all he had to do was wait for the British to leave; indeed, he progressively increased his expeditionary force back to 60,000, a disastrous decision as it turned out. As Bernard Mills, a British mercenary, recalled:

We (the Royalists) and the British Mercenary Organization) produced a situation where we'd won . . . the new British Government announced its intention to leave (South) Arabia. So we'd actually won the game, which is why I got so cross, we'd actually won the game and then it was given away politically because the Labour government was committed to a major defence cut.

The 'Voice of the Arabs' escalated its vitriolic threats against loyalist 'collaborators'. Encouraged by Egypt, the NLF, the Organisation for the Liberation of the Occupied South (OLOS) and other nationalist groups, except for the South Arabia League, merged into the Front for the Liberation of Occupied South Yemen (FLOSY), which established its headquarters at Tiaz. Local support for the Security Forces quickly disappeared as Adenis aligned themselves towards an uncertain future after independence and the British lost some semblance of authority. Patrols generally encountered resigned indifference, but terrorism kept Aden on the global public scene. The threat of assassinations continued, until only six Aden State Legislative Council representatives were prepared to sit on the 24-seat Federal Council. Indeed, it would not sit until August. The competence of the 'Cairo Grenadiers' had improved markedly. 'Double taps', later known as 'Come-ons' in Northern Ireland, drew patrols into ambush. Distraction look-outs were posted to cover attacks, escape routes were planned and, by late 1965, a second grenade was often thrown, designed to cause maximum casualties. The best defence against grenades thrown on to the spare wheels on Land Rover bonnets turned out to be dustbin lids. Leaflets promoted ways to disturb the life of British residents, such as rendering air conditioners useless, pouring sugar or earth into petrol tanks, puncturing tyres and setting fire to cars, the NAAFI and anything British that was inflammable. The riskiest element for terrorists was smuggling weapons past static sandbagged military checkpoints and roadblocks set up by patrols, at which the troops relied on experience and observation to identify suspects.

The murders of officials, representatives and prestige figures such as Special Branch members continued to sap morale. The majority of assassinations were now better planned, from selecting a target to picking a competent killer squad, to the disposal of the weapon and dispersal. The murder of Aden State representative Abdul Rahman Basewanda on 19 August led to the expulsion of 105 Yemeni 'undesirables'. The closure of the border with Yemen hurt Aden; however, the Federal rulers had lost confidence in London taking any action and, consequently, the British began to suffer more casualties.

In March 1966, 1st Cameronians (Scottish Rifles) took over from 1st KOYLI at Radfan Camp with security responsibility for Ma'alla, Tawahi and Steamer Point. The Cameronians had been described as the 'Poison Dwarfs' by a newspaper in Minden – perhaps because of their violent reaction after a Turkish taxi driver was alleged to have stabbed a soldier, perhaps because two soldiers were caught pouring fertilizer into the town reservoir.

As HQ Middle East Command began planning for Withdrawal Day (W-Day), the political aim remained to leave the fundamentals of a democratic state and transfer British military interests in South Arabia to elsewhere in the Middle East, notably Bahrain and Sharjah. Flexibility and inventiveness were crucial, and although a firm date had yet to be set, 1 January 1968 was provisionally selected as W-Day on the basis that the Ministry of Defence had to declare a firm date by 1 May 1967. A threat assessment assumed the final stages would be conducted in contact with an enemy in the form of either nationalists or Yemeni forces, and therefore there would have to be a defended perimeter. Aden had been a garrison since 1839, consequently the workload was enormous and only complicated by the Aden Emergency. Since Joint Service integration was critical, the Ministry provided a Quartering team to help prepare a detailed plan. This developed into a 15ft-long chart detailing tasks and timings and listing barracks, schools, hospitals and married quarters to be vacated, camps to be dismantled, ammunition dumps and supply depots to be emptied and stores and transport to be returned to UK or disposed of locally – a general principle being that heavy equipment would be moved by ship and light equipment and people by air.

An early decision was to fly out dependants direct to the UK six months before W-Day. Muharraq Aifield at RAF Bahrain was identified as the junction between tactical air operations affecting Aden and strategic operations in which troops would hand in weapons, shower and change into civilian clothes before boarding long-haul flights to the UK. It was crucial that RAF Khormaksar remained operational throughout; nevertheless, when concerns were raised that the runway would probably need to be resurfaced, the plan was rejected on the grounds of justified risk. Blast-proof shelters were constructed to protect aircraft and loading bays, and the ground defence was strengthened by the presence of 37, 48 and 51 Squadrons RAF Regiment. In the final stages, only aircraft that could take off on three engines were to be used. This did not apply to the 50 Squadron Shorts Belfast strategic freighters, which were then the largest aircraft to have entered RAF service, and a specialist engine-change team was therefore to be positioned at RAF Khormaksar.

So far, the ships of the Royal Navy at HMS *Sheba* had played a relatively minor role during the Aden Emergency. A Ton-class Coastal Minesweeper had had patrolled the coast, kept channels clear of mines and often provided shore patrols from ships docked in the naval base. Withdrawal would now require a substantial naval contribution to move heavy equipment and vehicles, as a well as warships to cover the final stages with naval gunfire, helicopters and a floating reserve.

Sir John Prendergast took over from Brigadier Cowper as Head of Intelligence in June 1966. Deciding to retain the Aden Intelligence Centre, he emphasised that he expected results, not excuses. When he asked Chief Inspector Jim Herlihy, an experienced Colonial Police Special Branch officer, to outline proposals for a counter-terrorist group, Herlihy placed his thoughts in front of Prendergast within twenty-four hours. This led to the establishment of B (Counter-Terrorist) Group as an alternative to the increasingly ineffective police force, to be assembled from within Aden Brigade with the prime roles of reacting to intelligence leads and taking the war to the terrorists. Included in B Group was the Fort Morbut Interrogation Centre, which was commanded by an Intelligence Corps major. Prendergast told Herlihy to ensure that there were no surprises emerging Fort Morbut that could embarrass Her Majesty's Government.

Herlihy returned to London for a short break and returned promoted to Superintendent. In his absence, his deputy, Flight Lieutenant Bob Laing, a former Kenya Special Branch officer, had organized a prefabricated building in the grounds of the Aden Intelligence Centre. The Deputy Superintendents recruited as Operations Officers were each supported by an Intelligence Corps corporal or lance corporal, who were responsible for establishing the veracity of interrogation and source reports. Corporal John Woolmore was with the

Group from October 1966 to April 1967 and supported Superintendent Jim Semple:

> At night they accompanied their respective Special Branch officer together with a dedicated Special Branch Infantry Platoon on the raids of premises that had been positively identified. These were mainly in Sheikh Othman, Crater and Ma'alla. A large quantity or arms and explosives were recovered in terms of F-1 hand grenades [a Soviet grenade nicknamed limonka, or 'lemon-like'], rocket launchers, landmines and a variety of small arms and ammunition. Booby traps were also used although these caused many more injuries amongst an inquisitive local population.

An Intelligence Corps major appointed by HQ Aden Brigade as the Military Liaison Officer was instrumental in cementing a firm relationship between the Army and the Group.

Brigadier Jefferies was committed to the B Group concept and instructed the three battalions in his Brigade to provide Special Branch Squads of an officer and ten soldiers, usually from the Recce Platoon, to be placed at the disposal of the Operations Officers for specific operations. One was on instant notice to move and the others available at short notice. Some squads were dressed in uniforms, others in civilian clothes, and they were armed either with 9mm Sterling sub-machine guns or 9mm Browning automatic pistol. The squads used apparently battered Land Rovers, complete with tassels hanging from their awnings, but their engines were regularly serviced and inside were a hidden radio, shovels, picks, crowbars and a hook ladder for searches. Sometimes civilian cars were used. To compensate for the loss of information, a Human Intelligence initiative increased the number of sources and informants. On the occasions when sources were debriefed, their security was preserved by covering them, in the vehicle carrying them, with a blanket that was only removed when it was safe to do so, usually inside a base. Under Operation Nina, the SAS also formed covert squads named 'Keeni Meenis', from the Swahili for an unseen snake in the grass. Their Fijian and some other members could pass as Arabs or Africans.

A typical B Group day would start at 7.30 pm with a 'Prayers' command briefing in Superintendent Herlily's office, at which the log of the previous twenty-four hours, reports from Fort Morbut and the state of current operations were reviewed. Prendergast then held an overview meeting in his office half an hour later, after which he attended the daily Security Policy Committee chaired by the High Commissioner – except for Sundays, when he attended Mass. Late afternoons and evenings were usually taken up with briefings and preparations for the night's operations. The use of covert patrols requires careful coordination to avoid friendly fire incidents; nevertheless, such encounters are high risk. In October 1966, a clash between the SAS and the 3rd Royal Anglians Special Branch Squad in Sheikh Othman resulted in a sergeant and a corporal from the Battalion being killed. Ken Connor, in his Ghost Force, wrote that he found it amazing that the Regular Army, without any experience, could conduct covert operations in an urban environment; but the SAS were no more experienced in such activities. Nevertheless, B Group took the war to the terrorists and proved effective in disrupting their activities by uncovering arms caches, finding nationalist propaganda leaflets and making arrests.

Any notion of the romance of resistance that guerrillas and terrorists may entertain frequently disappears when they are captured and asked awkward questions. Most answer such questions, thereby placing their colleagues at risk. During 1966, the nationalists employed tactics used by the Greek-Cypriot terrorist organisation, EOKA, during the Cyprus Emergency, and accused the Security Forces of brutality towards prisoners. Chief Justice Richard Le Gallais was instructed by the High Commissioner to investigate such claims and concluded the allegations were unfounded. The International Committee of the Red Cross (ICRC) had, and still has, responsibility for ensuring that regular and irregular forces conduct military operations within the Laws of Armed Conflict. Concerned about the reports, it sent a delegation headed by Dr Andre Rochet to review conditions in interrogation centres; but they were prevented from doing so on the grounds that the detainees were not prisoners of war or insurgents engaged in armed conflict, but suspects engaged in terrorism, which was a criminal offence.

In spite of protests from High Commissioner Turnbull that it was a philanthropic organisation that had no formal right to visit detainees, Amnesty despatched a Swedish delegate, the Arab-speaking Turkish gynaecologist, Dr Salahadin Rastgeldi, to investigate the allegations. Amnesty had been founded in 1961 by the lawyer Peter Benenson, a former Second World War Intelligence Corps officer employed at Bletchley Park, to campaign against abuses in the form of anyone 'imprisoned, tortured or executed because his opinions or religion are unacceptable to his government', under the Universal Declaration of Human Rights:

> Article 18. Everyone has the right to freedom of thought, conscience and religion; this right includes freedom to change his religion or belief, and freedom, either alone or in community with others and in

public or private, to manifest his religion or belief in teaching, practice, worship and observance.

Article 19. Everyone has the right to freedom of opinion and expression; this right includes freedom to hold opinions without interference and to seek, receive and impart information and ideas through any media and regardless of frontiers.

Rastgeldi was also refused access to detainees and during his visit between 28 July and 4 August was limited to interviewing those claiming to be former detainees and their relatives. Amnesty was gaining a reputation for supporting those whose opinions were unacceptable to governments; however, its credibility suffered when it emerged that its leadership had close links with the Labour Government, including receiving financial support. When Amnesty eventually published its report on 19 October, it was unbalanced and unconvincing, and referred largely to allegations of beatings and rough handling. The charges were denied in Aden, and it was pointed out that once a prisoner had betrayed his organization it was not unknown for him to attempt to ingratiate himself with colleagues by claiming coercion and torture. Nevertheless, in late October, the Foreign Office sent Mr Roderic Bowen QC to investigate the treatment of suspected terrorists. In early November, Abdul Mackawee embroidered the allegations at the UN, but this time the Foreign Office denied them and retaliated with descriptions of the brutal treatment of prisoners in Yemen, to which Amnesty was paying scant attention. Bowen published his Report on 20 December and, concluding that the Amnesty accusations were not proven, nevertheless recommended that the performance of three military interrogators between 18 October and 26 December be investigated. This duly occurred, and they were exonerated. Bowen concluded:

The mainstay of protecting the population and dealings with the terrorist falls upon military personnel and the police. I certainly gained the impression that speaking generally, they discharge their onerous duties with great restraint.

The ending of the Confrontation with Indonesia in September 1966 eased demands on the Army and, as the terrorism escalated, Brigadier Jefferies reorganized Aden Brigade into four battalion areas of tactical responsibility:

- Area North – Sheikh Othman and Al Mansoura
- Area East – Crater
- Area Centre – Ma'alla
- Area West – Tawahi and Steamer Point
- Force Reserve – Armoured Car Squadron

In October, 3rd Royal Anglians arrived from Tidworth and took over Area North from 1st Somerset and Cornwall Light Infantry in Radfan Camp after a six-month tour, during which it had lost two men: Corporal Roy Collins, killed when a mine blew up his vehicle in the Radfan, and Private Oakley, who died from grenade wounds to his head two days after the same attack. Sergeant Bob Bogan had led such a successful Special Branch Squad that he became a marked man and the subject of grenade attacks and an assassination attempt. As the Battalion arrived, the NLF was making a determined attempt to ensure that their supply of men, arms and ammunition from Yemen to Sheikh Othman and Al Mansoura was not interrupted. Mines damaged vehicles, anti-tank rockets were fired, patrols became involved in intense battles in the narrow streets and permanent checkpoints were attacked. The checkpoints were generally constructed from sandbags and were equipped with a GPMG. Overlooking Checkpoint Golf was an empty building often used as an OP. A Blindicide rocket directed at Checkpoint Golf, on the border between Aden and the State of Lahej, was immediately followed by a firefight in which terrorist AK-47 Kalashnikovs competed with GPMGs and SLRs.

The area opposite the derelict Scottish Missionary Hospital in Hunter Road was nicknamed 'Grenade Corner' – for obvious reasons. The hospital had housed No. 138 Combined Field Ambulance during the Battle of Lahej in 1915. On 3 November, a mine blew up the Land Rover carrying the commanding officer, Lieutenant Colonel Leng, shortly before he handed over to Lieutenant Colonel Dymoke. After a grenade attack seriously wounded a soldier on the 20th, Sergeant Allan of the Battalion Medical Team drove to the scene, without an escort, and treated him. He was awarded the BEM for gallantry. On 3 December, Captain Cox RAMC, the Battalion Medical Officer, was treating a casualty within three minutes of a grenade attack when another grenade exploded only five yards away. Undeterred, he continued, and was awarded the MBE for gallantry. Two days later, Radfan Camp came under fire from drainpipe mortars, but of the thirty bombs only five exploded inside the camp perimeter. The capture of a suspect digging holes in the road by a patrol under Corporal Jarvis led to arrests and the break-up of a mine-laying gang. On 30 December, the Special Branch Squad commanded by Captain Light, acting on intelligence, found arms and explosives in a house in Sheikh Othman. Although a prime target, the Squad was attacked just twice. In the first attack, a 'Cairo Grenadier' was shot dead, and in the second, three terrorists were captured before they could strike. By the end of the Battalion's tour, the Squad had seized 105 grenades, five automatic weapons, three pistols, two rocket launchers and a quantity of bombs, ammunition and explosives, and captured fourteen terrorists, including the FLOSY second-in-command and the FLOSY leader in Crater.

On 19 January 1966, a grenade thrown and shots fired from a taxi at 'Grenade Corner' at an Anti-Tank Platoon Land Rover developed into an hour-long gun battle between NLF and FLOSY. Patrols later found several dead terrorists and a wanted car containing mortar bomb fuses. At about 1pm, Checkpoint Golf came under fire from a gunman with an AK-47 located in the nearby Baayomi College grounds; however, a patrol was unable to trap him. At 7.15pm, after four mortar bombs were fired at the checkpoint, a patrol found that five mortars had failed to fire. On the 25th, a 'Cairo Grenadier' killed a child and two women and wounded another child and two soldiers. Shots and a rocket projectile were fired at the Al Mansoura Detention Centre. Private Rob Leonard was a section radio operator patrolling through a narrow street when an object he thought to be a stone bounced toward him. Then he realized what it was:

> I shouted or maybe screamed 'Grenade!' at the top of my voice, the whole patrol including me hit the deck fast. To my horror, as I looked back to where I thought the grenade had bounced past me, it hit the corner of a wall and it was bouncing back toward me. I automatically let go of the Sterling sub-machine gun I had been gripping vice-like, reached over my head as I lay on the deck and tugged hard on the top of the A41 radio, pulling it up to cover the back of my head. There was an almighty explosion as it went off less than a metre from my left foot. I didn't move for what seemed like ages but was less than three seconds, I was later told by the guy some 20 feet behind me. When I grabbed the Sterling and shouted to the section commander, the section was up and moving quickly down the side street to try and catch whoever had thrown it, but needless to say, he had disappeared rapidly, never to be apprehended . . . However, it was an awakening to what was to follow and made me realize that this was not a game but real life. [www.britains-smallwars/Aden]

After 1st PWO returned to Aden, C Company scored a significant haul when Privates Burgin and Ivan trapped a car that attempted to breach a roadblock, capturing an NLF sabotage team and several prepared explosive devices. Interrogations led to further arrests. In three weeks from 6 August 1966, 1st PWO suffered 18 casualties in Crater in six attacks, with Private Frederick Langrick killed and eight wounded, two of them seriously, when a grenade was thrown at a 14 Platoon patrol in a confined space. Langrick's father was a serving warrant officer.

In September, the Battalion handed over to 1st Royal Northumberland Fusiliers, commanded by Lieutenant Colonel Richard Blenkinsop. With a long history back to 1685, it had fought in the American War of Independence and was transferred to the West Indies, where it inflicted heavy casualties on a French attempt to seize St Lucia. Its soldiers then put white plumes worn by the French into their headgear. When in 1829, the Infantry were ordered to wear white plumes, the 5th Foot tipped their white plumes with red. This led to the legend that the Regiment had dipped the white plumes at St Lucia in French blood. During the Korean War, it formed part of the 29th Infantry Brigade during the 1951 Battle of the Imjin River. Fusilier Derek Kinne was awarded the George Cross for his courage as a prisoner of the Communists. His brother had been killed while serving in the Argyll and Sutherland Highlanders.

At the start of their tour, it was suggested that an Aden Grenade tie be awarded to any member of the Battalion who had been involved in a grenade incident. By the end of their tour, it would be awarded to every member. On 11 November, a mobile patrol commanded by Company Sergeant Major Bill Pringle was travelling up the Marine Drive along the coast when a grenade exploded alongside their Land Rover, tipping it over, throwing the men on to the road and wounding Pringle in the shoulder. A woman was also killed and several bystanders were seriously wounded. When Fusilier Reagan, a cross-country runner, saw the 'Cairo Grenadier' run from the scene, he caught him, floored him with his rifle and returned to the Land Rover with his prisoner. But the Fusiliers became the focus of press attention, with journalists and photo-journalists evidencing their criticism with photographs of 'brutal' soldiers kicking and threatening Arabs. Unsurprisingly, the journalists rarely included evidence of grenades being thrown. Blenkinsop insisted that his men were reacting with professionalism, considering that in most cases they had just witnessed the consequences of a grenade attack. The 'evidence' was equally distressing to the families.

CHAPTER THIRTEEN

The Final Year, 1967

In spite of the commitment by London to the independence of South Arabia, the New Year saw a sharp escalation in terrorism, with more gun attacks, the use of women and children to provoke the Security Forces, attacks on the police and civil servants and threats against pro-Federation politicians, all backed up by relentless propaganda in leaflets and by Radio Taiz threatening 'traitors to the cause who support Britain or her puppet Federal Government in any way'. On 10 January, Dr Cen Jones, a senior Federal Ministry of Health official, escaped an assassination attempt, but Deputy Superintendent of Police Niaz Hussein, who had just visited Jones, was murdered. Nine days later, a strike organized by the NLF to commemorate the 128th anniversary of the British occupation saw the local authorities and Aden Police lose control and Federal government authority weakened, as militants set out to demonstrate to world opinion that Britain was incapable of supporting the Federation unless it applied repression and brutality.

HQ Aden Brigade did not receive a request to assist, but when it became evident that police resolve was weak in the face of constant subversion and threats, the Federal authorities handed over security control to Brigadier Jefferies. Adopting a strategy of forcing the terrorists into the open and dealing with them from prepared positions, he reviewed the Standard Operating Procedures that conformed to the following principles:

- In the event of the Aden police losing control of situations, the Army would command internal security operations.

- There would be three States of Readiness:
  GREEN   Normal state
  AMBER   Probability of trouble
  - HQ Aden Brigade to take command and control with the Federal Armed Police under command.
  - Selected command posts and observation posts to be activated.

• Units on hour's notice to move.
• Support units, such the Armoured Car Squadron, engineers and transport, on four hours' notice.

RED
• Aden Brigade on 15 minutes' notice for a brigade deployment.
• Security Forces to deploy before disturbances break out and thereby gain the initiative. Much depended on the quality of timely intelligence and preventing crowds from turning into violent demonstrations.
• Key tactical areas to be seized to deny terrorists freedom of movement.
• Total or partial curfews and banning of vehicles in selected areas.

The Procedures contained detailed plans for transferring suspects to Fort Morbut and the handling of prisoners and detainees, including: ensuring that magistrates were available to dispense swift justice; ensuring the security of essential services, in particular water; the transfer of Security Forces and civilian casualties to hospitals; provision of transport for loyal employees; and the protection of markets and distribution of food supplies, including to Service families. To keep the Services abreast of the situation, 'Security Bulletins' were regularly broadcast on the British Forces Broadcasting Service.

Another procedure addressed dealing with improvised explosive devices (IEDs), which were developing in sophistication. A member of the High Commission, Robin Thorne, lost several fingers when a photographic album in a parcel exploded. Improvised mines appeared, such as Avgas containers filled with nails and explosive or grenades made from Spam tins. After several devices were found in bulky OHMS envelopes and police investigators sought forensic evidence, an X-Ray machine at the Khormaksar Beach Hospital was used to make mail safe. Shortly afterwards, X-Ray machines were installed in the Central Aden Post Office and suspicious parcels were regularly checked. Initially, the devices were simple, for instance constructed from stolen commercial explosive triggered by time-pencil and safety fuses. By 1966, IEDs were being used against strategic targets, such as the oil pipeline from the refinery in Little Aden to Steamer Point, and they included trembler and mechanical anti-handling devices, A device consisting of several slabs of TNT found in the NAAFI Families shop had been ticked as 'two bars of soap' at the monthly stock check. When a device was found outside an RAF Khormaksar married quarter, a blood trail led to a locked door and an injured terrorist. His arrest led to the smashing of a terrorist cell. Major John Elliott and Major G.C. Brownlee, of the RAOC, were both awarded George Medals, for each defusing about 150 devices, as was Mr 'Dickie' Bird, a Government forensic scientist sent from London. The bomb disposal teams usually had a briefcase containing a surgical scalpel, wire cutters, sticky tape, twine and fish hooks, and they had a knowledge of chemistry, electrical circuitry and explosives. Bomb disposal meant dismantling the device.

On 28 February, Mr Anthony Ingledow, a Political Officer attached to Middle East Command, and his wife were entertaining several civilian and military security officials to supper at their flat; at 9 pm, a bomb exploded in the dining room, killing an MI5 officer and Mrs Ruth Wilkes, the wife of Major John Wilkes (Intelligence Corps), who commanded the Counter-Intelligence Company, and injuring five men and six women. When Superintendent Semple and Corporal Woolmore attended the scene to initiate the investigation, it turned out that the NFL had kidnapped the mother of the Wilkes' houseboy and, after threatening to kill her, had given him a 'jumping jack' time bomb, which he concealed in the bookcase. Shortly before the guests arrived, Mrs Ingledow moved the furniture and the device fell over. A week later, a grenade was thrown at a dinner party of civil servants and police as they were drinking coffee inside RAF Khormaksar. While it was clear from both these incidents that NLF intelligence had good sources, Middle East Command was reluctant to impose restrictions on social activities in an environment of escalating terrorism; nevertheless, further security measures were imposed.

By 1967, the Ma'alla Straight of three- and four-storey, white-painted married quarters bordering the dual carriageway linking Steamer Point to Crater had become a target of rocket and grenade attacks and a dangerous place to live. When a patrol discovered that among the casualties in an attack on a bar was a WRAC, the soldiers were extremely displeased. Additional security was provided by off-duty servicemen rotated to conduct patrols around the 'patch' between 2 pm and 10 pm, armed with .38 Smith and Wesson revolvers for sergeants and above, .303 Lee Enfield rifles for the remainder and baseball bats and batons for civilians. John Middleton, of the RAF, describes a Sunday in late 1966:

Suddenly a grenade was lobbed over the breeze-block wall used to seal off the side road and bounced toward a British family on their way to church. The grenade exploded in the middle of them. The loudspeaker of a passing Land Rover cracked out, 'Throw some white sheets down!' Over the balconies came the sheets. The wounded were quickly dressed and the ambulance rushed the family to the Steamer Point British Military Hospital. The young daughter in the familiy, about eleven years old, was very seriously injured. [UKMAMS Old Bods Association]

At about 6 pm, after a grenade was thrown at an Army Land Rover from a white Opel, the vehicle commander broadcast the car's registration number on his loudspeaker, and those with weapons in the married quarters opened fire on cars they believed to be white Opels. Middleton suddenly realized that ricochets whistling past his windows were from other servicemen and it was time to take cover. Seven white cars were shot up and several people injured in crashes. Several weeks after anti-rocket breeze blocks had blocked side streets, in November 1966, the first phase of the Withdrawal began with Operation Relative: the first tranche of families, which included those seconded to the Federal security forces and civilians associated with the Armed Forces, were generally given fourteen days' formal warning to pack and prepare their quarter for handover to Barrack Services.

The Joint Services Air Trooping Centre played a vital role in ensuring that when they arrived in UK, the families had the option of either another married quarter near their husband's barracks or another chosen location or temporary accommodation. From January to April 1967, 2,691 dependants were flown out. When the winter term ended in the UK and boarders were looking forward to joining their parents for Easter, on 14 March, FLOSY issued a statement to the effect that while they did not intend to kill women and children, 'it is difficult to control the explosion of a bomb'. Although High Commissioner Turnbull advocated caution, opinion in HQ Middle East Command was that the presence of families remained important for morale. Two days later, about 400 children arrived in RAF 'Lollipop Specials' aircraft, straight into a period of the most hostile disturbances so far. Operation Relative was ratcheted up, with 6,605 dependants evacuated between May and 15 July. Meanwhile, 1,400 married quarters, 1,700 rented flats, six schools, NAAFI shops and medical centres were handed to local authorities, and with them disappeared a considerable military commitment to guard these premises. Local businesses lost sizeable incomes. To preserve the security of the lines of communication to Steamer Point, the Ma'alla flats were occupied by servicemen, normally eight to each flat. Some lacked air conditioning, and water was rationed.

Encouraged by the weak stand taken by the Federal authorities in

January, the NLF had set out to prove that the British could not govern effectively and declared the Day of the Volcano on 10 February throughout Aden and the Eastern Protectorate. Major General Willoughby pre-empted the potential for disorder by deploying troops before the expected trouble began, restricting the movement of traffic from 6 am and confining Service families to their married quarters. On the same day, Husain Ali Bayoomi, Federal Minister of Information, rejected the NLF's sentence of him to death for 'subservience to colonialism' and accused FLOSY and NLF of cowardice. By noon, Willoughby had deployed the Aden Brigade with orders under the Emergency Regulations to prevent demonstrations and gatherings. During the day, bomb disposal officers defused a mine buried at the Al Ittibad helicopter landing site and ten mortar tubes aimed at an area set aside to celebrate the eighth anniversary of the Federation. The lifting of the curfew at 8 am on the 12th was followed by disturbances after FLOSY called for a general strike, during which two people were killed and about 150 arrested. The Army reimposed the curfew until 5.30am next morning. For the first time in four days, Service families were permitted to leave their quarters. During the three days, British troops were attacked 66 times, resulting in 8 killed and 31 wounded, mostly in grenade attacks. Three NLF were killed, two wounded and eight captured. An effective curfew on the 11th was followed next day by riots. A show of force by Aden Brigade undermined the threat, but there now broke out the early stages of serious interfactional fighting between the NLF and the hardcore FLOSY offshoot, the Popular Organisation of Revolutionary Forces; this was in addition to the relentless terrorism against the Aden Police and civil servants, all aimed at ensuring that the British withdrawal would be seen as a victory for Yemen, Egypt and the NLF.

The next test for the Security Forces came on 27 February, when a bomb planted by the NLF at the house of the FLOSY leader, Abdul Mackawee, killed his three sons and three police officers. The NLF denied responsibility and blamed the South Arabian League and the rulers. The funerals next day developed from anti-British demonstrations into a mob that turned on representatives of the League and chased them into a mosque, where they were seized, hurled from the Crater mosque's minaret to the baying crowd and beaten to death, watched by the police. Although the Northumberland Fusiliers intervened to quell the disturbances, some believed that the troops were unable to maintain law and order – or unwilling to do so because of the Withdrawal – and consequently there was a significance collapse of confidence in the British ability to maintain control. The killings and that of Muhammed Said Hassan, a FLOSY supporter in Ma'alla, heralded yet more interfactional fighting as NLF turned on FLOSY, resulting in 32 murders in 35 days. Bizarrely, FLOSY activists sought the protection of the Army, and about eighty of them with British passports left the colony. Over 300 grenades were thrown, resulting in one British soldier killed and eighty-five wounded.

Deception, the use of surprise by B (Counter-Intelligence) Group, flares dropped from aircraft and air observation posts in helicopters were all used to detect and prevent acts of terrorism. In endeavouring to identify riot ringleaders and 'Cairo Grenadiers', who melted into cafés before a patrol appeared, 1st Lancashires, who arrived in February on a six-month tour in Tawahi, established OPs on Jebel Shamsan to guide patrols to grenade throwers.

In February, the UN General Assembly instructed that a mission should recommend measures to implement the previous Resolutions affecting Aden. However, it soon became very clear that the June 1966 resolution criticising the UK for shifting its responsibilities as the administering Power to the 'unrepresentative' Federal government would be a hindrance to trilateral negotiations. Meanwhile, the NLF and FLOSY continued to jockey for position to enable each to declare that they were, in fact, the true representative of the people; each then refused to meet the Mission until their claim was accepted. The Commonwealth Office, which been formed from the merger of the Colonial Office and Commonwealth Relations Office in 1966, hoped that the Mission would be flexible enough to identify a solution; but Venezuela, Afghanistan and Mali provided the senior delegates and, while hardly high-powered, were virulently anti-British at the UN. The Mission first went to London and then flew to Cairo, where it attended several receptions to meet parties interested in influencing their recommendations.

With the Mission expected to arrive from Jeddah on 2 April, HQ Middle East Command ordered State AMBER at 11 am on Friday 31 March, as intelligence suggested there might be demonstrations outside mosques after prayers. Since the Mission needed access to all parties, it would be escorted by the Civil Police in Aden and the FRA in the hinterland. On the day before the Mission arrived – April Fools' Day – a storm produced six inches of rain in seven hours and brought Aden to a halt. As usual, the troops helped with flooded homes and shops; nevertheless, as Major General Willoughby ordered State RED next day, the NLF called a three-day strike, during which gunmen used the cover of disturbances to snipe at patrols and throw grenades. FLOSY declared a seven-day strike to start the next day. The Mission arrived during the evening and were driven to their rooms at the Seaview Hotel, overlooking Khormaksar Beach, which had been fortified with sandbags and wire and was patrolled by the Armed Police. When High Commissioner Turnbull visited next morning, the Mission indicated they would only negotiate with the British and, accepting an invitation to lunch at Government House, were flown there by helicopter. They then acted undiplomatically by returning to their hotel and remained virtually incommunicado for the next 48 hours, except to accept a television, a radio, some books, a large bottle of orange squash and two bottles of champagne from Turnbull. They originally complained that, as Muslims, they could not accept the champagne, but the bottles were not returned. By the end of the day, the Security Forces had logged 71 incidents, 15 members of the Security Forceshad been wounded, a terrorist had been killed and 8 captured. The unrest was not as serious as anticipated because the rainstorm had disrupted telephone lines and atmospheric conditions had reduced the Voice of the Arabs to inaudible 'mush'.

The next day was troubled, however. The NLF strike brought Aden to a standstill, and since there was no public transport and no commercial activity everyone was free to join in the demonstrations. In Sheikh Othman, the Royal Anglians dispensed with 'Disperse or We Fire' banners and adopted street-fighting techniques. Some rioters were cleared by tear gas canisters dropped from helicopters. The besieged Sheikh Othman Police Station was liberated, but a QDG Saladin was damaged by a mine. The 4th was relatively tranquil, as the Security Forces avoided being enticed into incidents; nevertheless, two terrorists were killed, three were wounded and four arrested. Next day, after forty-eight hours confined to their hotel, the Mission visited the Al Mansoura Detention Centre; but when they arrived at about 5 pm, they were jeered by the 112 NLF and FLOSY detainees, who then refused to be interviewed. Outside, another interfactional gun battle broke out, and 13 Platoon, 3rd Royal Anglians, commanded by Lieutenant Brian Harrington Spier, bundled the angry and fearful delegates into a helicopter, because it was too dangerous to go by car. However, the helicopter was damaged by ground fire and 13 Platoon then transferred them to a Saracen, which was escorted to their hotel by B Squadron, QDG. The visit developed into further farce the next day, when Hussein Bayoomi, the Minister of Information, refused to allow the Mission to broadcast the purpose of their visit from his radio and television stations because they had denied the existence of the Federal Government.

While the NLF terminated their strike, FLOSY enforced theirs, with most staying indoors. On the 6th, the terrorists made a serious bid to seize Sheikh Othman in a day that saw 61 incidents. At about 9 am, 13 Platoon, commanded by Lieutenant Harrington Spier, was conducting a 'finger patrol' of the streets. Corporal Valentine and his section were near the Damascus main mosque when a grenade exploded. Through the smoke, Valentine fired two shots at the 'Cairo Grenadier' running towards the mosque and then set off in pursuit with his section; but, forbidden to enter mosques, they came under heavy automatic fire from roof tops. When the firing ceased, the section moved tactically from doorway to doorway past the mosque, ready to cross the road into Street 5. Half the section had crossed when it again came under heavy fire, including from the mosque, preventing the remainder from crossing. Sergeant Green's patrol tried to work their way round to give support. Lieutenant Harrington Spier and Platoon HQ had come under fire at the place where the grenade had exploded. Covering each other in short dashes, Valentine and Private Lanaghan searched for an exit from Street 5, but without success. Returning to his section, Valentine checked the section ammunition and found that Private Anderson had been slightly wounded by grenade splinters. After Harrington Spier had radioed for a QDG Saracen and Saladin to cover their exit, Valentine regrouped at the end of the street but then found that two men were still pinned down, As Harrington Spier took three soldiers to help them, a grenade thrown from a high building exploded near Private McCormick, but without causing casualties. The two privates were retrieved and the platoon moved from doorway to doorway, corner to corner, down to Street 11, then dashed across 200 yards of open ground to the safety of Company HQ and 14 Platoon. Harrington Spier was awarded the MBE for gallantry and Valentine the BEM, in circumstances in which they might have normally been awarded the MC and MM respectively. The inability of the Army to enter mosques strongly suspected of sheltering gunmen and stocking weapons was resolved when a 'mosque platoon' was raised by the FRA. Permission was also given to enter any house providing a terrorist firing position.

Next morning, in spite of requests from UN Secretary General U Thant to remain, the Mission departed amid quarrelsome jostling by journalists outside their hotel; the RAF VC10's captain refused to take off until they agreed to a search of their baggage. The alert state was dropped to AMBER at 5 pm on the 8th and then to GREEN at 11 am next day. In short, the UN Mission had been a complete, and inevitable, farcical failure.

The showdown during the first eight days of April had seen 280 incidents, during which eighteen servicemen were wounded and eight terrorists were killed and seven wounded. The British Forces Newspaper *The Dhow* listed several grenade attacks:

DATE	TIME	TARGET	COMMENT
1 Apr	19.30	British passengers from SS *Rosebank* in Tawahi	1 British woman killed, four injured and 5 Arabs injured
2 Apr	19.30	Crater. No apparent target	Car damaged
6 Apr	18.25	Military patrol	Arab injured
9 Apr	21.24	Tawahi. Not known	4 Arabs injured
11 Apr	16.50	Army lorry near Al Mansoura Detention Centre	
17 Apr	08.50	A car	Arab boy injured
19 Apr	19.10	Military patrol	
21 Apr	20.40	Military patrol in Sheikh Othman	2 Army and Arab girl wounded
23 Apr	20.25	Outside Bank of India, Crater	
24 Apr	09.21	House of a British teacher in Little Aden	
26 Apr	12.15 20.10	Army lorry in Sheikh Othman Mobile patrol in Sheikh Othman	
27 Apr	19.30 19.50 20.05	Mobile patrol in Sheikh Otham Sheikh Othman Police Station Mobile patrol in Sheikh Otham	Five Arabs injured
28 Apr	18.55	Three off-duty Servicemen in Tawahi	All injured

A week later, Lord Shackleton, the Minister for the RAF, arrived with a small delegation to repair the damage caused by the UN Mission; he suggested that if the nationalists joined a broad-based Federal Government and ceased their campaign, then the Emergency would end and the detainees would be released. But terrorism continued, with the murder of the father-in-law of a senior FLOSY leader by the NLF, the wounding of a British lawyer and a teacher and the blowing up of a school bus, killing the driver and six children and injuring fourteen others on 30 April. This generated a public outcry, with the NLF and FLOSY blaming the British and calling for three days of mourning, while the Federal Government blamed Egypt. The Popular Organisation of Revolutionary Forces distributed leaflets threatening Service families. On 2 May, Nasser declared that while the Egyptian Army would not cross the border, he would support FLOSY, thus isolating the NLF in its bid to take power after Withdrawal Day.

On 11 May, Major General Philip Tower arrived from Director of Public Relations (Army) at the Ministry of Defence and relieved Major General Willoughby on his retirement. Commissioned into the Royal Artillery in 1937, he had taken part in Operation Compass, which drove the Italians from Libya in 1940–1, but had been captured by the Germans at Bir Hacheim when his unit ran out of ammunition. Sent to a prison camp in Italy, he ignored the 'stand fast' order when Italy capitulated in September 1943 and trekked 500 miles through the Apennines, crossing into Allied lines but being wounded in doing so. He coordinated the 1st Airborne Division artillery at Arnhem and, escaping capture by crossing the Rhine, later accompanied the 1st Air Landing Regiment RA during the liberation of Norway. After 1945, he served in several high-profile postings, including commanding 3rd Royal Horse Artillery and 12th Infantry Brigade Group in West Germany, but had not seen active service since 1945. Seen as a safe pair of hands, he had visited Aden in 1965, and his most recent appointment seemed suitable preparation to handle the last few months of the British military presence in South Arabia. His reputation for flamboyance sometimes led others to underestimate his competence and experience.

On 20 May, at the recommendation of Shackleton, Sir Richard Turnbull was replaced by Sir Humphrey Trevelyan in a move that the Foreign Office described as a 'change of style'. Any reservations the Security Forces may have had about Trevelyan disappeared when he declared his first priority was to ensure the withdrawal was orderly and that the British left a viable country behind them. But the omens were not good. On 25 May, when 3rd Royal Anglians handed Sheikh Othman and Al Mansoura to 1st Para with C Company, 1st Kings Own Royal Border Regiment under command, it had logged 459 incidents since October 1966. The paras were commanded by Lieutenant Colonel Mike Walsh, who had commanded B Company, 3rd Para during the Radfan operation in 1964. B Company had passed out from Parachute Regiment Depot in April. During the handover, six Borderers were wounded in a grenade attack on a platoon, one having to have a leg amputated, Sergeant Colin Atkinson was awarded the Military Medal for his leadership during the incident, having sustained fifty wounds from the grenades.

Walsh planned to embed his men over the next fortnight, but no sooner had he bid farewell to the Royal Anglians' commanding officer than he received a radio message that the Aden TUC had called a general strike. Within 24 hours of the Battalion deploying, a patrol shot its first sniper. A second strike was announced for 1 June. At 2 am, D Company and a C Company platoon, commanded by Major Geoffrey Brierley, moved into Sheikh Otham and took over Company HQ at the Police Station and seven OPs dominating the Damascus mosque, principal streets and the road to Checkpoint Golf. Three 10-man quick reaction forces were on stand-by. As the sun rose at 6.30 am, the first incident occurred when a grenade was thrown at a patrol from a lorry near the mosque; this would herald a day in which the NLF made a determined attempt to seize the district. The Eastern Bank OP immediately returned fire, shooting two men running towards the mosque and another by firing through the window of a shop in which he had sheltered. A fourth man was captured hiding in the truck by a patrol. As the battle escalated, the distance between some OPs and terrorist positions was only the width of a street. A GPMG gunner was killed, a soldier wounded and the SLR of Private Yeoman shattered when a bullet entered its barrel. Two QDG Troops patrolled the narrow streets engaging targets. A broadcast from the mosque loudspeakers at 11 pm led the militants to cease firing. So far, D Company had been on the defensive; however, the pause gave Major Brierley an opportunity to seize the initiative, and when the battle began again, he ordered the OPs to fire short, intensive volleys at enemy positions, forcing the terrorists to withdraw to safer positions some 300 yards from the OPs. When one OP became untenable, armoured cars covered its evacuation at the cost of a para wounded in the foot. By the afternoon, ammunition in the OPs was running low and the paras constructed GMPG belts by connecting ammunition in the bandoliers using discarded links. When the Battalion second-in-command planned a re-supply operation of ammunition and water, it was led by the Intelligence Officer, Captain Edward Loaden, and completed by 6 pm. Shortly before last light, after a Russian grenade was thrown into the OP occupied by Corporal Tanner's section, followed by sustained, short-range fire, Tanner radioed a thoroughly relieved Major Brierley that his few casualties were merely suffering headaches. The terrorist position was blasted by fire from other OPs and a Saladin. By 9 pm, the firing had died down, and under cover of the darkness Walsh ordered HQ C Company and a platoon to occupy the Police Station, while D Company returned to Radfan Camp, having accounted for at least eight terrorists verified killed and five captured, three of whom were wounded, but at the cost of one killed and four wounded. Another clear message had been sent to the terrorists. C Company, 1st Kings Own Royal Borderers had ben attacked on about thirty-five occasions, mainly by automatic and rifle fire.

When the 5,000 men of the five FRA and four FNG 1 battalions merged to form the South Arabian Army (SAA) on 1 June, it was hoped that in due course the Hadhrami Bedouin Legion would join. Formed in 1940 and modelled on the Arab Legion in Jordan, it had distributed supplies during the 1944 and 1948 famines and operated from forts in the Eastern Aden Protectorate in counter-insurgency operations and in keeping the peace between feuding tribes. The army was commanded by Brigadier Jack Dye, who had previously commanded the FRA. His Chief of Staff was Lieutenant Colonel Richard Lawson DSO (Royal Tank Regiment), who had achieved international fame while serving with 3rd Nigerian Brigade with the UN in the Congo, when he had saved a Belgian priest by waving his swagger stick at a mob of several hundred Africans. However, historic tribal rivalry surfaced over the predominance of Aulaqis in positions of authority, including Colonel Nasser Bureiq as Deputy Commander and thirty per cent of the force's officers. On 3 June, eleven senior officers presented a petition to the Federal Minister of Defence, as opposed to Army Headquarters, highlighting their perception of the favouritism afforded to the Aulaqis. But the petition was left unattended on the desk of Brigadier Dye, who was on leave. At the same time, the Aden Civil Police, the 350 well-armed and disciplined Federal Armed Police and part of FNG 2, who were poorly trained and ill-equipped, were merged into the South Arabian Police (SAP). Although the British were scheduled to leave within 18 months, a few Army officers and other ranks had elected to compromise their personal security by passing information of disaffection to Dye and Lawson. The police had several grudges, in particular that the management of internal security in Aden had been devolved to British troops and that police vehicles were being searched for arms. Consequently, some had become susceptible to subversion in the meantime, and it was not difficult for the NLF to stoke up resentment.

When the Six Day War broke out on 3 June, Israel knocked out the air forces of Egypt, Syria and Jordan in pre-emptive strikes and launched ground offensives that sent the Arab armies reeling. Three days later, the 'Voice of the Arabs' set out to secure Soviet military assistance by accusing the US and Britain of supporting the attacks by providing carrier-borne aircraft and Canberra bombers, just as Britain and France, it was claimed, had supported Israel in 1956. British and US volunteer pilots were then alleged to be flying Israeli planes, and Israel was claimed to be using US-supplied Photographic Intelligence to plan its strikes. Radio Damascus added that a captured Israeli pilot had admitted that seventeen Vulcan bombers flying from RAF Akrotiri had arrived in Israel ten days before the outbreak of the war and had attacked targets in Syria and Egypt. The claims had an immediate impact. Several Arab countries severed diplomatic relations with the US and Britain, and Middle Eastern oil-producing countries announced oil embargos and suspended exports. On 6 June, Nasser heightened regional tension by closing the Suez Canal. Nevertheless, three days later, the Arab armies had been crushed in humiliating defeat, while Egypt still had 60,000 troops tied up in Yemen. The news was met with stunned disbelief from nationalists, while Federation supporters experienced a glimmer of hope and delight that Nasser had been humbled. FLOSY lost its way as its Egyptian support dissipated and Nasser withdraw his army from Yemen in order to replace the massive losses suffered in the war; consequently, the NLF grew in confidence.

However, the Six Day War had a psychological impact throughout the Middle East that has lasted until today. Nasser justified his second catastrophic defeat by accusing Great Britain and the USA of assisting Israel and constructing a psychological operations programme that became known as 'The Big Lie', Although Arab politicians and diplomats knew his allegations were false, such was the effect of the Egyptian rhetoric that diplomatic relations wavered. The Soviet Union had avoided any direct reference to supposed Western involvement but gave the 'Big Lie' credibility by broadcasting sympathetic reports from Cairo and Damascus. On 8 June, Israel released an intercepted telephone conversation between Nasser and King Hussein of Jordan, held two days previously, that suggested collusion between the two leaders. When Nasser resigned the next day, he claimed that the Israeli Air Force must have had outside assistance to achieve such success.

Washington and London reasoned that the 'Big Lie' would be exposed, and it was this belief that governed their response; but it had become 'fact' in the Arab world. A report by the British representative in Jeddah noted:

> Our broadcast denials are little heard and just not believed. The denials we have issued to the broadcasting service and press have not been published. Even highly educated persons basically friendly to us seem convinced that the allegations are true. Senior foreign ministry officials who received my formal written and oral denials profess to believe them but nevertheless appear sceptical. I consider that this allegation has seriously damaged our reputation in the Arab world more than anything else and has caused a wave of suspicion or feeling against us which will persist in some underlying form for the foreseeable future.

Nevertheless, King Faisal ridiculed claims by the Egyptian ambassador at a diplomatic function that Washington and London had supported Israel; and although Turkey and Jordan encouraged both capitals to regard the 'Big Lie' as a 'mistake in interpretation', such was its power that, by the end of June, London and Washington admitted that their counter-propaganda had failed. A British guidance telegram to Middle East posts concluded:

> The Arabs' reluctance to disbelieve all versions of the big lie springs in part from a need to believe that the Israelis could not have defeated them so thoroughly without outside assistance.

Two consequences were that Libya told Britain to evacuate its base at Benghazi and President Makarios demanded that Britain evacuate its Sovereign Bases in Cyprus.

The 'Big Lie' was a classic case of 'Tell a lie often enough and inevitably you start believing it'. It was launched, after a defeat, at a largely gullible mass fed on the idea that the Sykes/Picot Agreement carve-up of the Middle East had been a series of Western conspiracies and that Israel was nothing but a Western stooge. In short, the new state of Israel could not have won three wars without outside intervention and thus Arab nations had no need to be ashamed of defeat.

With strong anti-British sentiments evident, Lieutenant Colonel Walsh insisted that Sheikh Othman would not become a battleground and decided to enter the district in strength with the following plan:

- Battalion Tactical HQ and three platoons of C Company to locate in the derelict Church of Scotland Mission Hospital.
- The forth platoon to be located at the Police Station.
- Checkpoint Golf to be reinforced by placing a second company HQ on the roof of Bayoomi College. The move would lessen military traffic to Radfan Camp and the road to Dhala could be secured.

Everyone available at Radfan Camp filled hundreds of sandbags, and several soldiers from B Company collapsed after being struck by sandfly fever carried by flies buried in the sand.

When Brigadier Dye returned from leave on the 16th and read the petition presented by the SAA officers, he discussed it with British officials and concluded that he had no alternative but to risk of loss of esteem and suspend four of the colonels two days later on the grounds that they had used the incorrect channels to raise their concerns. He left his Deputy, Colonel Buraik, in post. Lack of urgency at the Federal Ministry of Defence and the impact of the Big Lie unsettled the SAA and SAP. Reports from the Bir Fuqum training camp in Little Aden and from Lake Lines indicated unrest and unease; and a plot by disloyal officers to seize the Bir Fuqum Armoury was compromised by a loyal officer and the keys sent to HQ 24th Infantry Brigade. Allegations of mutiny were rejected as spurious and not passed to Middle East Command. The consequences of these reports not being collated led to the most significant failure during the Aden Emergency.

Strikes led to the closure of the port, which quickly affected trade and the delivery and despatch of equipment for the civil community and the Services. This led on 19 June to the Military Support Organisation being formed under command of Commander, Royal Corps of Transport, HQ Middle East Command.

On the same day, Secretary of State for Foreign Affairs George Brown acknowledged in the House of Commons that South Arabia had been adversely affected by Egyptian ambitions and that defeat there would undoubtedly resonate throughout the Middle East and could also cause a breakdown of relationships between Arab states. He announced that the Federal Government had been informed that independence 'should come about on 9 January 1968 — this is the earliest practical date after 1 January because of the Moslem period of Ramadan and the religious events which follow it'. In a departure from government policy, he announced that after W-Day, a force of V-Bombers based in Bahrain and a Royal Navy squadron stationed in the region for six months would support the Federation. Based on this announcement, HQ Middle East Command set W-Day as 20 November, a notice of six months.

Dining with Major General Tower and other senior officers during the evening of the 19th, a dinner at which unrest among the Arab forces and police was discussed, was Lieutenant Colonel Mitchell, now commanding 1st Argyll and Sutherland Highlanders, which was normally part of 2nd Infantry Brigade and based at Seaton Barracks in Plymouth. After returning from a successful tour in Borneo, the Battalion was now threatened with disbandment. Mitchell had been in command since December 1966 and had arrived with an advance party of 126 men on 8 June, scheduled to rotate with the Royal Northumberland Fusiliers in Crater. He was determined that the Argylls would not be disbanded. His view on Aden had not changed since his visits in the spring and he criticized the internal security strategy in an interview on the British Forces Broadcasting Service, describing it as 'the least buttoned-up place I know'.

CHAPTER FOURTEEN

20 June 1967

A t 7 am on 20 June, as Algeria called for a general strike among Arab nations, the NLF denounced attempts by Britain to hand over responsibility for the security of Aden to the SAA and 'summoned Arab officers to resist this imperialist plot'. At about the same time, Sergeant Martin Forde of the QDG Air Flight flew Lance Corporal Jim Keighley and Fusilier John Duffy, both Royal Northumberland Fusiliers, to an OP on Temple Cliffs, overlooking Crater from the west, with instructions that they would be collected at midday.

Champion Lines

At about 8 am, three Bedford lorries containing 36 soldiers commanded by Captain Peter Godwin, from 60 Squadron RCT based in Normandy Lines, arrived at the Rifle Ranges half a mile east of Radfan Lines for their monthly practice and waited for a party from the RAF Regiment to depart. At 9.15 am, about half of the RCT had completed their practice and left in a Bedford. The rest of the squadron was on operations in Radfan.

Rumours had been circulating in the South Arabian Army Lake Lines, on the southern fringe of Sheikh Othman, that four colonels had been dismissed. They were, in fact, still suspended, but the psychology of the Big Lie had induced tensions resulting in tribal rivalries and the collapse of discipline. At about 10 am, as more rumours spread that an attack by British troops was imminent, about 300 FNG 2 police recruits in Champion Lines barricaded the gates, seized weapons from the Armoury and, distributing some of 15,000 rounds of ammunition loaded on a 3-tonner, then deployed to defend the barracks. When a Bren gunner sent to the base minaret opened fire on Radfan Camp and RAF Khormaksar, and Second Lieutenant Angus Young was killed while he was deploying the Defence Platoon provided by 13 Platoon, D Company, 1st Lancashires in Radfan Camp. Major General Tower, as Security Commander, instructed that fire was not to be opened unless absolutely necessary, just in case the news that British troops were shooting at Arab soldiers and police might lead to attacks on British civilians. In fact, rumours were already circulating that troops had opened fire. During the morning, Tower moved with a Tactical HQ to Seedaseer Lines. At about 10.15am, a police officer and his driver sent to investigate the disturbances at Champion Lines were shot dead, as was Hugh Alexander of the Public Works Department, as he was driving past.

The remaining RCT on the ranges had finished live firing, and when one of the two Bedfords could not be extracted from mud, three soldiers were left to guard it, while the remaining nineteen climbed into the remaining lorry; one man armed with a rifle rode shotgun behind the cab. The driver was following the metalled road to the junction in front of the main gate at Champion Lines, also taken by the two lorries earlier in the day, and when about 100 metres from the barracks firing was heard. Initially, this was thought to be from the new range inside the barracks, until Staff Sergeant Butler, who was para-trained, recognized that it was an ambush and ordered the driver to drive through. But the Bedford's engine was quickly damaged, and as it came to a halt, everyone except two wounded drivers baled out and took cover. About 20 metres to the left of the track were several hillocks of a Muslim cemetery. Since this offered some shelter, Captain Godwin ordered his men to use graves, but several were wounded as they scrambled for cover. Second Lieutenant Nick Beard recalled:

> I remained with the vehicle with a group of three men in order to get some ammunition off the vehicle. We took it round from the tail to

Schematic sketch of the ambush on 60 Squadron RCT on 20 June 1967 (Courtesy of Colonel Nick Beard)

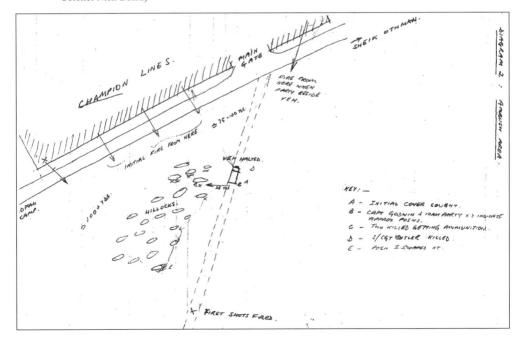

the right rear wheel to sort it out and also change mags. By now, we had come under enfilade fire.

Two of the men were killed and one was badly wounded. Beard threw a bandolier to the soldiers taking cover behind the graves, and Butler suggested that two men should make for Check Point Charlie. Beard again:

> I realized the best hope was for me to make my way to Radfan Camp since the hillocks were in that direction. I ran over to Capt. Godwin to tell him and took another another bandolier. As I reached him . . . I felt that I had been hit in the right thigh as my leg kicked back automatically.

Spread out among the hillocks, the RCT were under continuous automatic fire from three Bren guns and rifles being fired down from the 8ft perimeter wall of the barracks. Their hillocks were between 18ins and 3ft high, and anyone raising his head to take an aimed shot risked being killed or wounded. Captain Godwin later wrote that, in his opinion, the mosque loudspeaker was used to encourage those in Champion Lines:

> During this period when we were returning the fire, we received our maximum casualties. I therefore ordered those that were still able to reload and to stop returning fire and that they were to choose the best possible positions and keep still. From this time onwards, we received no further casualties or injured.

Loudspeakers from the camp mosque seemed to be directing fire, and helicopters flying from RAF Khormaksar at about 500ft about 20 minutes after the ambush ignored the soldiers waving their berets to attract attention.

Shocked by the reports from Champion Lines, the Federal Government requested HQ Aden Brigade to restore order and protect the lives of the seconded British and loyal Arabs and their families inside. Brigadier Jefferies agreed and, at about 10.30 am, Lieutenant Colonel Walsh instructed his Stand-By Company, C Company, 1st Kings Own Border Regiment, commanded by Major David Miller, to secure the Guard Room and Armoury at Champion Lines and gave him 5th Troop, A Squadron, QDG, commanded by Second Lieutenant Nigel Jenkins. Miller and his men dismounted from a Saracen intending to contact senior officers in Champion Lines, but came under fire. Fifteen minutes later, Walsh ordered C Company to move without Miller, but as the Bedford 3-tonners approached the perimeter, Private

Anthony Ferguson, the GPMG gunner of the leading vehicle, was killed and eight others were wounded. Although confused by the fact that police officers were shooting at them, discipline held as the soldiers found cover, still withholding fire. Major Miller appeared and instructed Second Lieutenant Tony Davidson, commanding 10 Platoon, to reinforce the defence of the Guard Room, which was near the main gate and in loyalist hand. Meanwhile, the Battalion Chaplain, the Revd Robin Roe, had driven the 400 yards from Radfan Camp intent on helping with casualties; however, when his Land Rover came under fire from Champion Lines, an officer told him to return to camp. Roe was an Irishman who had served as a priest in Dublin before joining the British Army. Sergeant Frank Roberts attended the casualties and, deciding that one needed urgent treatment by the Regimental Medical Officer, asked for volunteers to transfer him to Radfan Camp. Lance Corporal Vickers, an RCT driver attached to C Company, volunteered along with Private Dickenson, but their lorry came under fire and the latter was wounded. The remaining casualties were evacuated by 5th Troop. Meanwhile, Major General Tower had moved with a Tactical HQ to Seedaseer Lines.

There were other outbreaks of unrest. The Federal Operational Planning Committee was meeting in Al Ittihad when several junior police officers rampaged through the Government buildings, tore down the Union and Federal flags and threatened staff and visitors. The Minister of Internal Security, Sultan Saleh, quelled the unrest by summoning senior police officers and telling them to show leadership. As rumours escalated that the British had fired on Arab soldiers in Champion Lines, tension escalated and a mob stormed the prison in Crater, releasing several hundred prisoners, most of them convicted criminals. In the Armed Police Barracks next door, the police armed themselves and took up positions on the perimeter. Superintendent Muhammad Ibrahim, their commander, was absent, and a feeble attempt was made by Assistant Commissioner of Police Sayed Hadi to calm the situation. He had links to the NLF.

At about midday, the trapped RCT under fire from Champion Lines watched as a Saladin armoured car using the road in front of the barracks came under fire. About twenty minutes later, other armoured vehicles engaged Champion Lines which gave a few RCT the chance to fire a few rounds. At about 1 pm contact was made with an armoured car, which evacuated two wounded and lent a Light Machine Gun. Fifteen minutes later, the same Saladin returned, which drew fire from Champion Lines. At 1.30 pm, Captain Godwin refused an instruction from an Arab Army officer to lay down their weapons 'until such time as ordered by a British officer'. The mosque had been ordering 'Stop firing!' which was spasmodically obeyed. The arrival of

2nd Troop, Queen's Dragoon Guards had given Major Miller additional armoured support and by about 1.30 pm, C Company had broken into Champion Lines, without firing a shot, and in spite of provocation from the mutineers, had secured the armoury and restored order. At about 3 pm, a Saladin and three Humber 1-ton 'Pigs' commanded by Lieutenant Edward Loden, the 1st Para Intelligence Officer, then drove to the RCT and everyone piled into them. Beard:

> The scene inside on our way back round to Khormaksar Beach Hospital would have been like Dante's Inferno to someone from outside as we had bodies on the floor, but it was sheer bliss to be safe at the time! . . . Because of the numbers of wounded that day, several people could not be operated on until after midnight and the surgeons were operating after 3 am.

Seven RCT had been killed, including the inspirational Staff Sergeant Butler, and six were wounded. Driver Galsworthy, who had been shot in the stomach, died during the night. When the Bedford was recovered next day, it had 147 entry holes and 129 exits.

Crater

Meanwhile, the internal security situation among the Federal security forces had become sufficiently serious for Brigadier Jefferies to raise the Alert State to 'Red'.

At Waterloo Lines at midday, 1st Royal Northumberland Fusiliers were on the parade square for their farewell parade by Admiral Le Fanu, before formally handing over to 1st Argyll and Sutherland Highlanders. Indeed, the advance guard had left Aden and Z Company was in the gym, weapons handed in, wearing civilian clothes and waiting to board their long-haul aircraft at RAF Khormaksar. Supported by A Squadron, Queen's Dragoon Guards commanded by Major Tony Shewen, the Battalion had kept a firm control of Crater over the nine months and had recently established a series of sandbagged *sangars* at strategic junctions and positions to restrict terrorist movement, dominate the district and prevent rioting and arson. The picquet at Al Mansoura was attacked several times.

As Admiral Le Fanu arrived, Blenkinsop was advised from his Operations Room that the Alert State had been raised to Red. He immediately instructed Captain Nigel Robinson, his Intelligence Officer, to order Y Company, the Crater Operational Company, to regroup at the Crater operating base at the Marine Drive car park and to occupy Main Pass. Corporal Ken Coxon had

Tasks allocated to the platoons of Y Company,
1st Royal Northumberland Fusiliers on 20 June 1967

TIMINGS		7 Pl (Stand By)	8 Pl	9 Pl	Sp Pl	Recce	Remarks
06.30	13.30	Supreme Court Guard					
07.30	08.00	Civil Protection	Immediate Notice		15 Mins Notice		½ Tp QDG
07.30	08.30			Road Block Main Pass			
08.00	08.45	Immediate Notice when in camp	Anti-arson OPs and patrols		15 Mins Notice		1 Pig ½ Tp QDG
09.00	10.00				Leave 08.45 F + S Area NE Side, Queen Arwa Rd	APB	
10.00	11.00	Khormaksar patrols					O Group 11.15
12.45	18.30	Immediate Notice when in camp	Immediate Notice	Anti-arson OPs and patrols	15 Mins Notice		1 Pig ½ Tp QDG
13.30	14.00	Civil Protection					½ Tp QDG
15.00	16.00				Road Block Main Pass		
17.00	18.00		F + S Area E				
18.30	23.30			15 Mins Notice	Anti-arson OPs and patrols		1 Pig 5 RTR
21.30			9.30 Road Block Main Pass				
19.00	23.59	Cantonment Patrols					
23.59	06.00	Khormaksar patrols					

Source: Transposed from a copy of original document provided courtesy of Jim Carroll

just arrived on duty in the Battalion Operations Room, as one of two signallers, when Lieutenant Colonel Blenkinsop ordered his Battalion on his command net, 'Do not go to Armed Police Barracks. I say again, do not go to Armed Police Barracks.'

About the same time, as planned, Sergeant Forde collected the Temple Cliffs OP and, during the seven-minute flight to Waterloo Lines, had noted that buses were being used to barricade the entrances to Crater. Lance Corporal Keightley also reported unusual activity inside Armed Police Barracks to Battalion HQ.

Y Company, commanded by Major John Moncur, had been protecting the Jewish sector in Crater since the Six Day War from an expected backlash after the Arab defeat. It was supported by 4th Troop, A Squadron, Queen's Dragoon Guards commanded by Second Lieutenant Stevens. Attached to it was a small advance guard from D Company, 1st Argyll and Sutherland

Highlanders commanded by Major Bryan Malcolm. Accompanying 8 Platoon, which was commanded by Second Lieutenant John Davis, was Second Lieutenant Donald Campbell-Baldwin. The platoon was on 'Immediate Notice' for tasking.

Although Crater was generally quiet, Davis had earlier removed a roadblock. When he was instructed to remove two small buses blocking Queen Arwa Road near the Armed Police Barracks, he, Campbell-Baldwin and Fusiliers Harry Wiltshire and Phil Millan pushed them to the side; however, in doing so, Campbell-Baldwin cut himself badly. At the Marine Drive car park, Major Malcolm and his remaining three platoon commanders were gathered around in his Land Rover. Lieutenant David Riddick was commanding Support Platoon:

> Before John Moncur could brief us and give us our orders, we heard the voice of John Davis (on his radio) saying: 'The Armed Police are behaving strangely and several of them seem to have taken up positions on the rooftops overlooking Queen Arwa Road. I have spoken to an Inspector I know and cannot get an answer from him as to what is going on.'

When the 'Do not go to Armed Police Barracks' order arrived, it was acknowledged by Major Moncur, but not Davis. Riddick again:

> John Moncur grabbed the microphone and asked c/s 32 (Davis) to acknowledge last from 9 (the commanding officer). There was no reply, so John Moncur repeated his message. When there was still no reply, John then said that he must go and ensure John Davis had heard the instruction from the CO and was complying.

Under normal circumstances, if transmissions were not acknowledged immediately, the Operations Room signallers arranged for the message to be relayed through another call sign. With the surrounding volcanic crags and labyrinth of streets and alleys, communications in Crater were difficult. When Riddick later asked why the signallers had not organised this, he was told by a signaller that the commanding officer was manning the Operations Room radio. Meanwhile Davis had decided to return to Marine Drive by taking the safe route through Khormaksar, but this meant that radio transmissions were screened by the hills. Campbell-Baldwin returned to Waterloo Lines for stitches to his injuries.

With nothing heard from Davis, Moncur was anxious about him and instructed his Tactical HQ of three Fusiliers and a Recce Platoon Land Rover being used by Major Malcolm to mount up. To allow Corporal Bob Nesbit, normally Moncur's driver, to do some last-minute shopping before returning to England, the Y Company Sergeant Major Peter Hoare replaced him. With Malcolm in his Land Rover were two Argylls and Lance Corporal Liddell and Fusilier John Storey. Storey had handed in most of his kit and was standing on the veranda of his accommodation block when he was asked if he would join Moncur. Bored because the Argylls were now taking over from his Battalion, he changed into uniform and joined both vehicles shortly before they set off for Main Pass via Khormaksar.

Meanwhile, A Section, 8 Platoon commanded by Corporal Morris Dixon was making its way past the Armed Police Barracks toward the Main Pass, after a long patrol in Crater, intending to link up with Second Lieutenant Davis. As the two Land Rovers entered Queen Arwa Road from Main Pass at about 12.45, several occupants saw part of the section on one side of the road, and, as recalled by Lance Corporal Jim Carroll, the section radio operator, the soldiers waved at each other. Carroll was also a member of the Commander-in-Chief's close escort when Admiral Le Fanu visited the troops. Storey believes that Moncur, although not having seen Davis but assured that A Section was not near the Armed Police Barracks, then intended to turn around at the junction of Queen Arwa Road and the street leading to the Armed Police Barracks and return to Main Pass. But as the Land Rovers negotiated the junction, the Armed Police believed they were about to be attacked and opened fire. Moncur's vehicle careered into the corner wall of the barracks while Malcolm's crashed into the central dual carriageway island. Both caught fire. Trapped by crossfire from the barracks and gunmen in the married quarters opposite, the surviving soldiers stood little chance. Fusilier Storey, armed with a Sterling sub-machine gun, wounded in his left forearm and his side creased by a bullet, abandoned the slender shelter of the kerb and dashed into the married quarters and ran upstairs to the first floor where he dressed his arm with a handkerchief. He noticed that his colleagues were motionless, apart from a soldier still firing until he was shot. Making his way to the roof, he shot an Arab armed with a rifle. A second Arab took cover behind a wall.

Riddick was standing with Second Lieutenants David Waterworth and Jonathan Shaw, of 7 and 9 Platoons respectively, outside the Supreme Court when they heard the shooting. Riddick:

> David Waterworth and John Shaw then pointed out that if anything had happened to John Moncur, I was the senior officer and should take charge. This was a situation which I had never envisaged before and the reality of the situation took me by surprise.

His only remit was not to go to the Armed Police Barracks. Hearing nothing from Moncur, he then asked a Queen's Dragoon Guards lance corporal commanding a Ferret at the entrance of Supreme Court drive if he had heard anything from Moncur, but he had not. Acting quickly, Lieutenant Riddick assumed command and appointed his Platoon Sergeant, Sergeant Lowe, to act as Company Sergeant Major, then instructed Corporal Colin Pick, who had proven himself a natural leader, to take command of his Support Platoon. Davis then re-appeared in his Armoured Bedford and when Riddick flagged him down and told him of the gunfire:

> I asked him, as he had armour, if he could put his head round the corner and see if could see Moncur's two Land Rovers and to return immediately as I was assuming the worst and taking command of the Company.

He expected Davis to do this from the area of the Chartered Bank; however, Davis had arranged to meet Corporal Dixon's section at Main Pass and take them to Waterloo Lines. Riddick had just returned to Company HQ when Fusilier Duffy reported that the Sioux helicopter taking the OP to Temple Cliffs had crashed near the landing site and he had two casualties. Within a short time after returning the OP to Waterloo Lines, Forde was instructed to return it to the Cliffs and took off with Lance Corporal Keightley lying in the external wire basket and Fusilier Duffy inside with their A41 radio. As Forde flew over Queen Arwa Road at about 700 feet at about 12.50, he reported two burning Land Rovers outside the Armed Police Barracks and people throwing something into the flames; but as he approached Temple Cliffs, the Sioux staggered under automatic ground fire from below. Keightley:

> I looked up to the pilot when there was a big bang by my head. A bullet had gone through the canopy of the helicopter and shot the pilot through the knee. We were just about to land when somebody shot the rear rotor blade and, of course, at that point it went into a spin and we crashed into a gully. Both my legs were hanging off below the knee.

Although Forde retained control of the helicopter, a skid caught the edge of a ravine and it slid to the bottom of a gully on its belly and caught fire. Duffy pulled the pilot and Keightley from the flames and, recovering a rifle and the radio, reported the crash. The military artist, Terence Cuneo, depicted his actions. The pilot of another Sioux that passed overhead reported that no one could have survived the crash; nevertheless, a Wessex later landed several Royal Marines, who collected Duffy and the two wounded. Duffy was awarded the Distinguished Conduct Medal. Keightley lost a leg, not both as suggested in the Battalion Log. Lieutenant Riddick:

> This was beyond my ability to respond to and Battalion HQ were asked to undertake the recovery of all three, though I seem to recall that I was involved with Fusilier Duffy in trying to establish exactly where the helicopter had crashed.

In the belief that the Armed Police and the NFL were taking advantage of the situation, Riddick consolidated the security of Crater by sending Support Platoon to secure the Supreme Court and also insert OPs on Temple Cliffs. He instructed 9 Platoon to secure Main Pass while 7 Platoon was to support 8 Platoon patrols leaving Crater. He later radioed Captain Peter Marr, usually the Motor Transport Officer and acting Y Company second-in-command, for extra ammunition.

At about 12.20 pm, Second Lieutenant Davis had linked up with A Section at Main Pass, where Lance Corporal Carroll advised him of instruction from Lieutenant Colonel Blenkinsop not to go to the Armed Police Barracks. Almost simultaneously, heavy gunfire was heard from Queen Arwa Road, Without advising Lieutenant Riddick, when he had asked for volunteers from A Section to support Major Moncur, everyone volunteered. Leaving the section A41 radio with Sergeant David Holliday, his highly experienced Platoon Sergeant, and Corporal Dixon at Main Pass with orders to pass information to Company HQ, he and A Section mounted his Armoured Bedford, which was being driven by Fusilier Joe Wells. As Wells approached the Armed Police Barracks, it came under heavy fire and was hit several times, Davis stopped about 70 yards from the filling station opposite them, seemingly intending to return to his radio at Main Pass and wait for orders, but the wheels and tyres of the Armoured Bedford had been badly damaged and, probably following the military principle of keeping in contact with the enemy, he ordered A Section to dismount and instructed Lance Corporals Keith Kelly and Carroll to give close protection to the vehicle. Davis and Fusiliers Leslie Stewart and Thomas Smythe ran into married quarters while Fusilier Walter Crombie took cover near a post box.

The Supreme Court road block was also coming under fire. Riddick:

> Cpl Pick came on the radio and reported that Support Platoon were now in firing positions overlooking Crater and that he had clear observation of the Armed Police Barracks which seemed to be the focal point for the enemy, as well as the rooftops of the buildings either side of Queen Arwa Road.

The Platoon soon became engaged in several firefights against gunmen on rooftops in the vicinity of the Armed Police Barracks.

Meanwhile, Wells had coaxed his damaged Armoured Bedford past the Armed Police Barracks and returned to Marine Drive, where he learnt from Corporal Len Howe, from the Motor Transport Platoon, that Second Lieutenant Shaw was about to investigate what was happening at the Armed Police Barracks, rescue any survivors and recover any bodies. Wells replied, 'You deviant! Want to be going in there. It's just pure hell.' Wells had also driven the Armoured Bedford when Davis and his party had pushed the two buses left as a road block across Queen Arwa Road. At about 12.30 pm, escorted by Second Lieutenant Stephens in his Saladin and with a Ferret, Shaw entered Queen Arwa Road with members of his platoon in an Armoured Bedford driven by Howe. Passing the Chartered Bank, he was on the right lane of the carriageway while the two Queen's Dragoon Guards vehicles were in the left lane:

> When we drew level with the Barracks, we received heavy rifle and automatic fire. I was then ordered to drive into the petrol station opposite with the intention, I think, of dropping a patrol but the fire was so extreme, I was ordered to drive away from the petrol station without dropping off anyone. Bullets were coming through the hatches and bouncing round inside the vehicle. One burst right in front of me. As we pulled back onto the road, when Lieutenant Shaw and I saw metal bars across the road, he told me to drive straight through them which I did with caution, as I thought they may be wires stretched across the road. My wheels and tyres were completely shot out. I managed to make it to the Main Pass car park.

Although the .30in Browning machine gun and the turret cupola on Lieutenant Stephen's armoured car were badly damaged, his request to use his 76mm main armament in proportionate retaliation to suppress the fire from the Barracks was rejected by HQ Aden Brigade. The three vehicles pushed on past the Barracks and reached Main Pass where Shaw's men took up defensive positions. During the action, the Saladin took casualties from shots fired into the turret from above, and the driver drove straight to the RAF hospital at Steamer Point. Shaw's men and Howe waited at Main Pass for 90 minutes until Fusilier Sammy Lines, from the Battalion Light Aid Detachment, arrived to change the wheels and tyres. After Howe had then delivered Shaw back to Marine Drive, at about 3 pm, Lieutenant Riddick ordered him to return Main Pass and provide an armoured vehicle for a 45 Commando troop, who were now in control of Main Pass. He remained with them until about 6.30 pm, and when the Royal Marines were about to attack a Turkish fort, from which fire was coming, Howe asked the troop officer he could have an escort to Waterloo Lines; however, the Royal Marine was unable to provide anyone and therefore he returned on his own. At Waterloo Lines, he was met by a Regimental Policeman who asked him if he was aware of what had happened in Crater and, by the way, where was his escort? Howe's reply was 'very angry'. Howe then showed the policeman that the left hand side of his vehicle had been stripped of its paint by bullets and the inside pitted with skidding marks of ricochets.

The second attempt by 1st Troop, Queen's Dragoon Guards commanded by Lieutenant Everitt, ended when intense fire smashed the gun sight of his Saladin, the flying glass temporarily blinding him. The power steering and brakes were degraded when a hydraulic pipe was sliced by a bullet. The driver's episcope was also damaged.

Meanwhile, the Armed Police had captured Second Lieutenant Davis and his group. Fusilier Storey eventually ran out of ammunition. Unaware of the treachery of the Armed Police, he went downstairs and, seeing a policeman, called across the road to him, only for him to fire at Storey. Running upstairs and encountering an Arab holding a baby in a third-floor doorway, he entered the flat and marshalled some women and children into a back room. After several hours, an Arab warned him that the Armed Police were searching the building, and he hid in a ground floor alcove between the flats and cliffs but he was captured by a policeman, who shielded him from a hostile crowd by firing his SMG; he then took Storey into the Barracks where he faced further demands that he be killed. He was then put into the front of an Armoured Bedford, which was driven to the two smouldering Land Rovers, where several bodies were thrown into the back. When a crowd, which included a civilian carrying a GPMG, again demanded that Storey be killed, the police and the mob argued, until a burst of fire from Main Pass dispersed the crowd.

Z Company had been mobilised by Lieutenant Colonel Blenkinsop and at about 3.30pm, it passed through Y Company on its way to protect expatriates living at Ras Marshag, avoiding entering Crater by using the beach. Lieutenant Colonels Blenkinsop and Mitchell personally sought permission from HQ Aden Brigade to search for Second Lieutenant Davis and his patrol, however HQ Middle East Command was wrestling with conflicting political and military considerations.

At a tense mid-afternoon conference chaired by the acting Commander-in-Chief, Air Vice-Marshal Andrew Humphrey, the delegates knew the following:

- Nine soldiers, two police officers and a British civilian had been killed and seventeen wounded by fire from Champion Lines.
- 14 soldiers were missing in Crater.
- Crater was a 'no go' area.
- The credibility of the Federal Security Forces, in particular the Armed Police, lay in tatters.
- The fragility of the Federation had been exposed when the NLF ousted the Amir of Dhala.

Brigadier Charles Dunbar, Brigadier General Staff, advocated that Crater should not be entered, because he felt that a confrontation with Federal security forces would be disastrous for the future of the Federation, particularly as Middle East Command was working towards transferring security in November. In addition, an operation could jeopardize the safety of British expatriates elsewhere in the Federation and Al Hithad, and of 400 Service dependants still at Ma'alla. Indeed, rumours that the British had attacked Champion Lines had reached the SAA in Lahej and Mukeiras, and frantic efforts were being made to find and brief Brigadier Dye of the facts. The conference agreed the troops should be briefed on the situation, particularly as there was anger that Federal security forces had been 'the enemy'.

At about 6 pm, Captain Marr took command of Y Company from Lieutenant Riddick. At about 9.25 pm, during a truce agreed between Commissioner of Police Owen and Superintendent Ibrahaim, the Armed Police drove a flatbed lorry containing the eight bodies, the remains of three of them in tea chests, from the two Land Rovers and that of Second Lieutenant Davis to within 100 yards of the Chartered Bank. But as Squadron Sergeant Major Pringle, who had taken command of 1st Troop, warily approached it accompanied by a Saracen, a Blindicide missile glanced off his Saladin's glacis plate and a second one exploded in a shop. Corporal Pick proved particularly effective in ensuring his platoon put down as much covering fire as possible as the two vehicles withdrew under fire. Riddick:

> We immediately returned fire on the firing position and the Saladin and Saracen withdrew. We were now coming under fire and one of my men was hit in the arm. Colonel Blenkinsop came on the radio and asked me and my Platoon to stay there in position overnight. When I replied that we had just taken a casualty (hit in the arm) he ordered me to withdraw.

By midnight, the Battalion had regained control of Crater by blocking Main Pass and Marine Road. In the south, G (SAS) Squadron patrols lurking in

Jebel Shamsan dominated the main path. The Squadron had been formed in Borneo to give the SAS further flexibility and often drew soldiers from the Household Division. The water supply was cut. Inside, the NLF's control of the district had dissolved into anarchy as conventional law and order collapsed. Criminals released from the prison provided the NLF with a band of foot soldiers to neutralize and intimidate opponents. Schools, several banks and the Legislative Council were ransacked, and commerce ebbed elsewhere. Law and order, the disposal of rubbish and cleaning of streets ceased.

Second Lieutenant Beard recalled next day:

The BBC World Service had announced . . . that due to an unfortunate mistake, Arab troops opened fire on British [they thought were] attacking their camp. The idea that it was due to their thinking we were attacking them that resulted in the ambush, which seems to have been accepted by people, I find hard to understand.

CHAPTER FIFTEEN

The Reoccupation of Crater

Next day, at about 9 am, after a joint strike mission at Wadi Bana, four Hawker Hunters from 8 Squadron and two from 43 Squadron were instructed to conduct a low level 'flagwave' over the Armed Police Barracks before landing at RAF Khormaksar. One of the pilots recalled:

> Since during my first tour in Aden 1959–61 my family and I had lived in a flat in Crater opposite the Police Barracks for a month or so, I knew the place well and was keen to 'take it out', as although we had used our rockets, we still had plenty of 30 mm. However, we were not permitted to fire.

One aircraft suffered six hits from a Bren gun.

Lieutenant Colonel Blenkinsop thanked his soldiers and told them that he had been temporarily relieved of his command. He emphasized that the Armed Police and their families had been helped in various ways, for instance the Regimental Medical Officer had treated family members; yet their treachery had been unexpected.

During the afternoon, X Company, 45 Commando, under command of the Royal Northumberland Fusiliers, supported the Fusiliers and the QDGs by winkling gunmen from their positions in the volcanic rim above Crater, shooting four men as they ran from a Turkish fort. Corporal Terry Beal, of Y Company, was shot in the head while on High Mansuri Ridge; nevertheless, he recovered and stayed with his Battalion in a non-combat role, until he was discharged after twenty-two years' service. HQ Middle East Command authorised a Saladin to fire a single 75m round at a stronghold, and the Royal Marines used a Carl Gustav anti-tank launcher to clear a sniper from a house, a decision that raised the credibility of a headquarters that had lost some respect for its perceived inaction the previous day. The Royal Marines took over the Main Pass roadblock from 9 Platoon and spent the next four days checking 6,000 people and their donkeys, camels, sheep and goats, in order to deny the passage of weapons and suspects. The Royal Marines were supplied by 60 Squadron manpacking ammunition, water and rations. OPs on the rim watched the anarchy below unfold, as the NLF claimed that the '20 June Uprising' had shown that the Arabs, as a nation, had rebounded after the defeat of the Six Day War. Snipers such as Lance Corporal Tilley and Marine Harrison, using L42 rifles fitted with L1 Sighting Telescope, which gave accuracy up to 1,000 yards, dominated the streets and alleys and accounted for fifteen armed terrorists, at the cost of twenty-four rounds. The NLF responded by moving buses to provide cover and firing Blindicides at suspected snipers,

During the morning, after seeing Fusilier Wells leave in his damaged Armoured Bedford, Lance Corporals Carroll and Kelly turned up at Waterloo Barracks, after being thought killed. Concealed in rocks overlooking the Armed Police Barracks, they had seen Second Lieutenant Davis being dragged around Crater behind a Land Rover and the three missing Fusiliers, one of them unconscious, being taken to the fish market and dismembered on a slab. They made a pact not to tell anyone until the parents of the three had died. After it became apparent that a search party was not forthcoming, during the night the two NCOs made their way to Ma'alla where they then hijacked a taxi. They were debriefed first by Lieutenant Colonel Blenkinsop and then by Admiral Le Fanu and Major General Tower at HQ Middle East Command.

Meanwhile, Fusilier Storey had been located. An agreement reached between Commissioner of Police Peter Owen and Superintendent Mohammad Ibrahaim led to Flight Lieutenant Scott Russell-Martin, the duty medical officer at RAF Khormaksar, three RAF Nursing Attendants and an RAF Police corporal, reporting to the Main Pass car park where they were transferred to an Army ambulance. The Press were very much in evidence. Among the group was Nursing Attendant Corporal Donavan Slaven:

> We were escorted into Crater by a vehicle with armed men on board
> with their weapons trained on the ambulance. Being in the back of the
> vehicle with the Army medic, I could not make out what uniform, if
> any, the occupants of the escorting vehicle were wearing. On the way
> in, Dr Russell-Martin saw some armed men on rooftops and asked the
> RAF policeman, who had a Sterling sub-machine gun, to 'cover
> them'. The policeman refused and secreted the weapon . . . I felt that
> if the weapon had been discovered by one of our escorts, the outcome
> of this journey would have been very different. We were taken past
> the vehicles that had been ambushed which were still alight and
> smoking. We arrived at the Police barracks in Crater and pulled up
> next to two military trucks. The tailgate of the nearest truck to the
> ambulance was open and the bodies of the ambushed

Northumberland Fusiliers could be seen. They were very bloody and appeared to have been mutilated.

Russell-Martin then found Fusilier Storey and explained to a police officer that since he now had a wounded soldier, he could not take the bodies and attempted to negotiate their removal, but this was brusquely rejected. Meanwhile, a large, hostile crowd had appeared from a side street, some of whom flicked cigarettes on to the bodies. The Armed Police levelled their weapons and the crowd quickly dispersed. The medics were then escorted back to Main Pass where Storey was transferred to RAF Hospital Steamer Point in an Army vehicle.

After dark, during another truce agreed between Commissioner of Police Owen and Superintendent Ibrahaim, Armed Police left the flatbed containing the five bodies and three tea chests near the Roman Catholic School. Fearing a trap, a Saladin covered several Fusiliers in a Saracen, including Lance Corporals Carroll and Kelly, as a tow rope was attached to the lorry and it was dragged it a safer place. The bodies were then transferred to RAF Hospital Steamer Point where Lieutenant Colonels Blenkinsop and Mitchell formally identified them before RAF pathologists searched for cause of death. Second Lieutenant Davis was recorded as having died from a blow to his head. Assistant Commissioner of Police Hadi then reported shortly after midnight that the bodies of the three missing Fusiliers had been dumped outside the Zakku coffee shop in Maidan Square. At about 7.15 am next day, 22 June, Inspector Abdulla Yafai retrieved them from a lawless mob of men who had set them alight, and they also were taken Steamer Point where RAF pathologists had considerable difficulty in concluding causes of death. Identification was by a process of elimination.

It was now confirmed that twenty-two British soldiers had died on 20 June, four of them brutally murdered. The press corps, with its usual lack of sensitivity and little regard for the relatives, published sensational accounts of events in Crater. Two journalists claimed to have been inside the district. In spite of the outrage and political hand-wringing, discipline held, as it always did, and would do so in spite of political and media provocation. Lieutenant Colonel Blenkinsop explained why Crater was not being attacked in his *Background to Present Situation*:

It would obviously require a Brigade assault using all weapons to retake Crater under the present circumstances. This is unacceptable because of the enormous casualties that would be suffered by both military and ordinary peaceful civilians.

Fighting in built-up areas rapidly sucks in troops, as the Army would again discover three years later in Northern Ireland; however the events of these days had led to a near-total breakdown of trust in the reliability of the Federal security forces. Y Company remained at the Supreme Court for three days, with occasional returns to Waterloo Lines for a meal and replenishment of water. An Argyll sergeant defied his Battalion orders to remain in barracks by discreetly joining Support Platoon, usually arriving with a 'doggy bag' from the Argyll cookhouse. Even the Argyll RSM failed to intercept him.

In spite of indignant newspaper and television editors calling for retaliation, Major General Tower was determined that Crater was not a 'no go area' and calmly declared on 23 June, 'It is a deliberate decision by me that we are not going in at the moment, because I do not want to disturb the hot-pot – but we intend to go in some time'. Mindful of the regional politics, the weakness of the Federation and security threats to expatriates, he was aware that the Federal security forces, although collectively deeply ashamed, had been subverted by effective propaganda. Aden Brigade was also overstretched and would be off balance as several units were scheduled to rotate over the next fortnight. With the policy of the High Commission and HQ Middle East Command set at deep caution, Brigadier Dunbar discreetly opened negotiations with senior Federal army and police officers, in the knowledge that several were known to be sympathetic to the NLF, and elicited a promise that reoccupation would not be resisted.

In a moving ceremony on 25 June that received worldwide attention, 24 servicemen and one civilian were buried at the British Military Cemetery at Silent Valley. In addition to the 22 soldiers and one civilian killed on 20 June, a REME sergeant shot in Crater on the 16th and a 1st Para private shot two days later were also buried. The repatriation of dead servicemen to the UK had been possible since March; however, the delay in receiving the bodies and the effects of the heat meant that the burials had to take place immediately. To the sound of an Irish Guards piper playing a lament, the coffins, each covered by a Union Flag, were escorted by a party from the different Regiment and Corps to their graves. A poignant photo taken by the photo-journalist Terry Fincher of a Northumberland Fusilier biting his lip in sorrow was flashed around the world. None of the families were invited, and few have visited since, such is the instability in Yemen.

On the same day, Commissioner Owen spent two hours in Crater persuading the Aden State Police and the Armed Police to re-establish their authority, on the grounds that an initial inquiry ordered by High Commissioner Trevelyan had exonerated the Armed Police of the charge of killing British soldiers such was the political culture of appeasement.

This day, 20 June 1967, is a black one in post-1945 British military history but has long been forgotten, as have most sacrifices made in British counter-insurgency campaigns since 1945. While servicemen accept death and injury as a risk, few accept the mutilation of bodies. In spite of the police witnesses, no one has ever been held to account amid the pain for families, some of whom would never be able to visit the graves. More soldiers were killed that day than on any day since the Korean War, but not by an enemy. Lance Corporal Jim Carroll believes that more would have been killed outside the Armed Police Barracks had it not been for the courage of the APC drivers. Suggestions of a formal inquiry chaired by Aden Chief Justice Sir Roland Le Gallais never materialized; however, political damage limitation included statements not necessarily matching the recollections of some of 'those who were there'. Some statements are unsigned and are similar in style and language. Some have Foreign and Commonwealth Office reference numbers. The testimony of one officer dated 5 July is regarded by him as a concoction. The War Office released an account of events on 20 June, but omitted to comment on the poor radio communications in Crater. It was this factor that had set events in train; it was when Major Moncur had not heard Second Lieutenant Davis reply to his commanding officer's instruction not to go to the Armed Police Barracks that the sequence of events had been set in motion in Crater. The problem is that the official statements add credence to official views, as opposed to the reality, and therefore distort history.

Relatives remain angry but resilient. Mrs Mavis Hoult, the wife of Fusilier George Hoult, had just given birth to their daughter. The wife of Company Sergeant Major Hoare was awarded a widow's pension but it was insufficient to prevent her from having to return to live with her parents. The mother of Fusilier Stewart murdered in the fish market was awarded an annual compensation pension of 11 pence (in 1967), which she thought so derisory that annually, on 20 June, she sent an 11p postal order to the Ministry of Defence. When several soldiers were interviewed by journalists on their return to UK, they were accompanied by 'minders' describing themselves as Foreign and Commonwealth Office officials. Had the twenty-two dead been paraded in coffins covered by Union Flags through the streets of an English town and their deaths properly investigated by a coroner, one suspects the official reaction would have been less of a bureaucratic whitewash. Set against this was the policy of uncontested withdrawal.

Next day, as the Fusiliers formally handed over Crater to the 1st Argyll and Sutherland Highlanders, CSM Pringle advised his counterpart that there was no requirement to bring ammunition as X Company had sufficient to hand over. That afternoon, the Company expended so much in a firefight that the Argylls were advised to bring fresh supplies. Lieutenant Riddick's Support Platoon spent three days on the patrol base on top of a block of flats overlooking the Officers Mess. Riddick:

> I remember hearing a loud 'pop' and one of the sentries calling out that a suspected pistol shot came from the direction of the barracks. I looked at my watch, saw it was 18.00hrs and commented that it was probably Colonel Dick Blenkinsop opening a bottle of champagne to celebrate handing over. On looking down into the Officers Mess, sure enough Colonel Dick was pouring champagne into glasses in front of him.

At 7 pm on the 26th, 1st PWO, the Spearhead Battalion on 72 hours notice, was ordered to deploy to Aden – its third tour. Within three hours, Tactical HQ and C Company had left Colchester for RAF Lyneham, followed by the remainder of the Battalion at two-hour intervals. Major D.C. Hall, the Unit Emplaning Officer, helped RAF Movements with flight details, and at midday, four Transport Command Britannias left with the remainder of the Battalion; other absentees and 'sick on leave' following during the night. The Battalion moved into eight blocks of flats in Ma'alla Straight. The atmosphere was very different:

> We found a ghost town with rows of empty blocks of flats, windows banging in the wind, deserted streets and abandoned cars [*The White Rose*, October 1967]

Their arrival gave Brigadier Jefferies the opportunity to reorganize Aden Brigade as follows:

- Sheikh Othman – 1st Paras
- Al Mansoura – 1st Lancashires
- Crater – 1st Argylls and Sutherland Highlanders
- Ma'alla – 1st South Wales Borderers
- Tawahi – 1st Prince of Wales Own
- 45 Commando – reserve

One evening, Lieutenant Richard Fawcus, of 60 Sqn RE and supporting 1 Para, was working on a scheme to protect the Sheikh Othman tower from Blindicides. These rockets were fitted with a fuse on a stalk on their nose so that the correct angle to detonate its shaped charge head could be achieved. His roommate, Second Lieutenant Nick Beard, suggested that if a net was draped in front of the tower, rockets would either be caught in the net or detonate at such a distance as to do little damage. Fawcus developed the suggestion and designed and built a lightweight frame capable of being transported as an underslung load by helicopter and then lowered on to the tower roof with protective wire panels draped around it. This prototype was later developed to protect police stations and OPs in Northern Ireland and armoured vehicles in Afghanistan. Lieutenant Fawcus was awarded a Mention in Despatches for his initiative.

During the course of the next three months, a grenade thrown at a Recce Platoon patrol on 6 August caused several casualties, including Private Philip Davis, wounded so severely that both his legs were amputated. A fortnight later, a gunman murdered Lance Corporal Jeremy Holmes in a post office. On 14 October, when Battalion HQ and four A Company OPs at Tawahi Crescent came under sustained fire, Support Company evacuated the casualties and relieved A Company in contact with the terrorists; C Company then climbed Jebel Shamsan to dominate the district.

Lieutenant Colonel Mitchell was appalled at the humiliation suffered by the British Army and, unaware of the negotiations being conducted by Dunbar, found the appeasement frustrating. In 1965, his Battalion had seen action in Borneo, where Major General Walker had been allowed to attack Indonesian bases in Operation Claret. Instructed by Jefferies to prepare a plan to reoccupy Crater, Mitchell opted for a two-pronged night attack from Marine Drive and from Ras Marsag heights, intending to 'roll up' the commercial core of Crater south of Queen Arwa Road. In support on the high ground would be 45 Commando. Jefferies applied a few adjustments and then sent Mitchell to brief HQ Middle East Command. Major General Tower thought the plan too much for one battalion and, agreeing the Argylls should enter the commercial centre, suggested that 45 Commando should advance from Main Pass and neutralize the threat from the Armed Police. Mitchell thought that this risked friendly-fire incidents in the darkness. The same risk could equally have applied to the advance from Ras Marsag. Brigadier Dunbar intervened to say that he had been assured the Armed Police would not resist. On 29 June, Mitchell issued orders for the operation. H-Hour was set for 7pm on 3 July.

Before he returned to UK for a much-needed period of leave, Brigadier Jefferies issued written orders that recce patrols and OPs could be deployed on specific tasks, Mitchell organized an intensive patrolling programme on the fringes of Crater and concluded from the information collated by his

Intelligence Section that the intelligence picture supplied by Brigade HQ and HQ Middle East Land Forces was pessimistic. Next day, Jefferies transferred command of Aden Brigade to Lieutenant Colonel Peter Downward DFC, who was commanding 1st Lancashires and was the senior commanding officer. During the evening of 29 June, a Blindicide projectile hit a Turkish fort occupied by 5 Troop, Y Company, 45 Commando, temporarily deafening three Royal Marines.

Meanwhile, the Withdrawal was well underway. In January, the Port Security Force had been specially raised from UK-based Royal Military Police to enforce the security of the docks, search ships and dhows and detain rioters, who were usually taken to Little Aden and released for a long walk home. It was commanded by a Royal Navy officer. Naval Task Force 318 began assembling offshore. When another strike was projected to hit Aden, at dawn on 1 July, sailors, Royal Marines and members of the Joint Service Port Unit used Emergency provisions to requisition two tugs, four barges, and three other vessels by nailing orders to their masts or hatches. A second round of requisitions ten days later included water and oil barges. The four RCT Landing Ship Tanks, *Tern, Fulmar*, *Petrel* and *Grebe*, moving stores and vehicles to Bahrein and Masirah, were joined by four Royal Fleet Auxiliary ships, *Lancelot, Galahad, Bedivere* and *Geraint*, and another LCT. Sailors and Royal Marines detachments from Naval Task Force 318 were drafted to help with boat crews. Stevedores were provided by 51 Port Squadron, 45 Commando and the Irish Guards, until 518 Company, Royal Pioneer Corps arrived from the United Kingdom, where they had been unloading ships during the eight-week London dock strike. Unloading cargo nets and storing bales and crates in the holds of ships anchored offshore was hot, airless and uncomfortable work, particularly when the autumn monsoon in August ensured a heavy swell. As the cooler months arrived, shifts rose from four hours to eight. Admiral Le Fanu paid several visits to the port. It is said that on one occasion, when he arrived on a ship unannounced and wearing a shirt without rank badges, shorts, a Royal Marines stable-belt and 'floppy Joe' soft hat, the sergeant in charge of the working party thought he was a Royal Marine and sent him to hump ammunition in the lower hold. When the Admiral took a rest and removed his hat, thereby exposing his fairly red hair, a corporal reminded him, 'Oi, Ginge! Over 'ere! There's plenty of work to do!'

On 2 July, Mitchell decided to visit Corporal Grant's 1 Section, 7 Platoon, B Company, which was at the Supreme Court and in regular contact with the terrorists. Mitchell was driving his Land Rover with his Adjutant manning a GPMG and his bodyguard and two radio operators in the back. In the second vehicle were his escort and radio operators. As the two Land Rovers neared the Court, a trolley loaded with Coca-Cola bottles was pushed across the road behind them. Mitchell rapidly swung his vehicle through a U-turn and, smashing the trolley, launched several hundred spinning bottles, which smashed on the ground and punctured the rear tyres of the second Rover. About a month later, the authorities received a compensation application for 800 bottles of Coca-Cola.

On 3 July, Lieutenant Colonel Mitchell finalized his plan to 'roll up' Crater:

A Company (Major Ian Robertson)
Advance south along the causeway past the School, seize Sirrah Island and secure Banin Street, on which were Treasury and Grindlays Bank. Both buildings were usually guarded by Armed Police.

B Company (Major Patrick Palmer)
• Two platoons supported by A Squadron, QDG to form the Main Body and, using Marine Drive as its axis, to establish a demarcation line 400 yards into Crater.
• 5 Platoon (Lieutenant Hamish Clark) to provide observation reports and fire support from Aidrus Hill.
• 7 and Support Platoons commanded by Captain Buchanan to advance from Ras Marshag and seize the line of the old Turkish fortifications by Brown's House and the Cinema.

X Company, 45 Commando to remain in position. Under command was a troop from 60 Squadron RE, a 47 Light Regiment RA Sioux helicopter, a 15 Signal Regiment rear link detachment and 60 Squadron RCT. In reserve was B Company, 1st PWO.

During the morning, Lieutenant Colonel Downward agreed that Mitchell could push forward to the Aden Commercial Institute, about 400 yards from the Supreme Court and not far from the 'Coca-Cola' incident. When Mitchell suggested the time was ripe for deeper recce patrols of Crater to add to the intelligence collected by G Squadron, Downward referred the request to HQ Middle East Command; in response, Brigadier Dunbar emphasised Mitchell was not to penetrate further than his Phase One exploitation limit without his direct permission. During the afternoon, naval Wessex helicopters delivered the B Company platoons to Aidrus Hill and Ras Marshag.

Mitchell then reminded Major Ian Mackay, who had been promoted to replace Major Malcolm as the D Company commander and had previously been the Battalion Public Relations Officer, to organize press coverage. MacKay would carry the cromach (staff) of the late Major Malcolm. Under normal circumstances, the management of public relations was the Command responsibility, but when the press corps holed up in the Rock Hotel received a tip-off about the Crater operation, several journalists appeared in the quarry being used as a forming-up place. Mitchell then told them 'We are going into Crater', and they smelled a scoop. When asked for a name, he dubbed the operation 'Stirling Castle' in honour of the home of the Argylls. So far, most of the publicity had been about the perceived brutality of British soldiers; however, editors, who had spent thousands of words bullying the military performance, now had a new subject on whom to focus: a flamboyant regimental commander with a flair for public relations, who believed in a hard line and was possibly the last commanding officer of the Argylls. It was not difficult over the next months to create a legend around him.

At 7 pm, after the terrorists had used cars to conduct patrols of Sirrah Island, the Saladin drivers started their engines. After ordering B Company to advance, in an act that would come to epitomize the Aden Emergency, almost to the exclusion of everything else (as Bloody Sunday does for Northern Ireland), Mitchell introduced drama by instructing Pipe Major Kenneth Robson to sound the Regimental Charge 'Monymouth' and the Company March Pasts. The Terence Cuneo painting of the event shows Mitchell, in a blue shirt, standing by his Land Rover overlooking Crater on a moonlight night. Pipe Major Robson, also wearing a blue shirt, stands at the front of the vehicle. A QDG Saladin covering a column of Argylls advancing from the quarry is flying a red and white hackle from its antenna, in commemoration of those killed on 20 June.

Literally within minutes, two machine-gunners at the Sultan of Lahey's Palace opened fire at the leading platoon. Everyone dived for cover, except for Pipe Major Robson, who was oblivious to the bullets. Mitchell asked the leading Saladin commander to 'brass them up', which effectively silenced the machine guns, but not a sniper on the roof. Mitchell reminded his men, 'Play it cool'. The need for effective fire control was absolute. By 8 pm, B Company had reached the wrecked Legislative Council Buildings and the Chartered Bank. To the south, Captain Buchanan had descended Ras Marshag and was on the outskirts of the southern suburbs of Crater near the Cinema. One of several Arabs who failed to stop was shot. Meanwhile, A Company advanced past the Palace and raised the Regimental flag on Sirrah Island. The Treasury was known to be guarded by the Armed Police; nevertheless, Major Nigel Crowe, the Battalion Second-in-Command, and Sergeant Allison, an Arabic speaker in the Intelligence Section, demanded its surrender, with Crowe standing in the street covered by the Assault Platoon. The contents of the Treasury were now under British control.

The Battalion had reached its Phase One limit of exploitation, and when Mitchell radioed Lieutenant Colonel Downward requesting a 300-yard advance as far as the Civil Police Station in Phase Two to thereby undermine further disciplined resistance, Brigadier Dunbar agreed. Soon after Major Crowe's group had joined A Company, a Saladin fired on Company HQ, mistaking them for terrorists.

By daybreak, Phase One was complete. Mitchell established Tactical Battalion HQ in the Aden Commercial Institute on Maarif Road and named it 'Stirling Castle'. The Pipes and Drums announced the reoccupation of Crater from the roof of the Educational Institution with the 'Long Reveille'. At 10am, Major P. Wade, commanding B Company, 1st PWO, reported to Mitchell and noted the air of controlled confidence and the QDG Ferrets flying red and white hackles. He also noted a considerable number of press and television cameras. Mitchell told Wade that the Argylls could take Crater alone, that he should return next morning equipped with Carl Gustav anti-tank guns, mortars and plenty of grenades and that he should revise his fighting-in-a-built-up-area principles.

Major General Tower then arrived at Battalion HQ to review the final phase of Operation Stirling Castle. Lieutenant Colonel Mitchell felt that he was ill at ease and, in his autobiography *Once A Soldier*, accused Tower of sarcasm when the general said at the end of the meeting, 'This is just what I had planned'. Mitchell appears to have been unaware of Tower's and Dunbar's role in ensuring a low-risk reoccupation of Crater; consequently, they have never really been given due credit.

At about 5 pm, Major Crowe telephoned Superintendent Mohammed Ibrahim at the Armed Police Barracks, where the anxious police force were expecting retribution. Crowe, who generally liked Arabs, was not in a mood for 'soft diplomacy' and advised Ibrahim that if they interfered with the reoccupation of Crater, the Barracks would be destroyed. He also demanded that those directly involved in the 20 June murders should be surrendered. Ibrahim agreed to the surrenders but could not guarantee there would be no opposition. After Crowe had briefed Mitchell, the latter felt comfortable enough to advise Lieutenant Colonel Downward that the Armed Police would not interfere.

At 6.30 pm, Phase Two commenced with A Company advancing to the Haddadin Bazaar. Half an hour later, D Company occupied the subversive Aidrus Mosque, the Municipal Markets and the Bayoumic Clinic, thus controlling the principal routes into the centre of Crater. The NLF confined itself to circulating a tirade in its Blazing Hills newsletter, claiming that bullets and grenades would 'cause fear in the hearts of the Scottish red rats'.

At about 9 am on 4 July, D Company, 1st PWO relieved 45 Commando at Main Pass and took over the OPs. After High Commissioner Sir Humphrey Trevelyan had visited Crater at 11 am, Mitchell attended a meeting between Major General Tower, Brigadier Dunbar, Commissioner of Police Owen, his Deputy Said Abdul Hardi Shibab and Ibraham, at which it was agreed that the Armed Police would work with the Army to maintain law and order. Although reluctant to agree, Mitchell was sympathetic to Owen's predicament of having to police a colony with a force that had killed British soldiers. At 4 pm, an infantry and armoured car column reached the two wrecked Land Rovers outside the Armed Police Barracks, both of which were checked for booby traps and then towed away. Mitchell then drove to the Barracks and was saluted by Ibrahim. As he left to visit Major Wade at Main Pass, Lieutenant Colonel Downward and his Parachute Regiment escort drove into Crater.

The grip taken by Mitchell on the security of Crater was somewhat undermined on 5 July when Colonel Sharif Haidar, who had led the protest against the dismissal of the four colonels, apologized, saying that he never imagined his actions would result in tragedy. Even with forgiveness the flavour of the day, Mitchell emphasised that 'Argyll's Law' would apply, a prospect that induced hostility from the Aden Police, who usually had responsibility for law and order. When HQ Aden Brigade instructed that Crater was not to be isolated and the Main Pass and Marine Drive checkpoints were to be relaxed, the apprehensive residents and businesses realized that retribution was most unlikely. The reappearance of taxis and buses induced a semblance of civility, and refugees fleeing anarchy in Yemen indicated the relative stability of Aden; nevertheless, a one-way circuit and speed limits were enforced for all civilian traffic, and taxis were banned from beeping their horns because it was suspected that drivers were warning the NLF of patrols. The headlights of cars used to show up patrols rarely survived jabs from rifle butts. While there was no curfew, night was regarded as a cloak for terrorism and crime, and anyone on the streets was considered to be suspect. Patrols were not permitted to search the vehicles of Federal security forces, a factor that Mitchell regarded as increasing the risk of smuggled weapons and terrorists. In the event of major trouble, Mitchell developed 'Operation Portcullis' to seal Crater by reducing the movement of pedestrians and vehicles. Any males aged between 15 and 35 found in the vicinity of an incident could be considered suspect and transferred to Battalion HQ, where Major Crowe and the Intelligence Section were developing a large database from which nationalists were identified by photographs and fingerprinting.

When Major General Tower instructed the Argyll officers to attend a ceremonial parade at the Armed Police Barracks on 13 July, at which he would take the salute as part of political measures to rebuild the status and confidence of the police, it was poorly received, because some of those on parade had most probably been involved in the 20 June ambushes. Mitchell ordered kilts to be worn so that anyone not wearing a kilt and stepping out of line would be easily identified. Although the police band played 'Scotland the Brave', Mitchell and his officers were in no mood to shake hands with the Armed Police.

When a grenade was thrown at an Argyll working party from Lieutenant Jamie Graham's platoon who were filling sandbags, wounding Corporal Aucherlonie and three soldiers, it announced the relaunch of terrorism. Graham's father had commanded the 1st Battalion in Italy during the Second World War and later became Colonel of the Regiment. Mitchell activated Operation Portcullis, but three days later, the nationalists adopted the familiar strategy of undermining the security forces by complaining to the High Commission about the behaviour of the Battalion. An official within the Commission who referred to 'those Glasgow thugs' was reminded by Mitchell that his own mother had come from Glasgow and that he should support his Armed Forces. The official apologized, but the belief that the Army was full of bullies and miscreants was symptomatic of the anti-militarism of the late twentieth century.

Balancing political sensitivities against military necessity, Major General Tower felt that, under the circumstances, the principle of minimum force had been compromised. Indeed, Operation Portcullis was not being applied elsewhere. Although he was in Khormaksar Beach Hospital being treated for a painful leg ulcer, he summoned Mitchell to an informal meeting and asked him to 'throttle back'. Mitchell interpreted this to mean abandoning Operation Portcullis and scaling down early morning raids and house searches, actions that he felt would cost him the initiative and give the terrorists more confidence. However, he had little alternative but to accept the instruction and circulated a Special Order to his men:

ACTION IN CRATER

1. The methods we have used to dominate and pacify Crater have brought a flood of complaints from local nationals and the Federal Government authorities. We have been accused of stealing, brutality, wilful damage and arrogance. This is the 'Smear' campaign I warned you to expect. It was bound to come whatever we did and some of it

was bound to stick. The fact remains that for two weeks we have preserved the peace in Crater with only three incidents at a cost of four of our own men wounded, one Arab killed and another wounded, firing from the Aidrus Mosque.

2. I want all ranks to know how much I personally admire the way the Battalion has operated since arriving in Aden. I believe that our techniques and methods have paid off. If the day arises when we can use them again I know that they are the answer to the problem. 1 A and SH is justly famous for its tough line and I know that you have all been terrific. Well done!

3. However, I have now been ordered to 'throttle back' in the interests of a political settlement. The civil population has squeaked and I am reluctantly forced to modify or abandon some of our techniques. I am well aware of the disappointment this will cause to all of you but I too am a soldier under orders and must be 100 per cent loyal to my own superiors just as you to me.

4. Life will become a bit more dangerous now that we are prohibited from dominating the situation our own way. In the Argylls we thrive on danger so let us be even more alert – with fingers on the trigger for the good kill of a terrorist, which may soon present itself.

5. Company commanders are to ensure that this order is brought to the attention of ALL ranks in the Battalion by repeating it in Coy Detail.
Up the Argylls.

That night, a terrorist was killed near where the four Argylls had been wounded. Next day, after Major MacKay mentioned that the Civil Police were more surly than usual, Mitchell visited them and the Armed Police and returned with the impression that they knew he had been ordered to 'throttle back'. The increased terrorism predicted by Mitchell emerged on 21 July when Lance Corporal Willie Orr, a veteran of the Cyprus Emergency who had been promoted ten days earlier, was killed by two bursts of automatic rifle fire from a building, while he was inspecting his GPMG gunners in the Bazaar OP. An Arab who failed to halt while attempting to breach the cordon was shot. Brigadier Dunbar and Mitchell met during the evening to discuss operations in Crater. Next day, Admiral Le Fanu summoned Mitchell to HQ

Middle East Command, warned him that the Special Order had constituted disloyalty and told him that under normal circumstances he would have been removed from command. However, such a measure would be detrimental to his reputation and that of his Battalion and therefore he reprimanded Mitchell with a formal verbal warning. Mitchell advised his company commanders about the meeting.

HQ Middle East Command intelligence assessments indicated that several experienced terrorists had arrived in Crater and that terrorism would escalate during the last fortnight of July. The Treasury OP came under fire on several occasions. On the 26th, a soldier in the Gazeira Palace Hotel OP was wounded by a sniper. An assessment by the Intelligence Section suggested that the 'Cairo Grenadiers' were mainly FLOSY, who used mosques to escape into the network of alleys; but requests to Federal security forces for assistance was proving pointless. Mitchell therefore deployed snipers to overlook entrances to mosques, and within days three 'grenadiers' were shot as they raced for the sanctuary of mosques. To compensate for reducing the personnel of the OPs by redeploying the snipers, tailors' dummies, complete with Glengarries, took their place. Mitchell had earlier assured his soldiers that the Federal security forces were minnows compared to the Indonesians, said if there was an indication of a repeat of 20 June he would not abandon them, and instructed that, 'If you have no ammunition, you are to go in with bayonets'. A D Company patrol was questioning a suspect in an alley off Zafaran Road when he tried to grab a soldier's rifle. In the ensuing struggle the soldier knew that if he pulled the trigger the bullet could go anywhere, so he took the only other option and stabbed the man with his bayonet. Although Captain Tom Kenyon, the Regimental Medical Officer, treated the suspect, he died. The HQ Middle Eastern Command investigation concluded the response had been disproportionate and issued orders that bayonets were not to be carried on patrols. Mitchell disagreed, because he felt it degraded the deterrent effect of the military presence. A B Company patrol shot a terrorist armed with a Czechoslovakian pistol, and a RG-42 grenade thrown at a mobile patrol failed to explode. After three mortar bombs exploded around Battalion HQ in the Chartered Bank during the morning of 1 August, every available soldier at Waterloo Lines was employed to fill sandbags, as were several RAF personnel 'press-ganged' from the NAAFI, to the extent that the bank became known as the 'Sand Bank'. The defences were improved by 2 Troop, 60 Squadron RE, who fixed plumbing and solved several other problems. In what was perhaps an indication of his sense of isolation, Mitchell later wrote:

In Aden, the infantry for once stole the glory but this should never be allowed to obscure the part played by all the other arms and corps and, of course, the other two services.

Other Arms and Services would claim that the Infantry always stole the limelight.

Two days later, two RG-94s fired from spigots exploded near Mitchell's Land Rover and the next day, five mortar bombs landed near HQ A Company. RSM McKernen was dismantling several primed spigot grenades when a grenade set fire to his Land Rover. Four days later, Mitchell had just finished entertaining several visiting officers to lunch in the Officers' Mess when several mortar bombs hit the building, killing Pipe Corporal Jimmy Scott on the roof OP. His badly wounded colleague, Piper Oakley, described the probable location of the mortars, but searches proved unsuccessful. Two days later, a British 2-inch mortar of the type used by the South Arabian Army was found in a Public Works Department vehicle yard. The attacks continued throughout August and so did the flow of intelligence from interrogations, Human Intelligence and Documents Exploitation. Major Ron Smith, the Quartermaster, who had some experience of improvised devices in Palestine, reconstructed incidents and developed Weapons Intelligence from OP and patrol reports. On the 7th, Private Dickson, a B Company radio operator, was on patrol and about to transmit when he saw a 'Cairo Grenadier' and shouted a warning. The patrol dived for cover and the patrol commander was wounded. Dickson radioed the contact and requested medical evacuation for the corporal. The patrol then returned to base, and when Dickson said that he felt unwell, his colleagues discovered that he had also been wounded in the legs and arms. Royal Engineers fitted the window of Mitchell's room with steel shutters after a sniper had fired several shots into it. By the end of August, the Argylls had logged 117 incidents, at the cost of five killed and eighteen wounded, an estimated twenty terrorists killed and five wounded and five civilians killed and twenty-seven injured, most bystanders at grenade incidents.

On 8 August, as the UN Mission again endeavoured to find an all-party solution for the South Arabia Federation, the NLF issued a chilling statement:

We have no alternative but to strike harder at the enemy until we force Britain to fully abandon her stooge sultans, to recognize the revolution and to negotiate with it directly for surrendering power.

This was chilling because it was unequivocal – and yet Britain was preparing to leave Aden. However, the NLF was competing on two fronts, against the

Federation and FLOSY. By the end of June, the British units had largely withdrawn from the Federation amid a stream of contradictory instructions that confused junior commanders and led to this jingle in 45 Commando:

> Shoot 'em on Monday,
> Don't on Tuesday,
> Withdraw on Wednesday,
> Smile on Thursday,
> Don't on Friday,
> Shot at on Saturday,
> Crisis on Sunday.

On 9 August, the South Arabian Army amalgamated with the 1,500-strong Hadrami Bedouin Legion in the Eastern Aden Protectorate, and Deputy Commissioner of Police Hadi replaced Peter Owen as Commissioner. The Federation was already collapsing after an attempt to form a broad-based cabinet had failed when the names of delegates were withheld for personal security reasons. Next day, terrorists in Sheikh Othman made a second determined bid to drive out 1st Para C Company, Kings Own Borderers, based at Fort Walsh, logged over 80 incidents in two days. A mobile lured into a narrow street in Sheikh Othman by a suspect vehicle was ambushed from six gun positions, including two in the back of a lorry. Saladins of the Queen's Own Hussars destroyed several positions with their machine guns, but it had cost the infantry one killed and six wounded. The police reported twelve terrorists killed.

By the end of the month, the NLF had gained control of twelve states; then, on 3 September, it challenged FLOSY by claiming that it was the de facto representative of the people of South Arabia and established its headquarters at Zinjibar, a small coastal town in the State of Fadhali. There, Qahtan al Shabbi offered to discuss transferring power with High Commissioner Trevelyan. On the same day, the High Commissioner issued a statement from London preparing to negotiate with the 'nationalist forces as representative of the peoples', but without identifying who they were.

The NLF declaration heralded the first interfactional civil war with FLOSY between 6 and 11 September, the fierce gun battles amazing the watching British soldiers in Sheikh Othman and Dar Saad. When 1,000 Yemenis arrived at Sheikh Othman to reinforce the NLF on the 10th, the collapse of FLOSY resulted. After heavy casualties among the warring factions and civilians caught in the fighting, the South Arabian Army, which had dithered for two months, intervened on the 11th and took the lead in developing a solution.

CHAPTER SIXTEEN

Withdrawal

On 15 August, after 40 months of campaigning and over a thousand casualties, Aden State was finally declared to be an active service theatre, which meant that gallantry could be recognized with military awards.

Previously, such conduct had been recognized by Orders of the British Empire and Commendations of the Commanders-in-Chief. The problem was that the 1966 Army Act stipulated that medals could only be awarded for active service in a 'foreign country', which the Federation was but Aden was not, because it was a colony. The 1915 Naval General Service Medal (GSM) covered operations between 1909 and 1962 with sixteen campaign Clasps. The Army and RAF then issued the 1918 GSM covering 1918 to 1962 and also issued sixteen Clasps, one being 'Arabian Peninsula', covering the Border War between 1 January 1957 and 30 June 1960. Clasps of the tri-Service 1966 GSM, issued on 24 December 1962, included 'Radfan' and 'South Arabia' between 1 August 1964 and 30 November 1967, for operations in the Federation and Aden. The qualifying period was thirty days service in the Federation. Although twenty-five service personnel died between 1 July 1960 and 31 July 1964 and the Aden Emergency was declared on 10 December 1963, and those who served in the 1962 Brunei Revolt until 23 December 1962 received the 1918 GSM with 'Brunei' clasp and those who served in Brunei and Borneo from January 1963 to August 1966 received the 1962 GSM with 'Borneo' clasp, the Aden Veterans Association lobbied to fill the gap either by extending the 'Arabian Peninsula' Clasp to 24 December 1962 or backdating the 'South Arabia' Clasps to the same date. Unfortunately, their campaign was not successful on the grounds that Middle East Command concluded that

> The scale and scope of the border raids and terrorist attacks by dissidents in Aden did not justify the extension of the qualifying period for the medal.

Since the W-Day announcement, the service and civilian depots had been juggling requirements to ensure the Armed Forces had sufficient supplies and, at the same time, to backload stores and equipment of all shapes and sizes, or offer for local purchase by tender and destroy, where appropriate. All units also underwent the weeding of classified documents to ensure they had only the information they needed.

By the beginning of September, the service families had been evacuated by Air Support Command with its new range of strategic aircraft: Comet 4s, VC-10s and Britannias. Those married quarters no longer needed were handed to the Federal authorities by the Ministry of Public Buildings and Works. In the first major unit handover, on 13 September, Lieutenant Colonel Michael Hogge, commanding the Queens Own Hussars, handed Little Aden over to the South Arabian Army; as the Saladins drove through a guard of honour provided by the Camel Troop, they passed the Commonwealth War Graves Commission at Silent Valley. RAF Khormaksar now accommodated 3rd Wing AAC, and 45 Commando moved into the Ma'alla Straight married quarters in order to preserve the line of communication to Command Hill. Interfactional fighting between the beginning of September and the middle of October barely affected Aden Brigade, with no incidents logged in Crater.

The assault ship HMS *Fearless* arrived on 29 September and delivered two Michigan tractors, a Mexefloat, 170 soldiers, including a detachment from 10 Port Squadron, and several 25-pounder guns and ammunition for the South Arabian Army. On 10 October, the ship landed a force of Irish Guards at Hauf in the State of Mahra in the Eastern Aden Protectorate, from where the revolutionary Dhofar Liberation Front was launching insurgency into Oman. Twenty captured insurgents were flown to Salalah. Twice the ship then backloaded vehicles, equipment, eight Wessex helicopters, a Scout and a Sioux from Aden to Bahrain. On her third trip, she carried Support Company, King's Own Borderers to Dubai and unloaded 85 vehicles. In late October, the ship exercised landing Centurion and Chieftain tanks of 1st RTR and, in Exercise Falaise Fred gave HQ 24th Brigade some command post experience of controlling amphibious operations, in the event of a Yemeni attack. On 11 October, among the leading elements of Naval Task Force 318 assembling off Aden was the commando carrier HMS *Albion* from Singapore. On board, wearing Jungle Green uniforms, was 42 Commando, which been heavily involved in the Brunei Revolt and throughout Confrontation since 1962, Even though Intelligence was indicating that intervention from the NLF and Yemen was not expected, HQ Middle East Command remained concerned, aand the Commando took up positions on the Scrubber Line to ensure that air operations from RAF Khormaksar were not interrupted.

The NLF and FLOSY commemorated the fourth anniversary of 'The Revolution' by attacking the British. A mortar team was active in Crater. Six days later, when two 'Cairo Grenadiers' wounded an Argyll and two Arab bystanders, the soldiers killed one and wounded the other as he escaped. He was later killed by A Company when a taxi driver taking him to safety tried to breach a roadblock. Lieutenant Colonel Mitchell was visiting Crater Police Station and was near the Market Place when he and his escort saw a grenade thrown at Major Mackay's Land Rover by two terrorists. One soldier was blown out of the burning vehicle. While Mackay chased one terrorist, Mitchell, Corporal Mitchell, his driver, and Captain Thomson pursued the other into the meat market, where they split up to look for him, and Mitchell had to be rescued from a hostile crowd by Thomson. D Company flushed out the second terrorist, but he decided to resist. A RG-4 grenade was found in his full-length, loose-fitting *futah*.

On 4 November, Rear Admiral Edward Ashmore, the Flag Officer, Second-in-Command, Far East Fleet in Singapore, arrived to take command of naval operations and, under Operation Monitor, to support the British Embassy to the new republic. The Aden Naval Force, or Task Force 518, consisted of a fleet aircraft-carrier, two commando carriers, seven destroyers, two amphibious assault ships and twenty-three RFA and Fleet oilers. Ships' companies were kept abreast of the situation through the force's newspaper, the *South Arabian Sun.* Ashmore briefly returned to Britain when his daughter was killed in the Hither Green train crash. With the Suez Canal closed, the nearest safe fuel for the ships was at Kwinana in Western Australia. As far as water was concerned, the fleet tankers could distil their own, while the RFAs had to carry it. On the 7th, as the RAF began to thin out, the Sea Vixens on HMS *Eagle* helped with air defence, supported by Gannets of 849 Naval Air Squadron providing early warning.

On 2 November, the Ministry of Defence announced that W-Day would be moved from 20 November to 'by the end of November'; then on the 14th, it was announced to be 30 November, with H-Hour given as 23.59hrs. The original plan was to have all fighting elements clear by H-Hour, leaving a rearguard of an administrative tail to resolve any final matters; however, the deteriorating security situation led to orders that all units would withdraw through a shrinking, defended perimeter. The announcement prompted the third round of interfactional fighting between 3 and 6 November, mostly confined to Sheikh Othman and, to a lesser degree, Tawahi, where the NLF neutralized the FLOSY network. Crater became a refuge from the violence to the extent that one terrorist was disarmed by several Arabs before a patrol arrived. The Foreign Office concluded in its *British Policy Concerning Aden and the Beginning of South Arabia:*

> The NLF is clearly an influential force on the political scene . . . its political class seem singularly ill-informed . . . it has considerable support in Aden, controls half the trade union movement and has in recent months appeared to be gaining the upper hand of FLOSY in their internecine rivalry.

The South Arabian Army, standing on the sidelines, intervened on the 6th by declaring the NLF was the 'representative body' and then enforced a ceasefire with a firmness denied to HQ Aden Brigade, including firing a retaliatory shell at the FLOSY headquarters in Al Mansoura. With military support now assured, the NLF demanded that London recognize its authority and negotiate the handover of power, and then declared a ceasefire to start on the 8th. It was a tense time for the British. At about 11.30 pm, Lieutenant Colonel Mitchell and his escort were driving past the Armed Police Barracks when a grenade thrown over the wall exploded behind their vehicles, wounding Lieutenant Baty and two soldiers. A furious Mitchell instructed D Company to surround the Barracks, then he, Captain Thomson and Baty entered and complained to Superintendent Ali Gabir, who expressed suitable horror. Mitchell then addressed the police, assuring them that if it had not been for the discipline of his men, more blood would have been shed.

When the British Government failed to respond to the NLF demands, on the 11th, the organization generated a sharp burst of violence in which Argyll positions were mortared; in Tawahi, Marine Blackman of 42 Commando had the unenviable distinction of becoming the last British casualty in Aden, when he was shot in the head. Two days later, even though the prospects for a stable and democratic Aden were remote, London agreed to meet the NLF in Geneva. After the usual delays expected from terrorist leaders scenting victory, Qahtan al Sha'abi and his delegation of young, shadowy militants extracted £12 million in aid and an agreement, on the 22nd, that W-Day would be brought forward one day to the 29th.

In preparation for the disbandment of Middle East Command, some aspects of command and control were transferred the new British Forces Gulf in Bahrain. HQ Aden Brigade planned a three-phase withdrawal between 26 and 29 November:

• Phase One. By 26 November all Aden, except for RAF Khormaksar, to be transferred to the South Arabian Army.
• Phase Two. On 27 November, withdrawal into the RAF Khormaksar perimeter.
• Phase Three. On 29 November (W-Day) – withdrawal complete.
Floating Reserve – 40 Commando on HMS *Albion*.

Operational control was exercised through Brigade HQ and a Joint HQ inside RAF Khormaksar. Air defence centred on the Hunters of No. 8 Squadron and No. 4010 Flight and the naval air squadrons on board HMSs *Eagle* and *Hermes*. Defending the base was the RAF Regiment. In the largest operation of its kind since the Berlin Airlift, Britannias, Belfasts and Hercules had been flying a shuttle service between RAF Muharraq in Bahrain and Aden since August; then, between 5 and 30 November, Air Support Command lifted 6,000 troops and 400 tons of equipment.

Phase One began during the night of 23/24 November when, after logging 794 incidents in four months and with three killed and twenty-one wounded, 1st Para activated Operation Green Hackle by withdrawing from Sheikh Othman and joining C Squadron, Queens Own Hussars in hull-down positions. In prepared defensive positions along the Pennine Chain was 31 Battery, 45th Light Battery, to prevent interference from the district and Yemen, while 42 Commando had been moved to Tawahi. The operation was named in recognition of Brigadier Jefferies, formerly Royal Irish Fusiliers. Since 18 September, 3 Troop, 60th Field Squadron had been strengthening the Chain with weapon pits and several thousand sandbags. Several reporters reporting the withdrawal were roped in to load equipment, for instance Charles Douglas-Home, a former Royal Scots Greys officer and the *Daily Telegraph* defence correspondent, was unceremoniously asked to load an Elsan toilet into a lorry. In true para fashion, 1st Para marched in columns eight abreast through the perimeter wire of RAF Khormaksar, along the runway and into their aircraft.

At the same time, 1st Lancashires left Al Mansoura and the Mansoura Picquet without a hitch. The *sangar*, measuring 10ft square and 20ft high, covered the approaches to the Mansoura Detention Centre and had been attacked 254 times, twenty-three times on just one day. It had begun life as a simple covered machine-gun sangar.

As part of the ceremonial trappings of the transfer of power, High Commissioner Trevelyan reviewed Task Force 318 on the 25th, and then returned to Government House in the knowledge that an effective government had yet to emerge from Geneva. Most of the media corps also watched the

Review. During the afternoon, Lieutenant Colonel Mitchell issued orders for Operation Highland Clearance, the withdrawal from Crater. The Argylls had lost five killed and 25 wounded, more casualties than they had suffered in the past eleven years in Suez, Cyprus and Borneo. Senior Arab officers had toured his positions, seemingly most interested in ensuring that refrigerators, air-conditioners and carpets were left behind. Although Command Public Relations planned that groups of journalists should be attached to the three units withdrawing during the night and had organized a briefing at 10pm, it was poorly attended because camera crews and correspondents were focusing on the Argylls. When Major General Tower arrived at Tactical HQ outside the Chartered Bank he expressed exasperation at the focus on the Argylls, asking a journalist why he had not gone to Ma'alla. Mitchell instructed Captain Thomson to sidetrack Tower from the withdrawal because it 'was impossible to conduct operations with a disgruntled GOC and hordes of Press and visitors'. He later wrote:

> It was a pity that it had all worked out that way because we were leaving a town that we had fought to re-occupy and control in our own way and where five Argylls had died and others had been wounded. (*Having Been a Soldier*)

At 1.30 am on the 26th, as three battalions of the 'Armed Forces in Occupied South Yemen', formerly the South Arabian Army, entered Aden, the final stage of Phase One began. As the Argylls finished thinning from the 'Highland Line' through the Control Point at the Chartered Bank, the Regimental colours were lowered while the Regimental piper played 'The Barren Rocks of Aden'. A platoon from B Company, which had first entered Crater, provided the rearguard, and after Mitchell and Thomson had checked Crater to ensure all units were clear, Mitchell gave an Arab officer the box containing keys to every house, flat and occupied by his Battalion. He then radioed HQ Aden Brigade that Operation Highland Clearance was complete and replied to the acknowledgement with 'Up the Argylls'. The companies withdrew to RAF Khormaksar, and at 6.45 am, aircraft began flying the troops to Bahrain and onward to RAF Lyneham. Mitchell planned to fly on the last aircraft, but when Major General Tower switched him to an even later flight, he was suspicious until he arrived at Bahrain and was handed a signal from the Director of Public Relations (Army) that he would be met by the media. British newspapers had regularly run stories about 'Mad Mitch' and the Argylls. While there is no doubt that it had a major impact on saving the Regiment from disbandment, his approach cost Mitchell his military career and he was denied the DSO which all other commanding officers had received. He resigned, to make a new life as a commentator and, briefly, a politician.

As 3rd South Arabian Army took over Ma'alla from 45 Commando, Lieutenant Colonel John Owen handed over 100 keys to Ma'alla married quarter flats and was then escorted by a Queen's Own Hussars Saladin to RAF Khormaksar, where the Commando was in reserve. X Company took up positions along the Owen Line that stretched along the volcanic rim overlooking Crater to Ma'alla, to protect the left flank of the perimeter. Then 42 Commando handed over Tawahi and withdrew to Steamer Point without ceremony. Phase One was complete, without interference.

Next morning, as Aden awoke to streets patrolled by Arab soldiers, the people realized that Independence Day was imminent. With the violence temporarily forgotten, flag-waving NLF supporters declared that South Arabia had been renamed 'The People's Democratic Republic of South Yemen' and the Federal capital at Al Ittihad was now Medinat As Shaab, or 'the People's City'. High Commissioner Trevelyan formally cancelled the Emergency Regulations and, after ordering the release of detainees, left Government House and joined Major General Tower at his house. In an altogether more controlled ceremony at midday in Seedaseer Lines, Brigadier Dye formally handed command of the former South Arabian Army to an Arab colonel. On Jebel Shamsan fluttered a Union Flag and a White Ensign placed there by 42 Commando.

The 27th saw further constrictions of the British perimeter. After the High Commissioner left Government House and boarded HMS *Eagle*, C Company, 1st Kings Own Borderers transferred Steamer Point to 2nd South Arabian Army and withdrew with 42 Commando to the Pennine Chain, which was now defended by 8 (Alma) Commando Battery and A Squadron, Queen's Own Hussars. Tactical HQ was in the Polo Club. The next day was quiet. A short parade marked the independence of Aden, when a 24-man Guard of Honour drawn from 45 Commando, the King's Own Borderers, a Queen's Own Hussars troop and the RAF Regiment was inspected by the High Commissioner at RAF Khormaksar. The HMS *Eagle* Royal Marines Band provided the music and as they played the first verse of the National Anthem, a flight of No. 8 Squadron Hunters flew overhead and ended the Squadron's 48-year association with Aden. Then, in a gesture of irreverent British humour and irony, as Sir Humphrey Trevelyan stood on the steps of the Transport Command aircraft flying him to the UK, the band struck up 'Fings Ain't Wot They Used To Be', which brought a wry smile from the parade, most of whom were glad to be leaving. 'Auld Land Syne' would have seemed inappropriate. During the day, 1,300 servicemen were flown out in twenty aircraft.

As W-Day dawned on 29 November, relays of RAF Transport Command aircraft collected 1,000 more men from the shrinking perimeter, covered by Wessex helicopters from HMS *Intrepid* providing immediate support. An International Committee of the Red Cross medical team that had arrived in Aden found that the departure of the British meant that all of the seven hospitals in the former Federation now had very few doctors and clinical specialists. The former Queen Elizabeth Hospital in Aden, since renamed Al Gouriem Municipal Hospital, had lost its driving force of mainly British staff and was struggling to meet the needs of the 300,000 people. Only in Khormaksar Beach Hospital were the operating theatres ready were for use – staff prepared, instruments in bags ready for sterilizing and blouses and galoshes in place.

In the morning, 45 Commando ended its seven-year association with Aden, having spent 21 years of the last 25 years overseas. At noon, HQ Aden Brigade and the Joint HQ transferred operational command to Lieutenant Colonel Dai Morgan, who was commanding 42 Commando. At 1.40 pm, Major General Tower, Brigadier Dunbar, Brigadier Jefferies and Wing Commander Freddie Sowrey, the senior RAF officer watched as C Company, 1 King's Own Borderers were transferred by helicopter from positions at Radfan Camp to a C-130 Hercules; five minutes later, they formally transferred the defence of Aden to the South Arabian Army and boarded the last flight out, leaving the military airfield to become a fully functioning civil airport. Overhead circled two spare Hercules to cover any technical failures. Twenty British reporters covering the withdrawal were flown by helicopter to HMS *Albion*, where they were permitted to file a maximum of 1,000 words to their editors. They were then taken by fleet auxiliary ships to Djibouti and left to return to Britain under their own steam. At 2.50 pm, the rearguard of 120 men withdrew from the final seven defensive positions to the sandy 12th green of Aden Golf Club and were flown to HMS *Albion*. Major General Tower, who had spent the previous hour with the Tactical HQ 42 Commando, was flown to HMS *Intrepid*. At precisely 3 pm, as Lieutenant Colonel Morgan climbed into a Wessex with his Tactical HQ, Tower transferred command to Rear Admiral Ashmore, ten hours ahead of H-Hour at midnight. HMS *Albion* remained on station until midnight. High above Aden were two large ship's buoys painted in red, white and blue roundels and deposited earlier by an RAF helicopter. And at Main Pass was the badge of the South Wales Borderers carved into a rock in 1927 by the son of a veteran of the Zulu War, who had etched a similar tribute at Rorke's Drift.

While it is sometimes fashionable to describe the withdrawal from Aden as a retreat, that implies a degree of chaos. The withdrawal was, in fact, a meticulously executed operation, in which 56,643 tons of stores, 65 armoured and 2,148 other vehicles and 75,000 items were lifted by air and sea. Sapper John Collier, 50 Movement Unit (Embarkation), which had been heavily involved, noted, however:

> Unfortunately, when it came to calling forward items from the then MPBW (Ministry of Public Buildings and Works, later known as the PSA) they were never ready so we ended up scrapping together items to fill space, but never fully loading ships. This problem escalated the closer we got to final withdrawal as the MPBW then wanted additional space for items that should have been shipped earlier. The end result was that a huge amount of equipment had to be left behind. We did our best, however, to ruin it by smashing and burning as much as possible. [www.movcon.org – Aden1964–1966]

Members of 42 Commando recalled driving vehicles into the sea at Obstruction Jetty. The RAF had flown 24,000 Service personnel since April, 6,000 since 1 November, 2,000 within the last two days and 800 on the 29th. The RAF lost just one aircraft, when the crew of a 99 Squadron Britannia landing at RAF Khormaksar in October could not select reverse and it skidded into shallow water, causing several injuries. The aircraft was regarded as an obstruction and was therefore destroyed beyond repair.

As is common in states born out of revolutionary war, South Yemen descended into the chaos and brutality of the failed state that Yemen now is. Part of the problem was that the Suez Canal remained closed until 1975, and the NLF lacked the business acumen to confront the consequent collapse in trade. Corruption became endemic, inducing poverty and inadequate economic governance on a scale not seen under colonial leadership. In June 1969, a Marxist wing of the NLF gained power; six months later it reorganized the country into the People's Democratic Republic of Yemen and established close naval, military and commercial links with communist regimes such as the Soviet Union, China and Cuba. A short border war with North Yemen was resolved in 1972, with the understanding that unification would eventually follow; instead, both countries slid toward further hostilities that were resolved when both countries made another affirmation of unity. The resignation of President Abdul Fattah Ismail in favour of Ali Nasir Mohammed in 1980 saw South Yemen become less interventionist with North Yemen and its neighbour, Oman.

On 17 January 1986, Soviet intermediaries failed to resolve fighting between the rival Marxist factions and the ruling Yemen Socialist Party; such was their concern about the security of their expatriates that Great Britain, Russia and France sent ships to evacuate them. With British and Soviet diplomats coordinating transport, and the BBC World Service broadcasting the evacuation beaches, by noon next day, the Royal Yacht *Britannia* and RFA *Brambleleaf* had embarked about 450 people, irrespective of nationality, from a beach exposed to sniper and artillery fire. Next day, *Britannia* collected a further 200 people from a beach 30 miles east of Aden and transferred them to ships going to Djibouti. Heavy fighting the next day prevented further embarkations. On 20 January, the destroyer HMS *Newcastle* and MV *Diamond Princess* evacuated about 250 people from beaches near Al Mukalla, 300 miles east of Aden, and next day lifted 250 people from Little Aden. The ships were leaving the area in the belief that the evacuation was complete when a radio message was picked up that a further 800 people were 'running out of time, food and water'. The British Consul advised them to make their way to Little Aden, where HMS *Newcastle* and HMS *Jupiter* protected their embarkation on to the Royal Yacht, the survey ship HMS *Hydra*, RFA *Brambleleaf*, and MV *Diamond Princess.*

Against the background of the collapse of the Soviet Union, ten years later, North and South Yemen merged to become the new state of Yemen. President Salleh resigned in 2012, after a 33-year rule in which he had developed a government of patronage that managed to maintain a balance of power among tribes that collectively had more weapons than his Security Forces. He confronted internal threats, such as the separatist aspirations of the south, through fear and co-option and by rewarding tribal leaders. Nevertheless, Yemen has become a base for Al Qaeda and has seen several well publicised terrorist incidents, all of which means the country has been justifiably labelled a failed state.

CHAPTER SEVENTEEN

Conclusion

During the course of 128 years, British, Indians and South Arabians defended Aden and the Federation against spurious claims from north of the Protectorate border. The British left when the time was right. Unfortunately, it has become fashionable to describe the Aden Emergency as a military setback and it is a period not to be mentioned by the political set or the media, except in the context of abandonment, 'scuttling out' and retreat. All imply chaos. The withdrawal was, in fact, carefully planned and successfully executed in spite of nationalist violence, and was a diplomatic, political and economic necessity, as Britain transferred her colonial responsibilities. The United Nations failed to provide effective leadership or find a resolution to the conflict between those who wanted democratic and credible government in South Arabia and an Egypt determined to impose its version of Arab nationalism throughout the Middle East. It was thus inevitable Yemen should become a failed state, and one that has since exported and conducted terrorism within its borders, including in Aden.

There is no doubt that while many of those who served in the mountains and desert of South Arabia relished the environment, those who patrolled the airless streets and narrow alleyways of Aden and lived in the dusty cantonments, almost from the very start in 1839, were generally glad to leave. Many of the internal security procedures developed in Aden were applied three years later aand adapted in the Northern Ireland Treaties. The list of incidents below is extracted from Paget's *Last Post: Aden 1964–67* and is an approximate statistic covering typical breaches of internal security, including shooting, rocket and grenade attacks on Security Forces patrols, murders and assassinations, disturbances and arrests *only* in the State of Aden. Paget served in the Federal Security Secretariat for six months in 1965 and is a credible source. The statistic does not include incidents that happened in October and November 1967 because difficulties were experienced in separating attacks on Security Forces from the interfactional fighting between the NLF and FLOSY.

1964   –   36 incidents
1965   –   286
1966   –   480
1967   –   2,908
Total –   3,710

Throughout the years of the Aden Emergency, the Armed Forces, their associated civilian components and their family dependants in the Federation displayed resilient patience and persistent resolve that was frequently tested, no more so than on 20 June 1967. That active service in Aden was unrewarding is evidenced by the failure of successive Governments, over decades, to recognise the commitment and sacrifices of the Armed Forces. This is evidenced by the refusal, until very late in the Emergency, to recognise gallantry in Aden except by the award of medals normally associated with professional expertise and initiative, and by the refusal to extend the General Service Medal to cover the period 1960 to 1964, as lobbied for by the Aden Veterans Association.

The casualty statistics of those defending Aden and the Protectorates/ Federation are drawn from three principal sources: the Commonwealth War Graves Commission for the First and Second World War, the Aden Veterans Association Roll of Honour and Paget's *Last Post: Aden 1964-67*. Paget lists only battle casualties in Aden State. The Aden Veterans Association Roll of Honour stretches back to the First World War and after 1945 is comprehensive in listing those who died in theatre killed in action, those murdered by terrorists and non-battle fatalities, such as aircraft and traffic crashes, training, drowning, illness and natural causes. While the Roll does not give cause of death, few war memorials do. The Royal Garrison Church of All Saints in Aldershot lists 519 soldiers who died between 1839 and 1967.

In the Ma'alla Commonwealth War Graves Commission cemetery are buried 142 British, Imperial and Commonwealth servicemen who lost their lives during the First World War. This includes thirty-one moved from Sheikh Othman and eight moved from Holkat Bay. A Memorial commemorates ten servicemen transferred from the Christian cemetery on Perim Island and from Kamaran Island. At the Commonwealth War Grave Cemetery at Heliopolis, Cairo are listed 615 Adenis with no known graves. Also buried at Ma'alla are 157 Allied servicemen who died during the Second World War, all non-battle casualties from air operations, training and natural causes. A Memorial also lists thirty-three Indian Forces, twenty-eight British, including an airman from 203 Squadron buried at Kamaran Island, and five African soldiers, whose graves could not be found or could not be maintained for security

CASUALTIES 1914-1967

FIRST WORLD WAR SECOND WORLD WAR *(Commonwealth War Graves Commission)*	752 223				
BORDER WAR *(Aden Veterans Association)*	**01 Jun 57** 7	**1958** 12	**1959** 14	**30 Jun 60** 9	
ADEN EMERGENCY **British Armed Forces**	**10 Dec 63**	**1964**	**1965**	**1966**	**1967**
(Aden Veterans Association)	2	35	37	56	81
(Killed - Paget)	0	2	6	5	44
(Wounded - Paget)	0	25	83	215	325
Federal Security Forces					
(Killed - Paget)		1	9	2	5
(Wounded - Paget)			7	8	43
British Expatriates					
(Killed - Paget)	2	1	2	6	9
(Wounded - Paget)	0	5	28	19	31
Local Population					
(Killed - Paget)	0	0	18	32	240
(Wounded - Paget)	0	2	86	283	551
BRITISH ARMED KILLED IN 1967	**January** 6 **July** 2	**February** 0 **August** 8	**March** 5 **September** 6	**April** 0 **October** 0	**May** 7 **November** 0

reasons. Ma'alla also includes the graves of 381 Service personnel who died in South Arabia. Silent Valley was built by Royal Engineers in 1965 and contains 135 graves. Regrettably, the three British Military Cemeteries were desecrated after the withdrawal; however, the Commonwealth War Graves Commission rebuilt and refurbished them, in spite of serious insecurity in Aden, in time for a visit to Yemen in 1997.

Within two years, the Armed Forces were in Northern Ireland using some of the counter-insurgency and counter-terrorism techniques developed in Aden; the Military Reconnaissance Force and its successors developed by B-Group took the war to the IRA in their 'No Go Areas'. By 1974, the IRA had largely been defeated; however, an emerging progressive movement within republicanism had learnt from the Cyprus and Aden Emergencies and were successful in undermining political and military strategies. The result was a terrorist campaign in England and Europe that lasted thirty-seven years.

Appendix A

Royal Navy & Royal Marines

ROYAL NAVY AND ROYAL MARINES				
HMS *Norfolk III*	Naval Base	Jan 35	Apr 40	Steamer Point
HMS *Sheba*	Shore Base	Jan 40	Nov 67	1962 Flag Officer Middle East
HMS *Gambia*	Cruiser		1957	
HMS *Messina*	Landing Ship Tank		1960	Carried 1st Assault Sqn RM
HMS *Carlton*	Coastal Minesweeper	Apr 65	Jan 66	Guardship
HMS *Punchton*	Coastal Minesweeper	Feb 67	Aug 67	Guardship
HMS *Appleton*	Coastal Minesweeper	Feb 67	Aug 67	Guardship
HMS *Kildarton*	Coastal Minesweeper			Guardship
Task Force 518				
HMS *Eagle*	Aircraft Carrier			
HMS *Hermes*	Aircraft Carrier			
HMS *Albion*	Commando Carrier			
HMS *Bulwark*	Commando Carrier			
HMS *Fearless*	Amphibious Assault Ship			
HMS *Intrepid*	Amphibious Assault Ship			
HMS *Phoebe*	Leander Class Frigate			
LSL Galahad	Landing Ship Logistic			
RFA *Pearleaf*	Support Oiler	Aug 66	Dec 66	
RFA *Stromness*	Fleet Replenishment Ship			
RFA *Tidespring*	Fleet Oiler			
Fleet Air Arm				
815 Naval Air Sqn (HMS *Centaur*)	Wessex HAS-1 Anti Submarine Warfare	Dec 63	Jan 64	Op Nutcracker
826 Naval Air Sqn (HMS *Hermes*)	Wessex HAS-1 Anti Submarine Warfare			
848 Naval Air Commando Sqn (HMS *Albion*)	Wessex HU-5 Troop Carrier			
Royal Marines				
40 Commando			1967	Withdrawal - Floating Reserve
42 Commando			1967	Withdrawal reinforcement
45 Commando		1960	1967	

Appendix B1
Army: Cavalry & Infantry

ADEN GARRISON

Armoured Car Squadron			
Sqn, Life Guards	Jul 55		
Sqn, 15/19 Kings Royal Hussars	Apr 56		
B Sqn, 13/18 Royal Hussars	Oct 57		
Sqn, Life Guards	Sep 58		
1st Dragoons (The Royals)	Nov 59		
C Sqn, Queens Own Hussars	Feb 60		
C Sqn, 3rd Carbiniers	Nov-60		
11th Hussars	Nov 60		
A and B Sqns rotating, 17/21st Lancers	Oct 61	Oct 62	
Queens Royal Iirish Hussars	Nov 61	Nov 62	
9/12th Lancers	Sep 62	Jul 63	
D Sqn, 4 Royal Tan Regiment	Nov 63	Aug 64	
10th Hussars	Aug 64		
5th Royal Inniskilling Dragoon Guards	Dec 64		
4/7th Royal Dragoon Guards	Aug 65	Sep 66	
Royal Armoured Corps Parachute Sqn	May 05		
1st Royal Tank Regiment	Dec 65	Dec 67	
1st Queens Dragoon Guards	Sep 66	Jul 67	
5th Royal Tank Regiment	Jun 67		As infantry
Queens Own Hussars	Jul 67	Oct 67	

Tank Squadron Reinforcement from the Amphibious Warfare Squadron			
A and B Sqn rotating, Royal Scoys Greys	Oct 62	Nov 63	
Sqn, 16/5th Quuens Royal Lancers	Nov 63	Dec 64	

British and Indian Infantry			
1/6th Foot	1841		
17th Foot	1843		
94th Foot	1845-46		
78th Foot	1855		
57th Foot	1858		
! Kings Own	1860		
109th Foot	1862		
7th Foot	1866		
82nd Foot	1869		
3rd Rifle Brigade	1870		

3rd Kings Royal Rifle Corps	1871		
105th Foot	1872		
55th Foot	1873		
41st Foot	1874		
25th Foot	1875		
56th Foot	1877		
14th Foot	1878		
1st PoW	1879		
62 Foot/1st Willts	1880		
1st Seaforth Highlanders	1882		
1st York & Lancasters	1883		
22nd Bombay Infantry			
1st Essex	1884		
4th Bombay Rifles			
1st South Lancs	1885		
2nd Dorsets	1886		
9th Bombay Infantry			
2nd North Staffords	1887		
2nd East Yorks	1888		
3rd Bombay Light Infantry			
1st West Ridings	1889		
2nd Leicesters	1890		
17th Bombay Infantry			
1st Connaught Rangers	1891		
1st King's Liverpools	1892		
16th Bombay Infantry			
2nd South Wales Borderers	1893		
2nd Glosters	1894		
13th Bombay Infantry	*1894/96*		
2nd West Yorkshires	1895		
1st Worcesters	1896		
1st Royal Welch Fusiliers	1897		
1st Manchesters	1898		
1st Derbyshires	1899		
10th Bombay Light Infantry			
5th Bombay Infantry	*1890*		

Boundary Commission Operations 1900-1903

1st Royal West Kents	**1901**		
2nd Royal Dublin Fusiliers	**1902**		
1st Hampshires	**1903**		
1st Royal East Kents	1904		
123 Outram's Rifles			

3rd Rifle Brigade	1905	
102nd Bombay Grenadiers		
2nd Kings Own Scottish Borderers	1906	
116th Mahrattas		
81st Pioneers		
2nd Suffolks	1907	
1st Bedfordshires	1908	
113th Indian Infantry		
1st Queens	1908	
108th Indian Infantry	*1909*	
1st Northamptons	1910	
1st Linconshires		
1st Warwickshire	1911	
1st Middlesex	1912	
18th Indian Infantry		
1st Royal Irish Fusiliers	1913	

First World War - Aden Brigade 1914-1919

1st Lancashire Fusiliers	**1914**	**1914**
1st Royal Irish Rifles	**1914**	**1915**
1/1st Brecknockshires (TF) (4th South Wales Borderers)	**1914**	**1916**
109th Indian Infantry	*1914*	
1/23rd Sikh Pioneers (29th Indian Infantry Brigade)	*1914*	*1916*
28th Indian Infantry Brigade	*1915*	*1916*
51st Sikhs		
53rd Sikhs		
56th Punjabs		
62nd Punjabs		
126th Baluchistan Infantry (30 Indian Infantry Bde)	*1915*	*1916*
1/4th Royal East Kents (TF)	**1915**	
108th Indian Infantry	**1916**	
1/4th Duke of Cornwalls Light Infantry (TF)		
75th Carnatic Infantry		
69nd Punjabis		
129th Duke of Connaught's Own		
33rd Punjabis		
1/6th East Surreys (TF)	**1917**	1918
109th Indian Infantry		
Malay States Guides	*1917*	*1918*
1/7th Hamphires (TF)	**1918**	
62nd Punjabs		

1/7th Duke of Connaught's Own Rajputs		
1st Kings Shropshire Light Infantry	1919	
1st Brahmans		
2nd Royal Fusiliers	1920	
2nd Royal East Kents	1922	
1st Borders	1924	
1st Royal Scots	1925	
5/12th Frontier Force		
2nd Devonshires	1926	
4/11th Sikhs		
2nd South Wales Borderers	1927	
510th Baluchistan		
1st Welch	1928	1928

Second World War - Aden Brigade 1939-1945

3/7th Rajputs	*1940*	*1944*
3/1st Punjabs (Socotra Island)	*1942*	*1943*
Mewra Bhopal Infantry	*1942*	*1944*
Bikaniar Ganga Risala Camels	*1940*	*1942*
1st Rampur Infantry	*May 44*	
1st Hyderabad Lancers	*Nov 44*	
1st Patiala Lancers	*1945*	*1946*
1st Seafirth Highlanders	Jul 55	Oct 55
1st Kings Own Yorkshire Light Infantry	Oct 55	Apr 56
1st Durham Light Infantry	Nov 56	Feb 56
1st Gloucester Regiment	Apr 56	Sep 56

Border War 1957-1960

1st Queens Own Cameronain Highlanders	Sep 56	Mar 58
1st Prince of Wales Own Regiment of Yorkshire	Sep 58	Jun 59
1st Kings Shropshire Light Infantry	May 05	
1st York & Lancaster Regiment	Jan 58	Dec 58
1st East Kents (The Buffs)	Mar 68	Jan 59
1st Royal Lincolnshire Regiment	Jul 58	Sep 58
1st Warwickshire Regimnet	Aug 59	Apr 60
1st Northamptonshire Regimet	Jan 59	Jan 60
1st Royal Highland Fusiliers	Jan 60	Jan 61
1st Queens Royal Surrey Regiment	Jan 61	Jan 62

Aden Emergency and Federal Operations 1963-1967

1st East Anglians/ 1st Royal Anglians	Apr 64	Dec 64

'Radforce'

45 Commando	Mar 64	May 64	
C Coy, 3 Para	Mar 64	May 64	

39 Brigade

3 Para (less B Coy)	May 64	Feb 65	
1st Kings Own Scottish Borderers	Apr 64	Jul 64	
1st Royal Scots	Oct 64	Aug 65	

24 Brigade

2 Coldstream Guards	Oct 64	Oct 65	
1st Welsh Guards	Oct 65	Oct 66	
1st Irish Guards	Oct 66	Aug 67	

Aden Brigade

4th (Leicester) Royal Anglian Regiment	Feb 65	Aug 65	Ma'alla & Creater
1st Royal Sussex Regiment	Apr 65	Oct 65	Sheikh Othman & Al Mansoura
1st Coldstream Guards	Aug 65		
1st Kings Own Yorkshire Light Infantry	Aug 65	Sep 66	Tawahi/Ma'alla
C Coy, 1st Loyals	Jun 66	Aug 66	RAF Khormaksar
Dets, Royal Irish Fusiliers	May 05		
1st Prince of Wales Own Regiment of Yorkshire	Sep 65	Sep 66	Crater and Ma'alla
1st Coldstream Guards & B Coy, 1st Glosters	Oct 65	Apr 66	Sheikh Othman, Al Mansoura & Ma'alla
B Coy, 1st Yorks and Lancasters	Feb 66	May 66	Radfan Camp
1st Somerset & Cornwall Light Infantry	Apr 66	Oct 66	Sheikh Othman
1st Cameronians	May 66	Feb 67	Tawahi/Ma'alla
3rd Royal Anglians & Coy, 1 Kings Own Border Regiment	Sep 66	Jun 67	Sheikh Othman and Al Mansoura
1st Royal Northumberland Fusiliers	Sep 66	Jun 67	Crater
1st Lancashire Regiment	Feb 67	Aug 67	Al Manaoura
1 Para & C Coy, 1st Kings Own Royal Border Regiment	May 67	Nov 67	Sheikh Othman
1st Prince of Wales Own Regiment of Yorkshire	Jun 67	Aug 67	Tawahi/Ma'alla
1st South Wales Borderers	Jun 67	Nov 67	
1st Argyll & Sutherland Highlanders	Jun 67	Nov 67	Crater
42 Commando	Oct 67	Nov 67	Reinforcement

Appendix B2

Army: Artillery & Combat Support

ARTILLERY			
6 (Western) and 5 (South Irish Div) Bty	1885		
1 (Western Div) Bty	1887		
31 and 34 (Southern Div) Btys	1889		
5 and 15 (Western Div) Btys	1890-91		
13 and 26 (Southern Div) Coys	1898		
8 (Eastern) and 18 (Southern Div) Coys	1899		
Boundary Commission Operations - 1900 - 1903			
45 RGA Coy	1900		
30th Mountain Bty			
Camel Bty			
6 (British) Mountain Bty			Screw Gun
8 (Eastern), 18 (Southern) and 16 (Western Divs) Coys	1902		
45, 54 and 55 Coys	1903		
51, 60 and 70 Coys	1904		
69 and 76 Coys	1906		
76 Coy	1908		
64 and 76 Coys	1910		
62, 70 and 76 Coys	1912		
First World War			
61 Coy RGA	1914	1927	
62 Coy RGA (8th (Lucknow) Div)	1914	1918	
69 Coy RGA (4th (Quetta) Div))	1914	1918	
70 Coy RGA (Coastal)	1914	1927	
76 Coy RGA (Coastal)	1914	1927	
85 Coy RGA	1914	1918	
10-pdr Camel Bty RGA	1915	1918	
15-pdr Camel Bty RGA	1915	1918	
B Battery HAC (TF) (28 Indian Inf Bde).	1915	1916	15-Pdrs QF
Berkshire Bty, RHA (TF) (28 Indian. Inf Bde)	1915	1916	15-Pdrs QF

2/1 H (Devon) Bty			
1105 (H) Bty			
Malay State Guides Mountain			
Battery	*1916*	*1918*	*Screw Gun*
7 Heavy Battery	1924	1927	
Second World War			
5th Heavy Regt	08 Sep 39	01 Jun 40	
15th AA Bty HKSRA	08 Sep 39		
23rd AA Bty HKRSA	23 Feb 40		
24th Searchlight Bty	30 May 40		
9 Coast Bty	14 Dec 40	31 Dec 45	
5th Coast Regt	14 Dec	01 Jun 40	
5th Heavy AA Regt	01 Jun 40		
18th Mouintain Battery	23 Oct 40		
Post-1945			
Border War			
HQ 51 Coast Regt		1952	
1 and 5 Btys 14 Field Regt	Oct 58	Sep 60	25-pdrs
97 Battery, 33 Para Field Regt	Apr 58	Sep 60	75mm C, D
and J Btys, 3rd RHA	Sep 60	Jul 63	105mm Pack
Radfan and Aden Emergency			
D and J Btys, 3rd RHA	Jul 63	Oct 64	105mm Pack
170 Bty, 45 Medium Regt	Apr 64	Jul 64	5.5inch
Howizter			
I Battery, 7 RHA	Jul 64	May 65	105mm Pack
20 Commando Amphibious			
Observation Bty	May 64	Dec 64	
19 Field Regt	May 64	Sep 64	105mm Pack
F Para Battery, 7 RHA	May 65	Oct 65	105mm Pack
A, B and E Bty, 1 RHA	Sep 65	Jun 67	106mm Pack
3 and 31 Battery, 47 Light Regt	May 67	Nov 67	105mm Pack
8 (Alma) Battery. 29 Commando			
Regt	Oct 67	Nov 67	105mm Pack

Appendix B3
Army: Service Support

ARMY AIR CORPS
 8 Flight
13 Flight
653 Sqn

TRANSPORT
First World War
Det, 7 Mule Corps
18 Pack Corps
25 Camel Corps
26 Camel Coy
Porter Corps
No. 31 Divisional Supply Coy
No. 31 and 101 Brigade Supply Sects
HQ No. 55 Supply and Transport (Lines of Communication)

T' Supply Depot Coy
91, 92 and 321 Supply Sects
46 Supply Workshop Sect
631 and 634 Bakery Sects
7 Cattle Purchaising Sect
150 Tally Sect
Aden Water Column
Aden Local Transport

Post-1945
1 Sqn RCT
2 Coy RASC/2 Sqn RCT
2 Army Training and Selection RCT
10 Port Sqn RCT
16 Air Despatch Coy/Sqn RASC/RCT
20 Coy RASC
20 LCT Regiment
51 Port Sqaudron
60 Coy/Sqn RASC/RCT
90 Coy/Sqn RASC/RCT
Joint Services Port Unit

ROYAL ARMY MEDICAL CORPS
First World War
2 Sect, British General Hospital
No. 10 British Stationary Hospital
No. 10 Advanced Deport of Medical Stores
No. 10 British Staging Section Casualty Clearing Station

Sect B, 24 British Field Ambulance
Sect B, 26 British Field Ambulance
No. 80 Indian Stationary Hospital
No. 80 Indian Staging Section Casualty Clearing Station

Sects A and B, 26 Indian Field Ambulance
Two sects, 105 Indian Field Ambulance
Sects D and C 133 Indian Field Ambulance
Sects A and B, 138 Indian Field Ambulance
No 138 Combined Field Ambulance
Benares Ambulabce Transport Sect

Post-1945
10 Brigade Medical Company
15 Field Ambulance
16 Field Ambulance
25 Airportablew Field Ambulance
114 Parachute Field Ambunce (V)

ROYAL ARMY ORDANCE CORPS
First World War
Ordance Field Park
Ordance Advance Depot
Detachment Indian Ordance Depot

Post-1945

Ammunition Depot, Khormaksar			
Ordnance Depot, Aden			
24 Ordnance Field Park			
24 Airportable Field Park			
16 Para Heavy Drop Coy	Attached to 3 Para	1964	1964

ROYAL ELECTRICAL AND MECHANICAL ENGINEERS
52 Command Worshop (Aden
  Garrison)

1 Infantry Workshop	1964	
13 Armoured Workshop		1964
22 Engineering Equipment Workshop		

MILITARY POLICE
24 Brigade Provost Unit
Port Security Force

ROYAL ARMY PAY CORPS		Oct 64
MILITARY PROVOST STAFF CORPS		1967

PIONEERS AND LABOUR
First World War

Aden Labour Corps	1914	1918

Second World War

1401 (Aden) Coy	Somiland Campaign	Nov 40	May 41
1402 (Aden) Coy	Somiland Campaign	Feb 41	Apr 41
1422 (Sultan Saleh's Hadramaut) Coy	Socotra Island	Mar 43	Early 1944
2004 (Aden) Coy	Socotra Island		

Post-1945

518 Company	1967

INTELLIGENCE CORPS

4 Field Security Sect	1975
15 Intelligence Pln	In support of 39 Inf Bde Apr-64
Counter Intelligence Coy	

WOMEN'S ROYAL ARMY CORPS
28 Independent Coy

Appendix C
Royal Air Force

ROYAL AIR FORCE			
8 Sqn	1927	1967	Fighter Ground Attack
Abyssinian Crisis			
203 Sqn	1935	1936	Coastal recce
Second World War			
94 Sqn	1939	1941	Air defence
11 Sqn	1940		Bomber
39 Sqn	1940	1941	
3 (South African) Sqn	1941	1945	Air defence
203 Sqn	1940	1941	Recce and fighter
621 Sqn	1943	1945	General recce
1566 Flight			Meteorology
Aden Protectorate Flight			Air defence
Post - 1945			
21 Sqn	1953	1957	Transport
26 Sqn	1963	1965	Helicopters
37 Sqn	1957	1967	Maritime Recce
43 Sqn	1963	1967	Fighter Ground attack
73 Sqn	1957		Fighter Bomber
78 Sqn	1958	1967	Light Transport
84 Sqn		1967	Search and Rescue
93 Sqn	1953	1967	
105 Sqn	1962	1967	Medium Transport
208 Sqn	1961	1964	Fighter Ground attack
233 Sqn	1960	1964	Medium Transport
1417 Flight	1963	1967	Air Photo Recce
1426 Flight	1956	1957	Bomber
Aden Communication Flight			
Search and Rescue Flight	1957	1967	Light search and rescue
Aden Protectorate Flight		1967	Fighter ground attack and photo recce
RAF Regiment			
10 Armoured Car Flight	1955	1957	
HQ 20 Wing, RAF Regt			

66 Field Sqn	1955	1957	
62 Field Sqn	Jul 55	Apr 66	
58 Field Sqn	1956	1957	20 Wing
48 Field Sqn	Nov 62	Apr 63	
16 Sqn	Jun 64	Jun 65	Its Mortar detachment saw action in Radfan
37 Field Sqn	Dec 64	Apr 65	
27 Sqn	Sep 65	Dec 65	
34 Sqn	Sep 65	Dec 65	
2 Sqn	Nov 65	Apr 66	
37 Field Sqn	Apr 66	Oct 66	
66 Rifle Sqn	Jul 66	Nov 67	20 Wing
48 Field Sqn	Sep 66	Jan 67	
51 Field Sqn	Aug 67	Nov 67	
2 Sqn	Oct 67	Nov 67	

RAF Movements			
50 Movements Sqn	mid-1940s	May 05	Passenger and air freight within theatre and with UK

RAF Signals			
19 Signals Unit		1967	
22 Tactical Signals Unit	1961	1967	
123 Signals Unit		1967	
198 Signals Unit			
303 Signals Unit		1967	
402 Signals Unit		1967	
RAF Saltpans			Transmitting station

Maintenance			
114 Maintenance Unit			
131 Maintenance Unit	mid-1940s	Nov 67	

Marine			
206, 216 and 220 Air Sea Rescue Units		1952	
1152 Marine Craft Unit	1952	Nov 67	Maritime rescue

Medical			
RAF Hospital. Aden Steamer Point		1967	The General hospital for all Service and associated civilians
Khormaksar Beach	1965	1967	Stabilisation hospital for up country casualties

RAF Police **RAF Supply Depot**			
Airfield Construction 5001Airfield Construction 5004 Airfield Construction	1959	1966	
Aden Protectorate Levies 4001 Armoured Car Flight			

Appendix D
Protectorate & Federal Forces

ADEN PROTECTORATE LEVIES			
Aden Troop	1856		1967
Six plattons	Apr 28	1938	
Six plattons and Camel Machine Gun Tp			
RHQ, HQ Coy, Trg Coy, AA Bty, Siy Coy and			
10 rifle Coys			
Second World War			
Aden Home Guard	1942	1944	
FEDERAL REGULAR ARMY			
1st, 2nd, 3rd, 4th and 5th Battalions	1961	1967	
Training Battalion			
Armoured Car Squadron	1956	1967	
Signal Squadron		1967	
Motor Transport company		1967	
Supply Platoon		1967	
Workshop		1967	
Wing, Khormaksar Beach Hospital		1967	
Band		1967	

Appendix E
British & Turkish Forces, South Arabia 1914–1919

ADEN BRIGADE
Aden Brigade - November 1914
1st Lancashire Fusiliers, left in 1914
1st Royal Irish Rifles, left in 1914
1/1st Brecknockshires (TF) (4th South Wales Borderers)
109th Indian Infantry
Aden Troop
61st, 70th and 76th Coys RGA

Aden Brigade - November 1915
1/4th Royal East Kents (TF)
108th Indian Infantry
126th Baluchistan Infantry *(30 Indian Infantry Bde)*
1/23rd Sikh Pioneers (*29th Indian Infantry Bde*)
61st, 70th and 76th Coys RGA
5-inch Bty RGA
Aden Troop
3rd Bombay Sapper and Miners
5/1st Field Company
28th Indian Infantry Brigade
  51st and 53rd Sikhs
  56th and 62nd Punjabs
B Bty HAC
Berkshire Bty, RHA

Aden Brigade - November 1916
1/4th Duke of Cornwalls Light Infantry (TF)
75th Carnatic Infantry
33rd and 69nd Punjabis
129th Duke of Connaught's Own
1/6th East Surreys (TF)
109th Indian Infantry
Malay States Guides
Aden Troop
C & D Sqns, King George's Own Light Cavalry

62nd, 69th and 85th Coys RGA
Malay States Guides Bty
3rd Bombay Sapper and Miners
5/1st Field Company
23rd Fortress Company

Aden Brigade - November 1917
1/6th East Surreys (TF)
109 Indian Infantry
75th Carnatic Infantry
69th Punjabis
1/7th Duke of Connaughts Own Rajputs
Aden Troop
C & D Sqns, King George's Own Light Cavalry
62nd, 69th and 85th Coys RGA
Malay States Guides Bty
3rd Bombay Sapper and Miners
5/1st Field Company
23rd Fortress Company

Aden Brigade - November 1918
1/7th Hamphires (TF)
75th Carnatic Infantry
69th Punjabis
7th Duke of Connaughts Own Rajputs
1st Brahamans
1st Yemen Infantry
Aden Troop
B&C Sqns, King George's Own Light Cavalry
62nd, 69th and 85th Coys RGA
Malay States Guides Bty
1105 (Howitzer) Bty
3rd Bombay Sapper and Miners
5/1st Field Company
23rd Fortress Company

Source: Order of Battle, Indian Army Divisions & Paul Watson

VII TURKISH (YEMEN) ARMY CORPS
HQ 39th DIVISION - TAIZ
Lahej
1/117th Infantry Battalion
Detachment of 26th Cavalry Regt (Corps troops)
Artillery

Waht
2nd and 3rd Battalions, 115th Infantry Regt
3/116th Infantry Regt
2nd and 3rd Battalions, 117th Infantry Regt
Machine gun coy
Independent Engineer Coy (Corps Troops)
Artillery Bty (7 x 7.7cm and one mortar)
Howitzer Bty (2 guns)
2 Mountain Btys

HQ 40th DIVISION - HODEIDA
Subar
3/119th Infantry Regt (from 40 Div)
7 Model Battalion
2 x machine guns
Mountain bty

Sheikh Sa'id
1/120th Regiment
Mountain Bty
Two 10.5cm guns

CORPS TROOPS
26th Cavalry Regt
2 x militia battalions
Arab auxiliaries
Horse artillery battalion
4 x heavy batteries
9 x field and mountain artillery batteries
Howitzer battery
Rocket battery
7th Engineer Bn

Glossary

ADC	Aide de Camp
AIC	Aden Intelligence Centre
APB	Armoured Plated Bedford 3-ton Army lorry
APC	Armoured Personnel carrier
APL	Aden Protectorate Levies
BP	British Petroleum
Compo	Composite rations
CSM	Company Sergeant Major
DFC	Distinguished Flying Cross
DH	De Haviland
DSO	Distinguished Service Order
DZ	Drop Zone (for parachute troops)
FLOSY	Front for the Liberation of Occupied South Yemen
FNG 1	Federal National Guard 2 (Government Guards)
FNG 2	Federal National Guard 2 (Tribal Guards)
FRA	Federal Regular Army
G	The military G (General) Branch dealing with Operations, Intelligence and Security
GOC	General Officer Commanding
GPMG	General Purpose Machine Gun
HF	High Frequency
HQ	Headquarters
Jebel	Mountain/Mount
KOSB	King's Own Scottish Borderers
MBE	Member of the British Empire
MC	Military Cross
MiG	Mikoyan-Gurevich
MM	Military Medal
MP	Member of Parliament
NAAFI	Navy, Army and Air Force Institution
NCO	Non Commissioned Officer
NLF	National Liberation Front
OBE	Order of the British Empire
OLOS	Organisation for the Liberation of the Occupied South

OP	Observation Post
Pig	1-ton Humber Armoured Personnel Carrier
PSP	People's Socialist Party
PWO	Prince of Wales' Own Regiment of Yorkshire
QDG	Queen's Dragoon Guards
RSM	Regimental Sergeant Major
RAMC	Royal Army Medical Corps
RAPC	Royal Army Pay Corps
RASC	Royal Army Service Corps
RAOC	Royal Army Ordnance Corps
RCT	Royal Corps of Transport
RE	Royal Engineers
RHA	Royal House Artillery
RTR	Royal Tank Regiment
SAA	South Arabian Army
Sangar	Stone-walled enclosure
SAS	Special Air Service
Seil	A flash flood
SOE	Special Operations Executive
Sowar	Rider (cavalry)
SLR	Self Loading Rifle
TF	Territorial Force
TUC	Trades Union Congress
UK	United Kingdom
UN	United Nations
US	United States
USA	United States of America
VHF	Very High Frequency
Wadi	Valley
Wombat	Anti-Tank Gun
WRAC	Women's Royal Army Corps
WRAF	Women's Royal Air Force
Zenitnaya Samokhodnaya Ustanovka	Anti-aircraft self-propelled mount

Bibliography

Published sources
(Place of publication London, unless otherwise stated)

Blaxland, Gregory, *The Regiments Depart*, William Kimber, 1971

Campbell, Major Stephen Andrew, *An Exit Strategy not a Winning Strategy; Intelligence Lessons from the British 'Emergency' in South Arabia 1963-67*, US Army Command and General Staff College, Fort Leavenworth, 2012

Clayton, Anthony, *Forearmed: A History of the Intelligence Corps*, Brasseys, 1993

Cobain, Mark, *Cruel Britannia: A Secret History of Torture*, Portobello Books, 2012

Connelly, Mark, 'The British Campaign in Aden 1914-1918', *Journal of the Centre for First World War Studies*, Issue 3, Birmingham University, March 2005

Curtis, Mark, *Unpeople: Britain's Secret Human Rights Abuses*, Vintage, 2004

Edwards, Frank, *The Gaysh: A History of the Aden Protectorate Levies 1927-61 and the Federal Regular Army of South Arabia 1961-67*, Helion & Co, Solihull, 2012

Gavin, R.J., *Aden under British Rule 1839-1967*, C. Hurst & Co, 1975

Haswell, Jock, *British Military Intelligence*, Weidenfeld & Nicholson, 1973

Hincliffe, Peter, Ducker, John T. and Holt, Maria, *Without Glory in Arabia: The British Retreat from Aden*, IB Tauris & Co Ltd, 2013

HMSO: Indian Papers: Correspondence relating to Aden, 30 May 1839

Jones, Clive, 'Where the State Feared to Tread: Britain, Britons, Covert Action and the Yemen Civil War, 1962–64', *Intelligence and National Security*, Vol. 21, No.5, October 2006

Jones, Clive, *Britain and the Yemen Civil War 1962-1965: Ministers, Mercenaries and Mandarins; Foreign Policy and the Limits of Covert Action*, Sussex Academic Press, Bournemouth, 2004

Lord, Cliff and Birtles, David, *The Armed Forces of Aden and the Protectorate 1939-1967*, Helion & Co, Solihull, 2011

Macdonald, P.G., *Stopping the Clock*, Robert Hale, 1977

Mileham, P.J.R., *Fighting Highlanders: The History of the Argyll & Sutherland Highlanders*, Arms and Armour, 1993

Mitchell, Lt Col Colin, *Having Been a Soldier*, Mayflower, 1969

Monick, S., 'Operations on the Radfan May–June 1964', *South African Journal of Military Studies*, Vol 8, No 4, 1978

Paget, Julian, *Last Post: Aden 1964-1967*, Faber & Faber, 1969

Royal Air Force Historical Society Journal 18, 'South Arabia and the Withdrawal from Aden', 1998

Southby-Tailyour, Ewen, *HMS Fearless: The Mighty Lion*, Pen & Sword, Barnsley, 2006

Steer, Brigadier Frank, *To the Warrior His Arms: The Story of the Royal Army Ordnance Corps 1918-1993*, Pen & Sword Military, Barnsley, 2005

Stofford, Major D., 'Infantry Assistance from Outside Aden', *The Infantryman* No. 84, November 1968

Sutton, Brigadier D.J.*, The Story of the Royal Army Service Corps and Royal Corps of Transport 1945-1982*,Leo Cooper in association with Secker and Warburg, 1983

The Times obituaries
- Major General Philip Tower, 11 December 2006
- Brigadier Ian Mackay, 19 March 2007
- Brigadier Sir Louis Hargroves, 29 February 2008.
- Air Marshal Sir Ernest Sidey, died 18 September 2008
- The Reverend Robin Roe, 3 August 2010
- (Major) Mike Banks, 27 February 2013
- Major General Jack Dye, died 10 June 2013
- Colonel Edward Koden, died 7 September 2013

Thompson, Major General Julian, *Ready for Anything: The Parachute Regiment at War*, Fontana, 1990

Thompson, Major General Julian, *The Royal Marines: From Sea Soldier to a Special Force*, Sidgwick & Jackson, 2000

Young, David, *Four Five: The Story of 45 Commando Royal Marines, 1943-71*, Leo Cooper, 1972

Walker, Jonathan, *Aden Insurgency: The Savage War in South Arabia 1962-1967*, Spellmount, Staplehurst;, 2005

Warner, Philip, *The Vital Link: The Story of the Royal Signals 1945-1985,* Leo Cooper, 1989

The Internet

www.adenairways provides a useful directory of the history, development and culture of Aden

www.britains-small wars/Aden.

www.casemate publishing
  Capture of Aden
  Directory of units

www.keyhambooks.typepad *A Short History of the RAF Britannia*
www.mamsoba UK MAMS Old Bods Association; Gale, Tony, *RAF Khormaksar*
www.orbat.com/history.uk/aden Watson, Graham, *British Ground Forces Aden 1955-67*
www.psywar.org Friedman, Herbert, *PsyOps of the Aden Emergency 1963-1967*
www.radfanhunters.co.uk/Khormaksar Operations 1962 to 29 November 1967 and Khormaksar accommodation and amenities
www.4and7royal tank regiment.com/1961-1964 History of the 4th and 7th Royal Tank Regiment 1961-1964

Journals
Regimental Journal of the Prince of Wales' Own Regiment of Yorkshire, August 1958, February and April 1959, February, June, October and December 1966; October and December 1967; May 1968
Regimental Periodical of the Argyll & Sutherland Highlanders,1968
The Dhow, Journal of the Veterans Association, July and November 2012, March 2013

Unpublished Accounts
Beard, Colonel Nick, Personal account of the Champion Lines ambush
Godwin, Captain P.G.H., Incident Report (20 June 1967)

Index